Warren Chase

Forty Years on the Spiritual Rostrum

Warren Chase

Forty Years on the Spiritual Rostrum

ISBN/EAN: 9783337334833

Printed in Europe, USA, Canada, Australia, Japan

Cover: Foto ©Lupo / pixelio.de

More available books at **www.hansebooks.com**

FORTY YEARS

ON THE

SPIRITUAL ROSTRUM.

By WARREN CHASE.

A SEQUEL TO "THE LIFE LINE OF THE LONE ONE,"
AN AUTOBIOGRAPHY OF THE AUTHOR, AS

The World's Child,

WHO GAVE THE FIRST PUBLIC LECTURES IN THIS COUNTRY IN
DEFENCE OF MODERN SPIRIT INTERCOURSE, AND WHOSE
NAME IS FIRST ON THE LIST OF CALLS FOR COPIES
OF "NATURE'S DIVINE REVELATIONS,"
WHEN IN PRESS IN 1847.

———oo⚬oo———

BOSTON:
COLBY & RICH, PUBLISHERS,
9 BOSWORTH STREET.
1888.

PREFACE.

THE object in writing and publishing this work is not notoriety or money, as the author has plenty of the former, and will not long need the latter; but it is to follow the spiritual and intellectual footsteps of the author, and to mark the progress of what is called Modern Spiritualism in the United States and Europe, during the first forty years of its growth and propagation, the author having started with its inception as an exponent and been constantly advocating and defending it and the mediums as the instruments through which the spiritual world is trying to make itself and its condition known to the denizens of this world. But few of the personal vicissitudes and incidents of the author will, or can, be recorded in the work; but all who read this should read the "Life Line" of the author, which at the time of this writing is in its ninth edition, and should be in its twentieth, as it is a work all young persons should read and profit by, and is an appropriate introduction to this, which is an old man's legacy to his friends.

> "Pride often guides the author's pen,
> Books as affected are as men;
> But he who studies nature's laws,
> From certain truth his maxim draws."

NO INTRODUCTION.

NEITHER this book nor the author need an introduction to Spiritualists, and it is not expected that many others will read it. It is largely a continuation of the singular life experiences of the author as related in his former works, and is largely made up of original and borrowed thoughts, collected and expressed in the long path of earthly existence. It is void of theology, as the author never had any, and never took any interest in faith, never being able to prove anything by it. In the poetical selections will be found genuine poetry and rhyme and jingle of words, but gems of thought in all, some of which are not published elsewhere, though many are. The newspaper correspondence is original and embodies many of the author's radical ideas. Many articles which editors declined to publish were even more radical and critical than any contained in this volume. I could have filled out this book with descriptions of phenomena I have witnessed; but as our papers are full of such and tests constantly occurring, I decided to omit them.

CONTENTS.

CHAPTER I.

Internal and External Forebodings of Social, Political, and Religious Convulsions, Personal and General, resulting in a Social Effort by the Author 7

CHAPTER II.

Birth of Spiritualism — Failure of Fourierism — Political Career Opened, and Sketches on the Path of Life by the Crooked and Tangled Line — The First Spiritual Paper, *The Univercœlum*, and its Objects Explained 14

CHAPTER III.

Early Work — Boston *Investigator* — *Univercœlum*, *Spirit Messenger*, and Early Workers, etc. 30

CHAPTER IV.

Catalogue of Names and Short Biographical Notices of Early Workers and Persecutions 52

CHAPTER V.

A Brief and Brilliant Political Career 64

CHAPTER VI.

Threading my Way along the "Hard Road to Travel On" — Incidents and Events in the Path of Life 78

CHAPTER VII.

What I have learned from Forty Years' Intercourse with Spirits — Sexual Life in the Spirit World — My Social, Political, and Religious Creed, etc. 125

CHAPTER VIII.

Extracts and Scraps of Correspondence running through Many Years, with Various and Progressive Ideas on Spirit Life and Intercourse; with Scraps from my Scrap-book worth keeping and largely variegated 173

CHAPTER IX.

Poetical Selections from Various Sources, Personal and General — Good and Poor, but not Bad, greatly mixed, in Published and Unpublished Scraps 266

FORTY YEARS ON THE SPIRITUAL ROSTRUM.

CHAPTER I.

CLIMBING UP THE GOLDEN STAIR.

" Man was born into this world, poor, naked, and bare,
And his journey all through it is trouble and care,
And his exit from out it is, no one knows where;
But if well he do here, it will be well with him there:
No more could I tell you by preaching a year."

For several years before the advent of Modern Spiritualism, there had been internal forces working and fermenting in my brain, which, rightly interpreted, were the premonitory symptoms of a change. These might be attributed in part, if not all, to the study and such attention as I could give in my poverty and between my hours of labor, to the subject of phrenology, and later, to Fourierism and Mesmerism. Whether these were to produce a deeper-seated infidelity or agnosticism, or some change out of these, I, of course, could not foresee; but I never had, and never have, felt a leaning toward the supports of faith and hope which the Christian Church hold up. Phrenology led me farther away than astronomy and geology had previously done, and when Mesmerism and psychology and biology were added. I was entirely out of the reach and out of all sympathy with the creeds of Christians, however much respect, esteem, or love I might have for persons who I considered as surrounded by its fogs of superstition.

Reviewing the history of the past in all steps of evolutionary progress, and especially in religion, and still more especially in Christianity, there seems to have been some minds prepared for the reception of each new discovery and each new sect, as in each new step of any kind in human progress. Such was the case with Columbus, as with Luther and Melanchthon ; with John Wesley and John Murray ; with Darwin, John Stuart Mill, Huxley, Spencer, and A. J. Davis ; as well as with Swedenborg. Earlier still, Mohammedanism, like its older sister Christianity, although both were forced upon the people by tyrannical power with the sword and fagot and the most cruel persecution. Yet, undoubtedly, the ages and the people were largely ripe for them, as the older systems had become effete and outgrown. The Roman gods had lost their power over the hearts of the people, and the sun-worshippers of Western Asia had grown cold and careless in their devotions. Systems, like animals, become pregnant and bring forth new systems,—sometimes in single births, and sometimes in broods, as Catholicism did in its Protestant brood of children, and now grandchildren and several later generations, which, although most of them draw credal support from the old homestead, they do not go there to rest, but build new houses of their own for this world and the next.

The dreamers in the early part of this century began to " toss and sigh," and in the religious minds there were many premonitions of some great event about to be born near the middle of the present century. Some predicted the coming of their Christ and the final winding up of the temporal affairs of this world, with a general resurrection of the dead and a general judgment. Others predicted some astronomical and planetary as well as atmospheric change; and others, some great social change, such as a few spasmodic efforts in Fourier's system of social life started in this country, which soon failed because premature. False prophets all failed in their specific predictions, and yet a great event was born, and is yet in the hands of its dry-nurse, but rapidly growing and gaining strength, which in time will supersede all Pagan, Christian, and Mohammedan religions. In 1842 and 1843 many sensitive, honest, but ignorant Christians in our country who went by the name of Adventists, fully believed with abundant faith that the Scriptures were to be fulfilled in what they called a prophecy of the coming Christ and the end of this world in a general conflagration; and many prepared their white robes for an ascension to a higher and happier life. But of course, like all other Scripture prophecies and predictions, it failed to be fulfilled as predicted, and yet the trembling soul-impulse that went through these sensitives had a portent and was to all intents the forerunner of an event to come. This, like many others, was one of the pains that preceded the birth of an event that was destined to supersede Christianity and other religions, in a natural way, but not as a miracle or supernatural occurrence.

The writer was not affected by this religious tidal wave, never having been a Christian, and never having believed the Bible to be the "Word of God," or more sacred than other old books written in the ages of scientific ignorance; but he was taken on the social tidal wave of Fourierism and led into it by some very able and enthusiastic writers in the New York *Tribune*, then edited by Horace Greeley. Taking an active part in the discussion of this question in the Lyceum and public meetings in Southport, Wis. (now Kenosha), he became somewhat infatuated with the foreshadowed beauties of a higher and better social life than our competitive system, in which and from which he had suffered and still did suffer in a sort of "devil take the hindermost" race for homes and subsistence. I had by the hardest and severest trials and struggles, always aided and supported by every effort in the power of my feeble and faithful wife, who passed to spirit life in 1875, secured a poor little cottage home of one room, as fully and truthfully described in the "Life Line." From this uncomfortable, but to us comparatively comfortable home, I began a mental growth which has never ceased; and from important events which occurred there a new world finally opened to me, with which at this time, nearly a half-century later, I am partially as familiar as with this; for there lives the companion who struggled with me and obtained and occupied this home; there also are the other two members of our family who passed over from this home when to us that world was not known to exist, and when (in 1843) we did not know where they had gone, but supposed, and it seemed most likely to us, as we put their bodies in the little grave, that it was the last we should ever see or hear of them. One was a beautiful boy of nearly two years' growth, and the idol of its mother, uncommonly bright and promising; and it was a terrible blow to the feeble mother, then carrying another which prematurely hurried into this life and in a few months followed the other out of it. These two events, and especially the first, started a serious and somewhat painful train of thought and deep research into the mysteries of nature which seemed to bring children into this world and often hurry them out of it; but *where?* was the great question. Where did they come from? Where did they go to? Were they new creations in whole, or only in part, as the body surely was? If new creations, by what power created? Certainly not by the will of the parents. Could an involuntary action in a cell of inorganic matter produce such wonderful structures? But this was going into too deep water for one whose mind had never explored the metaphysical fields of thought, but who had ever been struggling with poverty and its burdens and trials in life, and yet with painful forebodings his thoughts would follow the dear little ones to the — *where ?*

In this eventful year, 1843, some experiments in Mesmerism led my mind into a tangled maze of curious experiments, but did not then open the spiritual world to my perception; for the more pressing and more promising socialism of Fourier took the precedence and led me into the organization of a Phalanx, instituted for the purpose of getting up a new settlement and better homes, which plan was carried out in 1844, as fully described in the "Life Line," and into which at first, in a still ruder and cruder home, the family was moved, the wife, sorrowfully but ever trustingly, as a faithful companion, going with the rest, bidding the old home and the graves farewell forever. Here, as related in the "Life Line," she and the feeble boy suffered a terribly severe attack of fever and came near the door that led to the home of the boys; but in my absence, extraordinary efforts and the best of medical skill and care saved both for future usefulness, and ably and faithfully did both perform the parts in life assigned them. She, a fully developed Spiritualist and medium before she passed over; and he as a surgeon in the army during three years of the war, and, as I write this, a skilful physician and leader in the cause of temperance, and among the Grangers of his native State of Michigan, and the father of seven as fine children as I have seen in my long journeys. Our daughter, two years younger, who tenderly cared for her mother in our joint home in Southern Illinois, and in whose presence her mother passed on to the higher life, is also one of the best of wives and mothers, with a beautiful family of six children, the eldest of which, as I write this, is editor of a paper in St. Louis, and professor of pharmacy in the college there. In the same city is also our other son, a bachelor, on the police force. He was born ten years after his brother, and in the Phalanx, and after the birth of Spiritualism inherited much of his mother, and is a universal favorite with all who know him. In closing this family picture I may as well say that in all of my family connections, including a second wife and her daughter and daughter's husband, not one of us uses tobacco or intoxicating drink, and none of my grandchildren use tea or coffee regularly; and none of us are poisoned physically with calomel, or mentally with sectarian Christianity. Certainly none of either were inherited from us by our children, and none by their children from them.

In the spring of 1844 our Fourierism culminated, and the Wisconsin Phalanx was born. We located it in an uninhabited township in the northwest corner of Fond du Lac County, Wis., and named it "Ceresco," changed to Ripon after we broke up and scattered, owing to the opposition of whiskey, Christianity, speculation, and popular prejudice against any and every reform that promised release to the poverty-stricken masses, who were kept down by these tyrants that caused nearly all such evils, and of which our Phalanx had none, as we were only social reformers. In the fall our little house was sold, and we all went there and lived in the new mode of life six years,— never fully satisfactory to either of us, less so to the wife than to me, but always hopeful of a better day, and the opening of a new heaven and new earth which was coming, but in an entirely different direction from that in which we were looking for it. Soon after our enterprise was started, one after another of the twenty or more Fourier associations in the States failed, till at last all were gone, the Brook Farm in Massachusetts, and the North American Phalanx in Red Bank, N. J., going last. All but ours were financial failures; ours closed a financial success, but a social failure. Before we closed out ours, a new light had dawned upon many of us in the SPIRITUAL PHILOSOPHY, and its new and crude phenomena. These references are made to the premonitory symptoms of a new birth to the world, because I was involved in them, and they were to me personally what they were to the country generally, as the half-century has shown. I need not follow farther the social problem, or my connection with it, as there are several records of it, all very imperfect ones, in the history of Fond du Lac County, evidently written in prejudice against me because I went into the spiritual field of labor instead of the spiritual world. A more accurate account was written by me in John H. Noyes' "History of American Socialism," but its author had strong prejudice against me on account of my religious views. A brief, and, so far as it goes, correct one may be found in my "Life Line"; and with this I leave the social convulsion, adding only that I believe there will be, at no very distant day, an entirely new and far better state of social life on earth.

CHAPTER II.

LAND AHEAD. — A REVOLVING LIGHT IN THE DISTANCE.

" Voyager upon life's sea, to yourself be true:
But if you would succeed, you must paddle your own canoe."

IN the fall of 1843 and winter of 1843 and 1844 I, with a few others, even during the Millerite and Fourierite excitements, began our experiments in Mesmerism in Southport. Whether we had then heard of the experiments with A. J. Davis, or of Laroy Sunderland, or of Cornell and others in Cincinnati, I do not now remember; but soon after our experiments we read in public and private circles evidence of the remarkable success of theirs, which was not unlike ours, only far more complete and more confirmatory of the few shadowy glimpses of the spirit world which came to us through the imperfect subjects we found in our experiments. Had not the more immediate and more pressing social subject carried us off in the spring of 1844, it is probable we should have opened there and then direct intercourse between ourselves and the denizens of the spirit world. That movement set us back, but did not extinguish the dim light we had seen; and a few of us in the Phalanx reached after and obtained all we could get of the published reports of experiments by these and other parties, until when, in 1847, the first book of A. J. Davis, now author of thirty odd works, was issued. I had an order long waiting for one dozen copies, to be sent, as soon as bound, to Milwaukee, where we could get them, that being our nearest express office. At this time the new impulse had shaken the liberal Universalist churches. T. L. Harris, S. B. Brittan, R. P. Ambler, William Fishbough, and John M. Spear had been taking in the spirit of the new age, and were coming out as advocates of a new religion. They were soon followed by many others from that and other churches. With myself and the few engaged with me there was no religious element in our investigations; they were purely scientific and metaphysical. Especially was this so with myself, who had been from childhood called an infidel, and long a reader of the Boston *Investigator*, it being the first paper I ever subscribed for, and to which I had been an occasional contributor. Hence I expected no help from God or the Holy Spirit, nor from prayers, and we had none of either. In the early experiments in these localities, and probably others not referred to, some astonishing developments were reached which have rarely been superseded, and never set aside, the most remarkable being a volume called "Nature's Divine Revelations," spoken through the organism of A. J. Davis while under the magnetic influence of Dr. Lyon, and written down as spoken by William Fishbough in the presence of others, all testifying that in no sense did it come from the mind of Mr. Davis nor from any of the minds of persons visibly present. When this book was published, the year before the rappings at Hydesville, N.Y., in the Fox family, had been recognized as coming from spirits or a spirit, it settled in many minds the origin of much of the intelligence received in other places and through other mesmerized persons. Especially was this so in my own case and those who with me had been experimenting and reading of the experiments of others with similar results. I have never doubted from that day to this the spiritual origin of the intelligence received through persons mesmerized by mortals or by spirits when the intelligence does not come from the mind of the medium.

The New York *Tribune*, which at that time as the organ of Horace Greeley, who was an active reformer and defender of the interests of the masses until he became a popular politician and partially, but not wholly, a monopolist, not only defended the investigation of Fourierism, but also of Spiritualism, until its present editor, Whitelaw Reid, got so much control of it as to make it become, as it now is, one of the most outspoken defenders of monopolists and political tyranny in the nation. This paper and Mr. Greeley did much to encourage the early experiments and investigation which has at last settled forever the fact of spirit intercourse. Much is due him and his paper, now so utterly lost to integrity and honesty even in politics. During those early experiments Laroy Sunderland published a highly instructive paper which we read with deep interest. In that paper he connected Mesmerism and psychology with spirit life and intercourse; but when he found that he could not monopolize the subject, and become its leader and the founder of its philosophy, he soured on the subject and abandoned it. His paper died, and he lingered in the cold fogs of agnosticism and doubt, and at a very old age passed out of this world in the faith of infidelity, but discovered at death a dim "light in the window," and put in an appearance on the other shore, I think, in the year 1885. His last years must have been gloomy, judging from his contributions to the liberal papers and in his bitter opposition to what he once proved to be true, and to a knowledge of which truth he helped others who have never backslid. The biography of those who gathered around Mr. Davis in that early time would be highly interesting, but as I was not one of them, although watching at a distance with deep interest the strange revelations, I am not the person to write it, but wish Mr. Davis would, as he could do it better than any one else.

There seems to have been no substantial benefit or permanent advantage to the cause of spiritual intercourse, or practical and scientific demonstration of the truth derived from any of these experiments, except through Mr. Davis. The far less important ones were at our Ceresco home in Wisconsin; Laroy Sunderland having turned his aside, and the experimenters in Cincinnati having tried to turn theirs into a field of speculation and failed in that part of it, most — though not all — gave it up. Old Major Gano and a few others having once gained the knowledge of spirit life and intercourse, never gave it up; but he retained it to a ripened old age and had it before him as a lighthouse on the other shore when he passed over the channel. At Ceresco most of us held out; some have passed on, and others like myself are still anchored in the knowledge partially gained before the Hydesville raps were discovered to be made by spirits, and subsequently by other modes of intercourse fully established.

Through the then wonderful manifestations in and through Mr. Davis, many were converted to a belief of their spiritual origin, and several popular preachers in Universalist churches left their pulpits and became public defenders of the new gospel. Among them no one held out better or did more faithful work than S. B. Brittan, who passed over too early to do all the good he could have done here with his masterly eloquence and trenchant pen, which was ever ready and active in the cause to the day of his death. T. L. Harris also came out about the same time, and exceeded Mr. B. in inspirational eloquence and poetic imagery, but lacked his firm stability of character and steadfastness, and after a few years of wonderful success as an inspirational lecturer and writer, especially of poetry, he ran into a wild fanaticism under what he evidently believed to be the Lord Jesus Christ, an imaginary person of whom none of the rest of us knew anything, and who as such imaginary person seems to this day to have exerted no influence except what is detrimental to true scientific spirit intercourse. Later, Mr. Harris, with the aid of some English capitalists who were converts, founded a colony at Brockton, N.Y., and later still sold out there and purchased and built up a grand and beautiful community house at Santa Rosa, Cal., which I overlooked, or looked over, in 1882, but could not see him, as he was sick, but not unto death, as he did not believe in dying.

William Fishbough, who also left his pulpit for the new cause, and who was the scribe of the great and grand volume referred to, although a firm believer to the day of his sudden and accidental death from a fall, had early grown cold for some reason never fully known to me, and did but little work in its propagation, although never opposing it. R. P. Ambler, another eloquent defender from the same sectarian pulpit, and who did a grand work in the early days when there was most need, later in the cause backed into his old church, as was asserted by his friends, because the support was insufficient for his family. Fanny Green, an able and eloquent writer of both prose and poetry, came early into the work, remained firm to the day of her death in California as Mrs. Fanny Green McDougal, leaving some works written and unpublished, but ever a faithful worker in the cause. From the legal profession, somewhat later, but still early, came Hon. J. W. Edmonds, Governor Tallmadge, Joel Tiffany, and Judge Larabee (all now gone over except Tiffany), and many others I cannot mention here. From the medical profession, Drs. Gray, R. T. Hallock, Lyon, Gardner, Nichols, and many others, most of them holding out; but Dr. H. T. Childs of Philadelphia, after many years of faithful work, took shelter in the Quaker church from which he had come out.

In 1847, when our Phalanx colony was three years old, I was nominated by the Democrats, to which party I had belonged since a voter, for the constitutional convention of Wisconsin, then a Territory preparing for State government. Fond du Lac County was entitled to three delegates, and I was elected by running ahead of my ticket, on which my two colleagues were defeated. In that convention my first speech was made against capital punishment, and it was the first and last I ever wrote out and read in any public assembly, as I found I was a better speaker than reader of my own writings. In that convention, when discussing the suffrage question in committee of the whole. I moved to strike out the word *white*, and had fourteen votes for my motion out of about one hundred and ninety members, and then moved to strike out the word *male*, and had one vote beside my own. I had then been for some years in favor of perfect equality between the races and sexes, and have had no reason to change my opinions on this subject since, and I believe my public and private life has ever been consistent on all of these questions of political, social, and religious reforms.

The work of this convention was not accepted by the voters, and the next year another convention was elected, to which I was returned as one of two for our county; and in this, by my motion, I secured equal rights to all citizens without regard to their opinions on the subject of religion; and the journal shows more references to me than to any other member, as I took a very active part and was chairman of the committee on banks and banking, then a very exciting subject, in which I opposed all banks of issue, as I have ever since. The work of this convention was accepted. In 1848 Wisconsin entered the Union, and I was elected to the State Senate for our county and Winnebago by the Democrats, and in the two sessions of my term took a very active part in the business, which it is not proper to record here. In the second session I was on the judiciary committee, a record very rare if ever found in the history of judiciary committees where a member was not a lawyer. There are still some of the reform measures that can be traced to me in the laws of that State, especially the divorce laws and the homestead exemption. I also got the usury laws repealed; but they were soon after reinstated and people deceived by them, as they always are. I introduced a bill to repeal all laws for the collection of debts, and still believe it would be good policy for any and every State, thus leaving all debts debts of honor.

In the State election of 1849 I received 3761 votes for governor of Wisconsin as the Free Soil party's candidate, as I had called the State convention of that party, presided over it, and drew up its platform; and I believe it was the first State convention of the party which eventually became the Republican party by a change of name. Nelson Dewey was elected by the Democrats, a good infidel governor. If the reader will pardon this digression from the historic line of this work, I will close out the Wisconsin political digression by noting that in 1852 I was on the electoral ticket for Hale and Julian, and one of the vice-presidents of the National Convention at Pittsburgh, that nominated them, and made the last of the four set speeches of that convention, Joshua R. Giddings, Gerrit Smith, and Fred Douglass preceding me. During this political work, and while writing constantly for several political papers in the State, I was steadily and constantly investigating, as best I could, the philosophy and phenomena of spirit life and intercourse; and also as one of the principal managing members of the Phalanx, was carrying out our social experiment, which we closed up in 1850 and 1851, paying off all our stock and its dividends and every dollar of debts, and making several dividends beside, so that no complaint was ever made of fraud or dishonesty in its business, all of which of a legal character was transacted by me.

In 1847 the long and anxiously looked for book from A. J. Davis put in an appearance, and no book was ever more welcomed by me, several members of the Phalanx, and others of my old friends at Southport, among them C. L. Sholes, who sent for a quantity of them, and as editor of a paper gave it a notice and supplied them, and when elected to the State Senate the same year I was, he brought them, and, we occupying the same double desk as the " David and Jonathan " of the Senate, we kept them on and in our desk, and often discussed the merits of the book, and defended its spiritual origin. This was in 1848 and 1849, when we knew little of the rapping at Hydesville, that had been recognized as spiritual and was creating great excitement, in which we were all deeply interested; and I expected much, but not as much as has grown out of it in forty years.

Previous to the publication of this book, "Nature's Divine Revelations," none of the believers in its spiritual origin had separated themselves from Christianity, but several had liberated themselves from sectarian bondage. I do not know the precise time that Harris, Brittan, Mumler, Fernald or Fishbough separated from their respective churches; but they all, and many others, defended the spiritual origin of this book, and the intelligence that controlled and came through Mr. Davis, and in 1847 twelve of them, including the above and Mr. Davis and Fanny Green, organized and started the *Univercœlum and Spiritual Philosopher*, with S. B. Brittan as editor-in-chief, and the other eleven as associates.

The first number was issued Dec. 4, 1847, about four months before the rappings were recognized at Hydesville. In this paper, every copy of which I have bound and sacredly kept, were many of the best written and most profound articles on our philosophy that have been written, and some of the best inspirational poems, by T. L. Harris and Fanny Green, that grace our literature. Mr. Harris was born in Stratford, England, May 15, 1823. He was brought to this country in 1827 by his father, and had to sustain, educate, and develop himself principally, as his mother died when he was a child. At seventeen he began to write for the press, and at twenty-one he left Calvinism, embraced Universalism, and preached it till he reached Spiritualism. In the spring of 1848 he had an independent society of Christians, with Spiritualism in it, in New York; but he never abandoned Christ, and hence became a fanatic and enthusiast, and tried to found a new Christian society at Mountain Cove, Va., in which attempt he failed, although claiming Jesus Christ as the guide and director of the enterprise. After that he became useless and worthless to the cause of Spiritualism, though he still claimed the divine inspiration and guidance. S. B. Brittan stood boldly out in defence of true Spiritualism, and began to defend it by lectures soon after I did, but neither he nor any other lecturer preceded me as a lecturer in its defence as a science or religion, separate and distinct from Christianity.

In the first volume of the *Univercœlum* I find but one article of mine, though I think several were sent to it; and though the volume closed the last of May, 1848, and the rapping excitement ran high, I find no reference to it as a sign of spirit intercourse, it being evidently considered of too low and obscure an origin to be thought worthy of notice in a paper taking so high a position in the literary circles; for the *Univercœlum* was really a paper of high merit and talent. It was evident, however, that it had too much dignity and too much Christianity to be, for any length of time, an exponent of Spiritualism, which was now coming as Christianity did, if it came in the time ascribed to it, among the poor and needy and despised, who had no popularity or dignity except the natural dignity with which all born children are endowed.

In the latter part of 1847, or early winter of 1848 (the exact date being lost), I held a discussion in the stone schoolhouse in Ceresco, with Rev. H. H. Vanamringe, on the origin and merits of "Nature's Divine Revelations," I defending its spiritual origin, and he opposing it and abusing the book and its author for not accepting Christ, in whom he was a firm believer. This was my first public speech in defence of the philosophy of spirit life and intercourse, and opened the new field of public speaking and writing in which I have labored ever since, and making, in the early part of the year 1888, my forty years. I thought, and most if not all of my hearers thought, I fully sustained my points, and I had one evidence in the anger and bitterness of my opponents, for, as James Russell Lowell says, "The fellow that first gits mad's most allers wrong." After this discussion, I availed myself of every favorable opportunity to give public lectures on the subject, taking "Nature's Divine Revelations" as my text-book, until others appeared, often putting in some of my own experiences. As I had none of the Christianity in my discourses, such as our Universalist come-outers kept and mixed in theirs, I often shocked church-goers, and sometimes frightened away good honest Christian inquiry. I always relied on science and nature, not on God or Providence or Christ, as the evidence by which I sustained the spirit life and its intercourse with us. Those who held fast to Christianity with one hand, and prayed and thanked God for spirit intercourse, believing it to be a developed phase of Christianity, were more popular as speakers, but did not do more or better, if as good, work in opening the new dispensation as I did, as the sequel has proved.

Until my work in and with the Phalanx was closed up I could not give much time to lecturing on this subject but my pen, which had been used extensively in defence of social, political, and religious reforms, was ready to take up this subject and cautiously put it over my name before the public. On page 343 of the first volume of the *Univercœlum* is the following, over my name and dated Ceresco, Wis., March 20, 1848, only ten days before the Hydesville phenomena, which was not known to us till sometime after their occurrence.

"THE PHILOSOPHY OF TO-DAY.

"It is by no means singular that the new philosophy which shadows forth a brighter day, indicating our connection in this physical sphere with a succeeding spirit life, should meet with strong and stubborn opposition from the tardy and conservative world of mind. The prevailing theology and philosophy of this age is the ultimate development of principles once new and strenuously opposed, but which contained more truth and light than the conservative world was prepared for at the age of their discovery. But they have nearly developed themselves, completed their circle, and finished their destiny. The evident signs which this age bears of a transition, show plainly that they must now give way to a new system, containing — as the greater circle contains the less — all truth and light which is within its sphere; thus rendering useful the little truth which past ages have discovered, and embracing in its wider range all knowledge contained in former systems.

"If the coming age, with its new philosophy, shall succeed in securing general happiness, by establishing harmony and unity in our moral, social, and political relations with one another, it will accomplish what formal Christianity and civilization have long preached, but never practised, — long taught in faith, but never realized in life ; nor, indeed, could it be, for the clergy have been the ' blind leaders of the blind.' The world has been progressing through every past age, and rapidly in the present age of civilization and refinement; but its head (the teachers of theology, divinity, and spirituality) has been cut off and accidentally put on with the face backward, and even then, it would seem, with the eyes bandaged, for they would not use even past experiences. It can hardly be righted without being again severed from its hold on the great body of humanity which will never fail to go forward in perfecting itself and completing its circle of circles, spirally winding forward and upward to the development physically of truth, harmony, mirth, and happiness ; and spiritually of life, light, liberty, and purity, and in both spheres, impelled by love acting by will and directed by wisdom.

" The materials of which our earth is composed doubtless passed through a long period of successive and continually progressive ages and changes before it could produce and sustain in the simplest form a vegetable. And science, as well as reason, teaches us that a long time was occupied in the process of production and reproduction, growth and decay, before the vegetable kingdom could develop either the flower or the fruit. Life in its lowest form is produced in the vegetable kingdom, and the flower is the highest development and the theology of that kingdom, corresponding to the spiritual development of humanity in its earthly sphere ; and by and through the fruit is its death or transition to a new and higher manifestation of its existence. It required a long time for the earth, through the medium of vegetable productions, to produce the higher types of animal and vegetable organization. The lowest type of animal may produce sensation, and the highest type, being man, exhibits mind in its simplest degree, which is the flower of the animal kingdom, the specimens of which as yet correspond only to the rudest and simplest flowers of the vegetable kingdom comparatively. Man is the only animal on this earth that brings forth a flower which is now evincing signs of a fruit that will be a true state of human life, guided, governed, and directed by the spiritual man. The outward form will die, and man pass another transition, to commence a new and higher and more glorious sphere of development. Every lover of goodness and truth will hail with joy the new philosophy, as the positive sign of 'a good time coming.' It shadows forth distinctly the approaching commencement of that condition of earth and man portrayed more or less vividly by Isaiah, Daniel, Jesus, and the Revelation, and by Swedenborg and Fourier. The animal kingdom has yet to produce its more perfect flower, or spiritual manifestation, and through that, its fruit, a true state of human society.

"The great body of mankind, guided and directed by the blind theology and philosophy of the past, is inclined to oppose, obstruct, and retard this onward march as much as possible; wandering in darkness, ignorance, and disorder, with the back to the light, seeking by competition, strife, and antagonism for peace and unity; seeking in filth and depravity for purity and beauty. If men continue to seek thus, they may and will find at last, but perhaps as ignorantly and unexpectedly as the fool found a Messiah. More light, more truth, more knowledge is what we want, is what we seek, and a concerted action to live a true life, as well as to embrace the faith of a true brotherhood.   WARREN CHASE.

"CERESCO, WIS., March 20, 1848."

Up to this time the door to the other life was only ajar, and in a few places only through mesmerized subjects had the dwellers in that life begun to talk to us, and tell us of their existence and their relation to this world. I had sent several articles before this; but as the board of editors were not entirely freed from Christianity, I was no doubt a little too infidel in my language; besides, I was but a poor man, a laborer.

With the third year of its existence, and third volume, the *Univercœlum* succumbed to the popular prejudice expressed in all of the religious, and most of the secular press, and uttered with the vindictive spirit of persecution from the pulpits of nearly all sects; in some instances even that of the Universalists, which had borne and nearly outlived the persecution of the orthodox pulpits, joined their persecutors in abusing us for being as far in advance of them as they were of orthodoxy. It was currently reported and believed by many that the twelve apostles of the *Univercœlum* and a few others wished and designed to found a new religious sect, and to retain Mr. Davis as the oracle, and that he rebelled and broke up the plans; and as the phenomenal intercourse opened at Hydesville, N.Y., and rapidly spread from Rochester, to which city it was soon removed, and the elder sister of the Fox girls, Mrs. Fish, was added to the mediums, largely augmenting the mental strength and mediumistic force of the movement, of course the monopoly was broken, and its forces scattered. Mr. Davis, Mr. Brittan, and others remained firm in support of the spiritual origin of the phenomena, while some of the early advocates switched off upon the side-tracks, and stood still till death took them, or are there yet. Other papers started up in defence of the opened intercourse with the unseen world, in various localities, and each in its turn, after a short life, gave way to the pressure; but each contributed something to the cause, and none of it was lost, as all was seed scattered by the wayside, and some fell on good soil, and was not burned out by the scorching fires of sectarian persecution, or the vulgar ridicule of the drunken rabble which always echoes the voice of the pulpit when it is on the popular side in its persecutions. This was the fate of all of the many papers that started till the staunch old BANNER OF LIGHT put in an appearance to stay, but for several years in doubt of final success.

Thus somewhat crudely, and perhaps prematurely, I began my ministrations in and for the new philosophy or religion, if it was a religion, in the autumn of 1847, and with tongue and pen, to the best of my ability and with increasing knowledge, have I continued it, without ever taking in any of the absurdities or fanaticisms of the Christian sects. As our facts increased and our numbers multiplied, and we thus became strong, having outlived their scandalous attacks and abuse, they began to lessen their bitterness, and some of the best men in the pulpits began to introduce into their sermons and literature some of our philosophy and facts; and many of our advocates thought they were coming to us. Yet I did not, and do not, for their conventions and resolutions are still outspoken against Spiritualism; while many of those who either know or fully believe in spirit intercourse, visit and support the churches which, if they could, would crush us out and utterly destroy every vestige of our facts and the philosophy we teach. Previous to the rappings, nearly all of the advocates who had learned the facts of spirit intercourse even through Mr. Davis, who did not join them, were quasi-Christians, and held to the Bible and Christ; and they might have founded another Christian sect, into which I should never have entered as a member, after the open warfare commenced with the rappings, which the clergy and leading Christians were determined to put down, even though it could only be done by denouncing it as the work of the devil. With the rappings began the "irrepressible conflict," in which, as in chattel slavery, the truth will ultimately prevail.

CHAPTER III.

"THE POWERS I HAVE WERE GIVEN ME TO COST."

"Stern alternation now follows, now flies;
As under pain, pleasure, under pleasure, pain lies."

"Revere thyself, thou art so near allied
To angels, on thy better side.
How various e'er their ranks or kinds,
Angels are but unbodied minds.
When the partition walls decay,
Men emerge angels from their clay.
Yes, when the frailer body dies,
The soul asserts her kindred skies.
* * * * * * *
Know, then, who bow the early knee,
And give the willing heart to me,
Who wisely, when temptation waits,
Elude her frauds and spurn her baits,
Who dare to own my injured cause,
Though fools deride my sacred laws,
Or scorn to deviate to the wrong,
Though persecution lifts her thong;
Though all the sons of hell conspire
To raise the stake and light the fire,
Know for such superior souls
There lives a bliss beyond the poles,
Where spirits shine with purer ray
And brighten to meridian day;
Where love, where boundless friendship rules
(No friends that change, no love that cools);
Where rising floods of knowledge roll
And pour and pour upon the soul."

Not much progress had been made in spirit intercourse through mesmerized subjects when the intercourse with the spirit world was opened on the 31st of March, in Hydesville, N.Y., in a family of Methodists, who were not aware that the house was what was termed "haunted" when they moved into it, and who for a time were greatly annoyed by the various noises that could not be accounted for from any known physical cause. So much has been said and written by the three Fox sisters and their friends, and by writers of the history (the sisters still living as I write, and good mediums), that it is not necessary to say more about it here than what connects it with my life and my labors in the cause, as I have known them all for many years, as I did their honest and faithful old mother in the earlier years, of my work. From my earliest story-reading and story-listening I had read and heard much about haunted houses, and knew full well that in most cases the causes of the disturbances were not in the reach of the most careful and scrutinizing and searching parties, and there always was a mystery about them unexplained, and could not be put out of the popular mind by the ignorant ridicule that explained nothing, and never found the cause; but as I then had no knowledge of spirits, or of spirit life, of course I could not account for them till this one case opened the door and let in the light that covered all of the phenomena of a mysterious nature. In my mind, as in many others, arose the question why these occurred in certain houses and places, and not in others, and until we found the cause, that remained as much a mystery and wonder to us as a rainbow or an eclipse was to the ancients before they found the law of causes. But at last this mystery was solved by the fact that instant and sudden deaths in fright and fear, as in murder, left an aura in the place that often for years enabled the spirit, or spirits, to visit it on certain occasions, to make physical manifestations of their presence by sounds and by moving ponderable articles.

When our friends had opened correspondence with spirits in Hydesville and Rochester, and had learned that certain living bodies contained the necessary elements for producing the sounds, or "raps," that these sounds could be utilized as language, the key to a great mystery was found, a haunted house accounted for, and the ridicule and gossip of the unlearned and self-styled wise ones was turned back on them. Nothing in the time of phenomenal occurrences was better established as a fact, not even the mirage, than it was that certain houses were haunted, some of which even at this time are tenantless after being repeatedly rented and abandoned. It was and is equally well established that certain places where murders had been committed, and occasionally in graveyards, were sometimes seen, in peculiar conditions of the atmosphere, floating and fleeting phantom human forms; and these still are occasionally seen, frightening the ignorant and superstitious who will not, or dare not, learn the cause that produces them, which is now known to be spiritual. For many years the learned, unable to explain, endeavored to suppress all belief in them by denying their occurrence; but the constantly increasing honest and candid evidence thwarted all efforts to prove facts to be falsities, and owners of tenements found it impossible to find occupants for their houses when they had a reputation of being haunted. A noted instance of haunted house was that in which Brigham Young died, in Salt Lake City. I was told as I viewed the stately mansion, completely furnished, that not one of his many wives could live in it because it was haunted, and as they did not believe he could be there in spirit, they supposed it was the devil, or some one from the infernal regions.

How long this remained, or how long he haunted it, I do not know. Our discoveries of and in spirit life and intercourse enable us now to account for, explain, and to rationalize all such phenomena without any aid of supernaturalism, and without denying or setting aside the vast amount of honest testimony given in witness of well-established facts.

Witchcraft, which so long puzzled and troubled the world, and which led to much persecution and the cruel murders of hundreds of thousands of innocent persons, is now fully accounted for, as also is obsession and possession of individuals by some outside influence; conditions that before these discoveries were strange and mysterious, and frightened those who witnessed them. The Christian churches were the principal persecutors in all of these cases, pretending to know all about the spiritual world, about which they really knew nothing, and do not yet, except as a few members have investigated the spiritual phenomena. From the days of Augustine to the present, this has been the greatest obstacle to, and most bitter opponent of, any and all discoveries that explained the phenomena of nature, of life, death, and the results of death. The black cloud of mental and moral ignorance and superstition that caused the historical dark ages, was naught else than a cloud of Christian darkness at a time when the Church explained all natural phenomena by a divine revelation, and prevented, as long as it could, any and all discoveries that tended to enlighten mankind; and it occupies at this time the same position toward this last and greatest discovery which enables us to meet our friends and converse with them about their homes and condition in the life after death. It is not strange that they should be even more bitter in their opposition to this than to astronomy and geology, as this takes from them all power over the destiny of souls, and proves that they know but little about what they assume to know so much, and spend much time, talent, and money in darkening rather than enlightening their fellow-men.

Our discoveries of spirit life and the power of our spirit friends to communicate, and to diagnose disease and precribe for it through mesmerized subjects did not give us the key to unlock the mysteries of haunted houses and graveyard apparitions; but the physical phenomena at Hydesville and Rochester did, and hence the appropriate celebration of the 31st of March as the day on which, in 1848, the justly celebrated Fox girls began to converse, very imperfectly, with the intelligence that haunted that house, which has gone into history. I and a few friends at large had no sooner heard of these phenomena, than we sought eagerly everything published about them, taking the side at once of the spiritual origin and wondering greatly at the tardiness and neglect of the subject or apparent ignoring of it by our spiritual paper, the *Univercœlum*. As this paper did not publish my letters except the one already copied, up to the end of the first volume, May 29, 1848, and had not given us what we wanted to know about the new and great excitement then at Rochester, and called in ridicule the "Rochester knockings," we began to suspect its managers of designing to make a new religious sect, founded on natural divine revelations, and step out as far in advance of Universalism as that sect was in advance of Calvinism. We soon, however, learned that neither Mr. Davis nor the spirits that controlled his mental organism could be drawn into it, and that Mr. Brittan and several others were ready for a general and universal progress, instead of founding a new church. Fernald, Fishbough, and Ambler soon left us; but others took their places, and the work went on in a general and universal movement all along the line. To me it was ever evident that ultimately it would leave the old superstitions of the churches all out, and give us an entirely new system of belief and knowledge of the future.

Up to 1850 the lack of a Spiritual press through which I could express my convictions of the truth of spirit life and intercourse, without pandering to Christianity or its Bible, induced me to send the following article to the Boston *Investigator*, which never had and never has refused my articles, however strongly tinctured with Spiritualism, which it does not advocate.

"The Immortality of the Soul.

"Mr. Editor: This is an interesting subject when written upon with candor and argued with reason; but ridiculed egotism is neither interesting nor useful in this nor any other subject. I am glad to say it is less common in the *Investigator* than in most other papers. This subject seems to narrow down to a few important points: —

"*First:* Is the soul of man material? If it is, it seems to me few will deny that it is immortal in some form or forms, as every philosopher's mind must grant all matter to be. If it is not material, it is nothing, and hence it is neither mortal nor immortal, and it seems a waste of words to talk about nothing.

"*Second:* Is it a unit, or a combination of different material substances? If a unit, it is reasonable to suppose it may endure eternally, and not dissolve; if a chemical combination, it is reasonable to suppose it may dissolve and decompose, and hence lose its identity, as we know our bodies do after death.

"*Third:* Is it in human form, or in the form of our bodies, or has it an ambiguous form, as is taught by theology? In either case it will be likely, if composed of a simple substance and being a unit, to continue its form, for aught I can see, forever.

"*Fourth:* Is the will and intelligence in man composed of or connected with the soul, or are they appurtenances of the body? If the former, we may knowingly continue to exist; if the latter, it is of little account what becomes of the soul, or whether there be any such or not.

"I know this is filled with *ifs*, but there is little to be said in these days, without an *if*, except the positive assertion of some person, and that is not proof. Some will say these positions are all based on the assumption that man has a soul; but this question is involved in the first query, and leaves those who deny in whole or in part with the large majority of Christians who teach the immateriality of the soul. I have met with many of this kind of reasoners, and some of them logical ones; but they all admit that there is a *principle* of life. Some call it the vital fluid, some a nervous fluid, some a magnetic medium, some one name, and some another; but all admit that there is something or *a nothing* which keeps our bodies from decay during life, and by which this something moves the arm or leg, and moves other substances by using the arm and hand, etc.

"To me it seems absurd to say that *nothing* can perform these feats, or that an immaterial principle which has power to raise the arm, and by the arm and hand to operate against attraction. To me it does not seem reasonable, even for infidels, to believe that man (and perhaps the brute) possesses a soul, and that it pervades every part of the body, and hence is in human form; and that through and by this material medium the will, which is to the soul what the head is to the body, controls the motions and actions of the body; and since we all know there is a mysterious principle about us and our existence, I cannot see why this may not be invisible and yet material, why it may not be composed of electricity or some other of the infinite variety of material substances — imponderable, refined, and yet eternal in its form of existence; nor why that form may not be the human form as well as any other. To ask what life is, or what soul is, forms no argument. It matters little by what name we call it. It may be a substance for which we as yet have no name in chemistry or philosophy. One person may give it one name, and another some other name, as we already seem to do, while we do not differ more about its properties than its name. But is there life? Is there soul? Has *it* properties? Are they one or more? Or is life a property or a manifestation of the soul, which can separate from the body? are the more important questions.

"Nature, reason, and investigation will bring out and make plain the truth, in this science in due time, as in every other; but men's minds are generally in a poor condition to reason in this age of superstitious folly. They are more engrossed with such unmeaning words as 'supernatural,' 'immaterial substance,' 'heaven,' 'hell,' etc. It is more difficult to determine whether the soul is composed of one or many materials, than it is to determine its existence and identity, separate from the body. If it is composed of a combination of materials, nature teaches us that the chemical affinities will not always last and hold the parts together, and hence it may be subject to other changes like the death of the body after its separation from the body, but it may retain its form and identity after its separation from the body.

"To treat these theories as visionary or fanciful creations of the mind, is not to treat them with that candor and fairness which is to be expected from infidels. It seems to me to be about as much of a strain on natural powers to create a vision in the mind of man as for the minds of some to perceive and comprehend facts and existences which other minds do not. If the mind of man has power to create unreal scenes (which I doubt), and to dwell in them for a time, why not sustain them and dwell in them for ages? The vision of a night's or a day's sickness may be prolonged for aught I know, when the body has a sounder sleep or a final one, and at least I must have more than the cry of humbug to convince me that immateriality, whether in vision or by vision, ever assumes forms or paints scenes on the brain, so as to exist in memory when they do not exist in fact. It is to me some evidence of a real existence, material of course, when the mind perceives a form.

"In an infinite universe of materials of infinite variety of forms, I cannot conceive of one new form the mind of man can create, or that may not really exist; as for materials I should be very much narrowed in my ideas if I supposed man could take cognizance of all the matter that exists, or all of the materials of the universe of matter. To me it is at least an agreeable belief, that I possess *naturally* the power of mental perpetuity and individual identity. If I lose it, I shall never know my error; and if it be a vision of the mind, I shall certainly try to continue it after I have done with this life, which seems fully as much a vision."

The above was signed by me, and dated Ceresco, Wis., Sept. 14, 1850.

Up to the date of this letter I had seen very little of the physical manifestations and heard in only two or three instances of raps by spirits, but had repeated evidence of spirit life through communications and clairvoyance by mesmerized subjects, one instance of which nearly settled my mind and freed it from all doubts. While canvassing and speaking for the new political party, then called the Free Soil party, which by change of name became the Republican party in 1856, and of which I had called the first State Convention and presided over it in the town of Watertown, Wis., I stopped at the house of a friend who knew I had experimented in Mesmerism and advocated Spiritualism. While there he told me there was a school-teacher, a young lady, five or six miles from his house, with whom his family were acquainted, who had been mesmerized, and often saw strange visions; that she sometimes went under the influence herself. He said he would go and get her if I was desirous of seeing her, which, of course, I was, and it being Saturday, she could come. He went with horse and sleigh and brought her in the evening; but as she did not come into the parlor, I asked for her, and I was told she had a severe headache and was not able to sit for us. I remarked that I often cured headache, and perhaps could relieve her. Thereupon I was invited into the room where she was, and introduced to her, an entire stranger, having never seen her before or since to my knowledge. Making a few passes over her head, she apparently fell asleep, and I seated myself to await results. Very soon she turned to me, apparently asleep, or with closed eyes, and said, "Two little boys are here and call you *papa*." I asked, "Is any one with them?" and she said, "Yes; a young lady; and they say *auntie*." My two little boys, as before stated, had passed out of this life, preceded by a sister of their mother. I asked for their names, and she said, "The largest one says Martin [which was his name]. The other I cannot clearly understand; I took it to be Noys; he shakes his head, but it sounds like Noys." I asked, "Is it Norris?" and she at once said, "Yes; he confirms it." She then gave correctly the aunt's name, and they answered, as well as could be expected, my questions. The influence passed off; her headache was gone; she joined us in the parlor, and we spent a very interesting evening, with some general results confirming the fact that spirit life is a reality and within reach of our senses by proper and natural means. The facts stated by her could not have been known to her, and I know they did not go from my mind to her, for they were not in my mind at the time. I only cite this as one of many cases by which I became convinced before the physical phenomena had been much witnessed by me.

From 1847 to 1851 I had much to occupy my mind, as I had largely the settling of the affairs of the Phalanx, the cancelling of its stock, and dividing its surplus, and also had a large and leading interest in the affairs of the new political party, being its candidate for governor of Wisconsin at its first share in the elections; but amidst all of this I found time to investigate the spiritual phenomena, and was able and willing to defend the facts I witnessed, with both tongue and pen, and often did so, giving lectures whenever I could find a place, and interest enough to·bring an audience.

Among the early converts from the ranks of agnostics like myself was Apollos Munn of Springfield, Mass., who had his curiosity and intellect awakened, not by experiments, as I did, but by reading Mr. Davis' first book, and following up his interest by visiting the Fox family, and finally taking one (Margaretta) home with him, by and through whom he became fully convinced that the intelligence through the raps came from disembodied spirits, and that such beings did exist. Mr. Munn was an enthusiastic man; and while wearing away with consumption, became deeply interested in the new discovery. About the time of his conversion (if it could be called such), his sister, Angeline Munn, became a medium, and for many years did a good and faithful work as a medium, till her physical system was exhausted; and as I write these lines, January, 1886, she is still living, an aged and yet faithful worker in the cause, but too feeble to give more séances as a medium. Through her mediumship Dr. George Haskell of Rockford, Ill., was convinced, and became a faithful and excellent worker in convincing others, spending most of his time and a handsome fortune in the cause, a part of which he spent in publishing a paper in Rockford, Ill., and more in efforts to get up a school where spiritual truths and philosophy should have an equal chance with theology and physical science. He passed over to the other life from Ancora, N.J., where he made his last effort to found a school, with a very partial success for want of sufficient help and interest, which result he greatly deplored. For many years he did much to assist me in my work of explaining and extending the truth of spirit intercourse. Many others can trace their satisfactory evidence to Angeline Munn, as I found her doing a good work in my first visit to Springfield, and patiently waiting, as I saw her in 1886, for the messenger to take her over to a waiting husband and parents and brothers in the land she had so often described, and from which so many had come to her to be identified by their friends still lingering here.

In the summer of 1850 Apollos Munn and R. P. Ambler started the *Spirit Messenger*, the first really spiritual paper wholly devoted to the work of making known the fact of an open intercourse between the two worlds. Mr. Ambler represented the religious side of the subject; and Mr. Munn, the rational and natural side, which was the vital element of the paper. A. J. Davis was a constant and extensive contributor, and it contained much valuable matter from his pen. At the end of six months Mr. Munn was compelled to leave the work, as consumption, with its white hand, was already clipping the last threads that connected him with his body; and soon after (in 1851) he passed over to the other shore, when the paper fell wholly into the hands of a Christian Spiritualist, and soon died, as have all of that class of papers, the elements of the two never harmonizing, as they never can coalesce nor be wedded to each other. R. P. Ambler tried for a time to sustain himself by lecturing; but it was too hard and the pay too meagre for one who had been a clergyman, and he slid back into his old society of Universalists, repented of his heresy, and ever since has been preaching for them, and as little known and of as little account in the great cause of reform as a farmer in the mountains of Pennsylvania. Several others have since followed his course, and backed into the liberal churches as preachers, or, like him, been lost or worthless to the great cause, but secured an easy living, and shutting out the new light of spirit intercourse, ceased to grow and ceased to give light to others. A diluted Christianity is worthless, and a diluted Spiritualism is little better than none, as years of experience have proved.

In September, 1850, the following article from my pen appeared in the *Spirit Messenger*, which, like the others I have copied, shows the caution with which I advocated this new discovery and philosophy, and how strenuously I then tried, as I ever since have, to keep Spiritualism out of Christianity, and Christianity out of Spiritualism, having ever looked upon the dogmas of Christianity as the only poison Spiritualism was likely to take which would destroy its usefulness, if not its life. In this view many of its ablest defenders have agreed with me, among them Profs. Hare, William Denton, Henry C. Wright, Dr. Hallock, A. J. Davis, and Dr. H. F. Gardner.

"IDOLATRY.

"It will scarcely be denied by the candid and impartial observer of past and present religious history, that this is decidedly an age of idolatry. When we write for a civilized and Christianized condition of society, we need not allude to the worship of images of wood and stone, made in the forms of men or animals, of monsters or of ridiculous idols, for all will acknowledge that they who worship such images or supplicate them by prayers are idolaters. It is to another class of intelligent beings, nearer home, that I wish to call attention, and see if the charge can be made to bear against them. Is there not in our very midst, and comprising a large and respectable class of worthy and moral, as well as unworthy and immoral, citizens, many who have crucified reason — the true saviour — and, with a blind devotion, superstitious fear, and constrained belief in the Christian Bible, set up that as an image, to which they pay their devotions in the same manner as do the heathen to images of wood and stone, — make the literal reading of the so-called sacred book the test by which the truth of every discovery in science must be tested, and reject every truth unfolded by God's true act, the book of nature, unless they can see it confirmed by the language in this image of perfection to them? It is true they are divided into sects, and can partially see the idolatry of each other in all except Bible worship, which contains all of their doctrines, and in devotion to that they are nearly all agreed. The Protestants can see the superstition and folly, if not the idolatry, of the Catholics in their worship of the cross and image of the 'Holy Virgin,' of relics, etc. The early Methodists could see the blind folly and ignorant devotion of the Church of England to its written prayers and pompous ceremonies, its costly churches built by the forced labor and pilfered earnings of the suffering producers of all wealth, whose souls were of little value in the scheme of salvation. The Unitarians could see the folly of Trinitarians in the worship of a God born of a woman, and at the same time the creator of countless millions of worlds, which had been revolving in space for countless ages before our world had existence as a planet; and they could see that the teachings, being true, could call for no worship of the teacher. The Universalists could see the folly and absurdity of teaching the love of a God who held his children in submission by the fear of hell and never-ending torments for those who do not believe the absurd stories, while belief is involuntary. The Quakers could realize the error of those who were governed by the Word and outer signs, and neglected the promptings of the monitor within; but all, with many other sects of worshippers, each rejecting some error of its neighbor, remained in blind devotion to the idol of the Christian, the infallible Bible. With them, reason must not criticise its sayings; nature must not be allowed to introduce new truths, to conflict with any statements therein: if it did, nature is wrong. Geology must bind her stupendous truths and have them cramped into the Word, even though it destroy them and the science. Phrenology must be put down, for it conflicts with the Bible. Mesmerism, clairvoyance, Spiritualism, with all their light, must be crushed out by the law and religion, for they are infidelity, and will surely destroy the worship of the Book if allowed to spread, even though they teach truths which, if adopted or lived, would bring about a higher and better life than any truths revealed since the Nazarene taught the poor fishermen in the open air among the hills and along highways, when he struggled with poverty, unheard, except by a few mendicants, on the burning sands and frosty hills of his rude and rocky country, scarcely known and little heard of for hundreds of years after he lived, *if he lived at all.*

"That the Bible contains some truths none will deny; that it teaches some good lessons none will deny; but so does the Koran, so does the Zend Avesta: yet this does not teach either of them worthy in their entire contents the confidence of the human mind. If any one supposes all truth is contained in the Bible, it is a childish error, unworthy a progressive mind. If it does not, how can it be worthy the devotion of mankind? Truth is worthy of our confidence and adoration, but a truth is no better in the Bible than in a novel or an almanac. If we examine closely, we shall find very few truths in the Bible of importance to man's happiness in this life or the next, and they may be found elsewhere, and its historic statements are not to any great extent reliable, being mixed with fables and unacceptable marvels. All churches, however wide apart in creeds and doctrines, have the same sacred and holy Bible, filled with the errors of all the creeds, as each can see them in its neighbors. Reason must not criticise nature, and reason must not conflict with its infallible words. The truth is, the Bible is the idol of all Christian sects, or rather their earthly idol; and there can be little progress in a human mind till this idol is given up to reason and criticism, and tried for its truths by reason and science and history, and these will utterly ruin its claim to authenticity. It is a truth none can deny, that the fear of hell has made more converts to Christianity than the love of God or the early beauty of Christian teachings. Most have not been led by love, but driven by fear, to a doctrine, to the book, and the churches. When the time shall come, as it surely will, that every intelligent and honest person will abandon the worship of idols of all kinds, and be governed by reason, then will all truth be collected and arranged to compose a guide for human actions, bring happiness to mankind, and destroy sectarianism. The blind idolatry of this age has a stronger hold on the human heart than most people are aware of, but it is beginning to weaken. The rope of sand will soon break asunder; the penetrating light and heat of science and true revelations shall penetrate it and crumble it to pieces. When the crucified saviour REASON shall rise again, it will lead the nations from their idols of wood, or stone, or priest, or heaven-pointing spire, or Bible book of huge proportions occupying some conspicuous place in the Christian church or Christian family. W. C.

"CERESCO, WIS., Sept. 2, 1850."

In the first number of the *Spirit Messenger*, Editor Munn, who found in "Nature's Divine Revelations" what I did, says of the book: "It needs only to be read consecutively, carefully, and analytically, to carry to the mind irresistibly the conviction of its perfect philosophy and intrinsic truth. It may be denounced, but its arguments can never be refuted. Its facts and its philosophy, appealing directly to reason and the superior faculties of the soul for credence, have obtained a firm foundation in the very heart of humanity, thus furnishing an impregnable fortress for the faith that is in us, against whose imperishable walls of truth, error will dash itself only to fall mutilated and powerless to earth." Editor Ambler says in the same number: "'The beautiful sentiment standing at the head of our columns will be at once recognized as forming the leading sentence in the preface of that stupenduous work, 'Nature's Divine Revelations.' It is, 'Brethren, fear not, for error is mortal and cannot live, and truth is immortal and cannot die!'" In this paper William Fernald is advertised to lecture on the Harmonial Philosophy; but when through the rappings and tippings and other rude forms and modes of manifestation the spirit world sent its messages to "publicans and sinners," he soon turned back to the "flesh pots" of the New Jerusalem Church, as Ambler did later to those of the Universalist Church. H. D. Barron, still an able and faithful defender of the truth, and who, with E. H. Capron, published the second truthful pamphlet record of the spirit rappings at Hydesville, is mentioned as an agent of the *Messenger*. John H. W. Toohey, who did a good work tardily and is still with us, but greatly slackened in that element, which was always too slack, is also mentioned as an agent. My old and highly esteemed friend, and publisher of several of my works, Bela Marsh, then on earth and on Cornhill, Boston, is mentioned as an agent. I see in the *Messenger* a communication from Dr. Webster and Dr. Parkman, the two celebrated murdered men in Boston, — one murdered by law, and the other without it, — through the elder of the Fox sisters, in which they announce themselves as reconciled. In the issue of November 2 is a notice of spiritual messages through the raps in Athol, Mass. Also a notice that in seven or eight places in Providence, R.I., the spirits were communicating to mortals. Another earnest and faithful worker, long since gone, T. S. Sheldon of Randolph, N.Y., is registered in the *Messenger*.

In these early years of spirit intercourse, and for fifteen or twenty years of my first public advocacy, it was all a person's reputation and almost all a person's life was worth to publicly defend it. As the other world was discovered to be a veritable fact instead of a fiction, as it was in the hundred thousand temples of our country, dedicated to the unknown gods, and was putting knowledge into the possession of the people in place of the blind faith and hope which were taught in these temples by the seventy thousand ordained clergymen, who obtained their salaries by keeping up a belief without knowledge in their varied and various theories, no two of which were alike, and in presenting pictures of heaven, hell, god, and devil; and as they knew this knowledge would finally supersede all of their theories, of course it aroused all of the bitterness and malignity in their natures, and many of them were not lacking in this quality of mentality. I had abandoned a most flattering political prospect, neglected all financial pursuits, and was giving my time and talents to this new discovery, which seemed to me to be of the greatest value to our race. This I did because it seemed destined to remove the necessity of supporting the enormous expense of the churches, by substituting a knowledge of another life beyond the veil of death, and to prove that the churches had saved no souls, had never taught any correct theory of another life, or even proved there was any soul or life after death, and now seemed unwilling we should. Among the meanest and most rabid of these clerical opponents who took it upon himself to silence me was a Rev. Henry Drew, of whom a bad report followed from the East. He came to Ceresco and found a few Methodists and more enemies of Spiritualism, and began his lying and scandalous abuse of me and kept it up with tongue and pen for years, greatly to the annoyance of my family and friends. Covered with his cloak of religion and clerical title, he was able to find plenty of opportunities to work his social mischief and feed his corrupt mind on the popular prejudice against all who took part in defending the new truth. He had the advantage of me, as I was much of the time away from home, while he was working up his lies about my actions during my absence; but I proposed a discussion with him in his own church, to which he consented provided I would take the Bible to defend it, which I did successfully, as the audience plainly recognized. On one occasion when in a sermon he was telling some falsehood about me, my son, being in the meeting, spoke out and said, "That is a lie, sir," to which he made no reply, as he had told plenty before. He tried hard to make people believe I was socially and morally what he was himself, and it took me many years of toil and trial and trouble to outlive his lies, which would not have found believers had I not been advocating the unpopular teachings of Spiritualism. I only allude to this one of many enemies because he attacked me at my home, while in many places where I went to lecture, letters were sent before me by unknown parties, warning the people against me as an outrageous infidel and social renegade, who had left his family to suffer, when no family was more devoted to a husband and father, and no husband and father more faithful in providing than I was, as they always have borne testimony. During all these trials nothing but an indomitable firmness and consciousness of the valuable truth I had in my possession could keep me in the field; while no scandal or persecution could drive me out, and no political allurement draw me from it, for both forces were about me, and the lies and scandal of the preachers would have been no obstacle to my success politically if I would have given up to it and abandoned my public defence of spirit intercourse. Neither in that early time of trials and mental suffering, not always exempt from physical, nor in later years, when political promotion was open to me, did I for a moment give up my devotion to this cause or neglect it for any work that would prevent my public defence of spirit life.

During these early years of my itineracy I went over much of the settled portion of Wisconsin, of Northern Illinois, and into St. Louis, having good meetings in the latter city, by the aid of A. Miltenberger, John Mellen, Mr. Hedges, Mr. Freleigh, and Dr.. Britt and Mrs. Britt (since Mrs. Spence), who has been one of our ablest speakers for many years, and done much for the cause. Thomas Gales Forster I also found early in the field at St. Louis. He was one of our best trance-speakers, and did a noble work for many years, until his health forced him to retire from the rostrum. In Chicago I found D. A. Eddy and a very few others, and there I hired a hall and gave a course of lectures. Being very poorly paid everywhere, I felt severely the deficit of $12 in the receipts to cover expenses, but remarked to my friends that it would come back in time; and surely it did, when a crowded audience in the largest hall in the city paid me $25 a lecture through the week; and to some less conspicuous extent the same was true in many other places. In my early visits to New York City I found T. L. and Mary Gove Nichols, Stephen Pearl Andrews, Dr. Hallock, Dr. Gray, Judge Edmonds, Dr. Dexter, and a few others, but not acting in harmony, as the Nicholses and Andrews had some unpopular socialisms; yet all admitted that spirits had opened intercourse with this world, and that was my theme. The Nicholses and Josiah Warren had started a colony for their social views at Modern Times, L.I., and were anticipating great results from their extreme social radicalism; but the popular prejudice was too strong, and it had to be abandoned. It was at this settlement I first met our champion writer and speaker, Emma Hardinge (now Britten), and before she had taken the pen or the rostrum in defence of our cause. She was a remarkable medium, but I never knew that she sympathized with the settlement at Modern Times. I had then been several years on the rostrum, and had then, as I have at this writing, January, 1886, given more lectures in small places on the subject than any one else, and up to this date have never failed to meet an appointment from sickness or personal cause, and only a few times been snowed in so I could not reach the place. Very few persons have done more for our cause with the pen, and not many with the tongue, than Emma Hardinge Britten; but in her history of Spiritualism in Europe and America she has shown the failing so common to mortals of personal likes and dislikes, and probably had me in the dislikes. Not from my early acquaintance with her, but probably because I defended Victoria C. Woodhull, as I would any man or woman that the churches tried to put down. As I had never had any domestic troubles, I felt able as well as willing, in this and every case, to sustain, so far as I justly could, every victim of social tyranny, and every one who tried to reform society by exposing its corruption in high places, and this I considered the work of Mrs. Woodhull. And when the fight came with the churches and popular corruption, I defended her; and as Emma wrote largely for the Christian Spiritualists, it would not do to give credit to an infidel Spiritualist, however much he might have done; and especially one that defended the persecuted socialists, even if he did not indorse their theories to the extent they proclaimed them. She could not have failed to know I had been the first to take the rostrum in defence of spirit intercourse, and that from the first publication of a paper in its defence my pen had been writing for it, as it has in some published article nearly every week since, and that I had been several years an editor as well as speaker. But it does not hurt me to be left, and only hurts the party by leaving out items of value in a history.

CHAPTER IV.

"Beware of desperate steps. The darkest day
(Live till to-morrow) will have passed away."

"Reason's whole pleasure, all the joys of sense,
Lie in three words — health, peace, and competence;
But health consists with temperance alone.
And peace, O virtue! Peace is all thy own."

"Deeper than all sense of seeing
Lies the secret source of being,
And the soul with truth agreeing,
Learns to live in thoughts and deeds;
For the life is more than raiment,
And the earth is pledged for payment,
Unto man for all his needs."

IT is doubtful whether any person not schooled in adversity and suffering, as I had been, and as related in my autobiography, "The Life Line," would, or could, have withstood the oppositions met with in the early years of public defence of our glorious gospel of good news to all people in all ranks and grades of life, and which the churches so bitterly opposed because it came to all people and could not be controlled by the priests. The buffetings of Satan were as nothing to the buffetings of the churches, backed by all the scandalous gossipers who are ever ready to aid them in their efforts to put down and out any new discovery that will deprive them of any part of their control over the people. I seemed to have been designed for my work, or consecrated to it by my introduction into this life, or by the death of my mother and her work as a spirit, for I was early and ever in the advance guard in all public reform measures; ever opposed to war as a barbarism unworthy of, and a disgrace to, any enlightened nation, as there could be no civilized nation with a military power; ever opposed to capital punishment as utterly barbaric and only worthy of a religion that advocated an endless hell as a part of its "plan of salvation"; ever opposed to the administering of oaths, as a piece of nonsense with no sacred obligation in it. I have ever been in favor of perfect equality of the sexes in and out of marriage; and long before Mrs. Stanton or Miss Anthony began their good work I had borne the sobriquet of "The Ladies' Advocate," because I advocated female suffrage and other rights for the sex. I was ever opposed to land monopoly, and among the early advocates of land limitation with titles confined to occupancy. I was ever opposed to chartered banks and laws regulating money, and in favor of the most rigid restrictions in all chartered corporations, to prevent monopoly; ever in favor of having the government make all of the currency, and supplying an amount for the business, so that people could pay as they purchase, and prevent the excessive usury and Shylock robbery; ever in favor of taxing church property the same as the property of other corporations and individuals; ever opposed to all laws for the collection of debt and imprisonment for debt; ever opposed to the employment of chaplains in Congress, in legislatures, and in the army and navy; ever in favor of temperance and every measure calculated to prevent dissipation, and opposing all license laws as wrong in principle, and advocating the prohibition by law of the importation of intoxicating liquors and the suppression of distilleries by the national government. In many other lesser reforms my tongue and pen have been active for the forty years of this public pilgrimage, among them an unswerving opposition to tobacco in all its forms, as one of the greatest curses that encumber our social life. Standing out on all of these reforms, mostly in opposition to the churches, and then publicly defending the spiritual phenomena and the mediums, made me a target for many shafts.

Among those who volunteered and enlisted in this cause during the first five years of its existence as distinctive Spiritualism, and who may be said to have answered the first call for volunteers, and who, as I write this in January, 1886, just after passing my seventy-third annual mile-stone, are still living on this stratum of earth with me, as I now recall them, is John M. Spear, the prisoners' friend, as he was called when I first found him in Boston. A medium and a more faithful and devoted servant of the spirit world has not been found in our ranks. He held on to this life at that date (he has since passed over), but had passed his working days, which were taken up by his faithful wife. Mr. and Mrs. A. E. Newton I also found at the same time, and two more honest, conscientious, and indefatigable workers we have never had with us. C. L. Sholes, who was with me in the Wisconsin State Senate in 1848–49, was with me in defence of this cause with his able pen, as early as it was a cause, and he still holds on to it and to life in Milwaukee, Wis. Joel Tiffany, than whom the cause had no abler public advocate for ten years or more, is to-day still bound for the same haven, but has taken passage on a legal boat. Jeremiah Hacker, former editor and publisher of the Portland *Pleasure Boat* and *Chariot of Love*, all his life a reformer and good worker in the reforms, is still lingering, now in his ninetieth year, and is now in New Jersey raising sweet potatoes and writing poetry, but too deaf to hear the angels whisper, and has some doubts about a real future life. Dr. Dillingham, of Boston, is well known to the old pioneers, and still lives.

R. P. Ambler and T. L. Harris, they, with many others, backed out and into the Christian army when the shots came too hot and heavy from the pulpits; but both have lived to see their errors, I think, though they may not acknowledge it. A. Miltenberger, of St. Louis, and Mrs. Spence are still with me, and have lived to see, as I have, their highest anticipations realized in the cause. John S. Adams and his wife Hattie — she an early and excellent medium — are still in the good work on our side of the death line. Parker Pillsbury, who in the anti-slavery controversy had found the Christian church on the wrong side, found it the same on this subject, and is still defending truth and justice on the rostrum. Cora L. V. Scott, now Mrs. Richmond, came in among the early mediums when quite young, and through her mediumship brought her parents and many others into the ranks. She is still one of the best speakers and mediums we have, and has done as much as any one in her work to advance the cause. The three Fox sisters, Leah, Maggie, and Kate, are all with us yet, and as faithful and good as ever. Of course I need not say they were the first to open, through a haunted house, the intercourse with spirits that haunted it, and thereby opened a more general intercourse. Rachel Lukens, now Mrs. Chase, — daughter of the late David Lukens of Morrisville, Pa., — near Trenton, N.J., and one of the early defenders of spirit intercourse, is still efficiently engaged in linking the two worlds together, after many years of faithful service as a medium, in which work she began about the same time the Fox family did. Anna M. L. Potts, M.D., at present a very popular lecturer on physiology, hygiene, and kindred subjects, was also with Miss Lukens, an early believer, but her popularity in other fields of public service has prevented her from saying much about it. Dr. H. T. Child, of Philadelphia, came in very early, and is still advocating it in the meeting of the Society of Friends, to which he returned to escape the entanglements of Spiritualists and their discords. His old friend, H. B. Diott, for many years a faithful worker in the cause, partially fell from grace in later years, or became spiritually paralyzed; while Mr. Wren, another of the Philadelphia pioneers, lingers, leaning toward agnosticism. Dr. John Mayhew came early into the cause and did faithful service many years, and does yet, in his private way, connected with his office in Washington, D.C.

There are many more still living here who joined us in the first campaign during the first five years of my public work, and who were and still are known to me, but whom I cannot register, as I only intended to name a few of those well known to the public by their public labors; but I should be glad to have justice done to all such noble and faithful workers as dared to face the host of enemies in those trying times. Many who came in later, and have won a well-deserved fame in the cause, did not have to endure the trials and hardships of these early pioneers whose names should be preserved in the true history of Spiritualism.

I must add a few from the list of pioneers who have gone up higher, yet are still in the good work as earnestly as ever. Of these I speak in each case from my personal knowledge, so far as their belief and interest is concerned, but leave their public records to other history and friends. Among those best known to the public are President Abraham Lincoln, Vice-President Henry Wilson, Senator B. F. Wade, Senator Howard of Michigan, Ex-Senator and Ex-Governor Tallmadge of Wisconsin, Hon. Gerrit Smith, Hon. Joshua R. Giddings, William Lloyd Garrison, Judge Edmonds, Judge and Colonel Charles H. Larrabee, who was burned to death in a palace car on the California Southern Pacific Railroad, Dr. R. T. Hallock, and Dr. Gray of New York. Dr. Hallock was one of our ablest speakers. Dr. H. F. Gardner and Rufus Elmer of Springfield, Mass., Drs. Samuel and Abel Underhill of Ohio, both among our first workers and never flinching before any foe. Professor Hare and Professor Mapes were not personally known to me. Lydia Dennett of Portland, a very intelligent old lady, who for years furnished a home for reformers, as A. J. Davis, Parker Pillsbury, and myself can testify, deserves notice as having done a good work for the cause. Judge Lawrence of Ann Arbor, Mich., was early and faithful in the cause. Judge Boardman of Illinois did early and faithful service in Waukegan, whereof J. C. Smith, now of Washington, D.C., early became an open advocate, and is yet. Seldon J. Finney, an early medium and eloquent speaker, who started in Ohio and died in California. Dr. O. H. Wellington of New York, a very early advocate. Mrs. Semantha Mettler, first of Buffalo, N.Y., and later of Hartford, Conn., deserves more than a passing notice in a history of Spiritualism, as few among those of us who have "blown our own horns" have done more real good and successful work than she did. Mr. Alvin Adams, founder of the Adams Express Company, who early provided myself and others a home of elegance and refinement, through her obtained much valuable information relating to both worlds and fully appreciated it. A Mrs. Spaulding of Waukegan, Ill., was one of our earliest mediums, the first one reported as having writing come out on the arm, and the first one I saw before Charles II. Foster had that phase of wonderful mediumship, and in which he wore out his life and did much to convince the world of the truth of our cause. The father and mother and other relations of Cora L. V. Scott came early into the work, and never deserted it. There was a Mrs.

French of Pittsburgh and St. Louis, and last of New York City, who did a good work, and was for some years a sort of patron saint of Emma Hardinge, but seems to have been left out in the cold in all notices except this. Fanny Burbank Felton came out early through Mrs. Metler, and was many years a faithful worker and a good one. Fanny C. Allyn, still on the rostrum, was early in the field, and has left many subjects for thought among her listeners in her wide and long course of lecturing. An Ex-Reverend Averill of Battle Creek, Mich., came early in and worked faithfully till he went over. He helped out A. B. Whiting, a brilliant speaker, and also Dr. Slade and Mrs. Emma Tuttle and Emma Jay (since Bullene), and a faithful and good public worker. In Michigan and Wisconsin the cause started early and had many advocates in the first campaign. Francis Barry of Philadelphia deserves much more than I can say for his good work; and Lucretia Mott, a faithful friend of Mrs. Chase, then Rachel Lukens, and now a glorious spirit, glorious for the good work she did here. Mrs. Hattie Huntley of Paper Mill Village, N. H., a good medium and speaker, stepped out boldly to the work, and was soon stricken down by heart disease and passed over, and is nearly forgotten, but should not be.

Among those who volunteered, in the last half of the first decade of Spiritualism, were many noble workers who have gone over to the other life, and many who are still with us in the work. Our grand and noble sister, Achsa W. Sprague, whose brilliant career was short, Mrs. M. G. Townsend Wood, still in the field, Dr. Wellington, Dr. Buchanan, Dr. Dutton, Dr. E. A. Smith and his noble wife, Fanny Davis Smith,— all active workers yet,—with many I cannot name, equally entitled to be remembered. Emma Hardinge Britten is perhaps as extensively known as any one, through her pen and lectures in this country and England. Dr. Slade came into this class. Dr. J. V. Mansfield entered on his glorious public world-wide work, and Dr. H. B. Storer, who deserves a heaven if any one does, and scores whose names are not recorded, and who are forgotten at this early date except by a few relatives, and soon will be by them; even their graves will be forgotten, and the good service they rendered in this cause only remembered by themselves or in the spirit world. Visiting Louisville, Ky., in 1886, I found traces of a good work left there in some minds by one of our ablest but short-lived mediums and speakers, Mr. A. B. Whiting, who was even then almost forgotten in his native State of Michigan, where he attained his mediumship, which was remarkable and of a highly intellectual order. In that same year I found in Connecticut many precious recollections of the eloquent discourses of Mrs. Charlotte Tuttle, another of Michigan's early mediums, who lost her life by her over-exertions in our cause, and left her body at Winsted, Conn. At this time of writing, still another of Michigan's good workers is in the form, — Emma J. Bullene, who was known to me when a child, and for many years was a faithful wife and mother, as well as lecturer in our field. I cannot here recall and record more than one in ten of those I knew in these early years of my labor; but their names and labors are still sacred to me, as far as I can recall them. In the fall of 1886 I lectured in one of the meeting-houses in Somersville, Conn., built by and presented to the society of that place by our elder, Brother Hall, with several thousand dollars to support it, — a worthy example for others more able than he was.

Among the comets that have blazed through the horizon of Spiritualism with a brilliant, fiery trail and moved on into space, Mrs. Victoria C. Woodhull was the most conspicuous on record, and Thomas L. Harris the next. Laroy Sunderland was, no doubt, the third. Then came lesser and more transient visitors,—T. L. and Mary Gove Nichols, Charley Hayden, F. L. Wadsworth, W. F. Jamieson, who did a noble work and is not doing badly now, but has drifted into the shades of agnosticism, and does not give any spiritual light. Cephas B. Lynn and Brother Houghton seem to have been small comets or meteors, as their light has gone out with Brother Ambler's. J. M. Peebles also proved to be a blazing religious comet in our horizon, but left a permanent light in some valuable books. Capt. H. H. Brown shone brightly, but ran under a Unitarian banner for protection from the scorching sun of persecution, that dried up the financial fountain too much for his support. Thomas R. Hazard did a noble work in the cause with his tongue and pen, and never relaxed till he passed, an octogenarian, to the higher life, following the scores of my old friends and co-laborers whose names even I cannot now recall to record here ; and, as I cannot do justice to them, I may as well pass on to my personal narrative of an active and closing life on earth, but not till I name Henry C. Wright and Jesse B. Ferguson, brilliant fellow-laborers, and from whom I often get messages that encourage and strengthen me in my work ; and I should mention here that the first work published explaining the rappings in Hydesville was issued by E. E. Lewis of Canandaigua, N.Y., in 1848 ; and the next by Capron and Barron, which had a large and rapid sale. Dr. O. H. Wellington and Charles Partridge introduced the rappings and the Fox girls in New York City, and John S. Adams and his wife Hattie got up the first lectures in Boston, assisted by Dr. A. B. Child ; and also for me the first in Chelsea, Mass.

During the first ten years of my labors in this field and on the rostrum, closing with 1857, the items and incidents of importance are recorded in my autobiography, "The Life Line," and need not be repeated here, as every reader of this book ought to read that, and read it first. Those who can get files of the first papers devoted to our cause, and copies of the first books, will find much in them that I could not record here from memory, or copy if I had them; but I regret that there has been no library kept by any one in which these early records have been preserved, as they should have been sacredly, and the names of the early members and many martyrs sacredly recorded; but they have gone over with our blessings, and been received on the other side as martyrs for the glorious gospel of good news to all men and women on earth, and their works do follow them for their reward. Only a very few of the early pioneers who took an active part in the first decade of this cause are with us yet in earth life, but among them are Capron and Barron, the early publishers, whose works antedate any newspaper devoted to it, but not the articles in the New York *Tribune*, then owned by Horace Greeley, but which now, under Whitelaw Reid, has degenerated into a tool and servant of the most oppressive aristocracy and tyranny. During those early years of my labors in the cause, no tongue can now tell and no pen can now write the terrible ordeal of persecution through which I passed socially, from the scandalous falsehoods circulated about me, and often taken up and extended by prejudiced Spiritualists who had some personal end to accomplish; but by the aid of my spirit friends I continued on my course and in my work, always assured by them that I should outlive it all, and rise to the plane of life I have now reached.

Among the best and noblest early workers in spreading the new gospel, and one who lived up to its highest and purest teaching, was William White, who came in early to the support of Brother Luther Colby, with financial aid to the support of the *Banner of Light*, which must have gone under in the pressure without his aid, as Brother

Colby could not support it without financial aid; and no person could better appreciate the assistance rendered by this good man than did Brother Colby at this time, and until his sudden departure to the higher life in April, 1873, of which event the following brief note informed me: —

"Boston, April 28, 1873. — BROTHER CHASE: We are in the midst of sorrow. Brother White is dead — gone home to live with the angels. He died suddenly in a horse-car to-day. 'In the midst of life we are in death.' Yours truly, LUTHER COLBY."

No one out of the office and the home circle felt this loss among our able and faithful workers more than I did, for we all loved the one so suddenly taken from us. In the autumn of 1887 Dr. Abel Underhill and John M. Spear, two octogenarians and early workers, left us and followed the many who had preceded them to the better life, soon after followed by our venerable and universally esteemed Allen Putnam of Boston, whose works will long remain to testify to his faithful labors in our cause. His years neared the close of eighty-six, as he passed on in the fall of 1887, preceded by his last wife, long a faithful medium, once Fanny Remick. Each of these aged workers passed gloriously through the gate of death, as the friends testify who were present at the change. Just now, as I write this, at the close of November, 1887, the earth is fresh and new over the body of John Tarbox of Worcester, an octogenarian, and one of the earliest and most faithful devotees of our cause to the last. A large family had preceded him to spirit life, where he joined them a few days ago, passing out of this life by cancer. I often wish I had kept a record of the many prominent workers who took part with us, and also a record of what changes took place in their lives. It would show many martyrs among the mediums who deserve the crowns they wear in the other life. Seth Hale and wife, now in Worcester as I write, aged and able, intelligent and faithful to the knowledge they have, are doing what they can, as are many others here and in many other places. Early in December, 1887, Horace M. Richards, an aged and faithful worker in New York, passed on; and at his funeral reported his safe arrival in spirit life, as many others have since this mediumistic door has been left ajar.

CHAPTER V.

THE POLITICIAN.

"It is indeed an easy task
To hide behind some pleasing mask,
And mingling with the swelling crowd,
Shout what they shout both long and loud."

"They are slaves who fear to speak
For the fallen and the weak;
They are slaves who dare not be
In the right with two or three."

"The times demand new measures and new men.
The world advances, and in time outgrows
The laws that in our fathers' days were best.
The time is ripe, and rotten-ripe for change.
Then let it come; I have no dread of what
Is called for by the instinct of mankind,
Nor think I that God's world will fall apart
Because we tear a parchment more or less.
Truth is eternal, but her effluence
With endless change is fitted to the hour;
Her mirror is turned forward to reflect
The promise of the future, not the past;
For men in earnest have no time to waste
In patching fig-leaves for the naked truth."

AFTER the long and weary years of toil and struggling with poverty, as related in "The Life Line," at the age of thirty-three a new line of life began to open before me. I was then in the Wisconsin Phalanx, trying the Fourier system of social life, which did not prove to be adapted to the American people at that nor at this time, for reasons I shall not present here. In that year I learned that I was, and had been for fourteen years, poisoning my system with tobacco, and I left it forever, and its use has never been acquired by any of my descendants to this time of writing. In this year, 1846, I was elected by the county of Fond du Lac, Wis., to a constitutional convention, as before stated. I was politically sound as a Democrat. I had written articles on land reform, partially advocating what Henry George has so ably set forth in his late works, and there had some of them been translated into German, and published in a paper in that language in the eastern end of our county. This gave me the extra votes that elected me; it was my radicalism that elected instead of defeating me. I went into that convention (which gave me place as one of the fathers of the State in later years) a novice in legislative political life, but with a capacity for public speaking somewhat developed by publicly advocating the rights of colored persons and women as equal before the law in States where slavery did not exist and was not protected by the Constitution, and by working up the social question to a point where we began our experiment, as also by academic declamations and lyceum discussions. In that turbulent convention, whose work was too radical for the conservative condition of the people and had to be defeated by them, I found myself with the most liberal and radical minds, and often in advance of them, as in the matter of woman suffrage, which I introduced in committee of the whole and had no supporters; but on negro suffrage I had a dozen votes with me, and all of them Whigs, as no Democrat but myself dared to vote for it. My first speech was against capital punishment; and on the rights of married women to property which came to them from others than their husbands, I took active part, and this more than any one article caused the defeat of our work. I also opposed banks and banking, and, as far as possible, all monopolies and extra powers for them. The active part I took on the side of the people in this convention, and my articles in the papers, for which I wrote often, rapidly made me quite popular with the laboring classes, and the poor and oppressed, which popularity I have never lost, and in which I have never ceased to sympathize and labor in public and private, with tongue and pen.

In spite of our efforts this constitution was defeated. Out of over one hundred and ninety members, only six were returned to the convention in 1847, to prepare a second; but my county returned me by a large vote, though it gave a meagre support to the labor of the first. The leading politicians who were anxious for the offices were now very anxious to get into the Union of States and Congress, and urged us to be sure and not encumber the new work with objectionable articles, as it was desirable to get into the Union in time to have a vote in the presidential election of 1848. In this convention the journal shows more references to me than to any member of the body, and by it more than by memory I know that I did my share of the work, even as before, on the reform and radical side of every question; and I think some of my work is still a part of the fundamental law of the State. My pen was as active as my tongue, and several papers were open to my articles and glad to get them, and by them I identified myself more and more with the laboring and oppressed classes, to which I had all my life belonged. Our work this time was readily accepted, and the State at once admitted into the Union. State machinery was at once put in motion, and Fond du Lac and Winnebago Counties, being a senatorial district, nominated and elected me to the Senate for the two years' term to which it was entitled. During all this time I had steadily refused to be sworn into office or as a witness or juror, in which capacity I had served, but affirmed, as the Society of Friends do, believing the oath a farce — which opinion

THE SPIRITUAL ROSTRUM. 67

I still hold—and of no value, except for the penalty of telling an untruth, and utterly worthless in qualifying an officer. Later in life, though considering it a useless farce, I accepted it and qualified with others.

At this time I had become fully satisfied that spirit life was a reality and spirit intercourse opened, and never failed to advocate and defend both in public and private, never discovering that it injured me politically. In the two sessions of the Senate I took a very active part in all its business, seldom missing a session or a vote any day; and in the second session I was one of the committee of three on this judiciary, though not an attorney at law. I was an advocate of many reforms, some successful, and some considered Utopian by our conservative body. C. Latham Sholes and myself, both Spiritualists, were called the David and Jonathan of the Senate, as we had joint desk and seats, and boarded and roomed together, and usually voted the same way. In the second session we adopted the commissioners' report of revision of the statutes, adapting them to state government, and I had much to do in the changing and adapting the report. I secured a complete change in the divorce laws and several other important items. I also secured a repeal of the usury laws and defeated the license law for the retail of liquors, but supported the act making the retailer responsible for damages. I advocated land limitation and the repeal of all laws for the collection of debts by a gradual process. Homestead exemption and the rights of married women, which defeated the first constitution, we secured in the statutes, and were at once accepted by the people who, by the discussion, had been educated up to the acceptance.

In 1848 Lewis Cass was nominated for President, and his celebrated Nicholson letter caused me and my friend Sholes and many others to leave the Democratic party; and, as we could not go into the Whig party, we, with others, began a new party, with the name of "*Free Soil*," afterward changed to Republican, and I issued the first call for a State convention of this party, which met in Watertown, Wis., with some thirty odd members. This was the first State convention of the party held anywhere, the next being in Maine, soon afterward. This call I issued from my home in Ceresco (now Ripon), and I drew up its platform. My Democratic friends were very much offended at my leaving the party, as they had intended to send me to Congress from my district; but my conscience not being as pliable as those of many Christians, I could not and would not accept a position that would restrain my tongue and pen on any subject I considered needing advocates — and by this time I had become satisfied the cause of the spirits did. In all this and subsequent public life, I opposed all laws for organizing and arming militia, believing all such to be opposed to civilization and the best interests of our own and every other country claiming to be civilized. At the expiration of my term in the Senate, I, of course, could not be nominated by either of the old parties, nor elected by the new one; but still I had many friends, especially among the producing classes and laborers, whose interest I had everywhere defended and advocated with tongue and pen, and largely through the press. During the second session of the Senate we had copies of "Nature's Divine Revelations" on our desks. Brother Sholes kept them for sale; and we defended spirit intercourse whenever the subject came up, which was quite often. The work I did, the measures I advocated, and the correspondence I kept up, during the two sessions, are now nearly forgotten, but, at the time, made me popular with the people, and unpopular with political rascals and time-servers, as well as with monopolists. The newspapers of the State contained at that time many articles of mine, some with my name, and many without. Of the latter was a series of letters closely criticising, analyzing, and delineating the political and social character of each member of the Senate ; and no one knew who wrote them. If I had copies of all this correspondence, a valuable volume for the State library could be made from it. The volume entitled "The Fathers of Wisconsin," published by Tenney & Atwood, and distributed by the State, contains a very just, though brief and imperfect, account of my life and services in Wisconsin.

In 1849, when our society had decided to close up the social experiment at Ceresco, I procured the necessary legislative change in our charter which I had lobbied through the territorial legislature when we began the experiment. I also did all of the legal business of the society as notary public and in drawing up papers and closing up, and later made out the deeds with the new form of blanks which I had got adopted by act of legislature in place of the old, with less than half the printed matter to record, and which are still used in the State. I had also done much of the town business as chairman of the board of supervisors, in laying out roads, etc. During all these busy weeks I often found time to lecture on Spiritualism, including the "Rochester Knockings" and intercourse through mesmerized subjects. In 1849 the new party, which I had taken an active and leading part in starting, — then the "Free Soil," now the Republican, — nominated me for governor in the strongly Democratic State of Wisconsin, where the Whigs were as stubborn and conservative as the Democrats. In the election of November 6th of that year I received 3762 votes ; Nelson Dewey (Dem.), 16,649 ; and A. L. Collins (Whig), 11,371. I received a plurality in two counties, Walworth and Racine (then including Kenosha). and we had a plurality of votes for colored suffrage, but not a majority of all votes cast ; so it was lost. At the end of his two years' term the nominating committee in our State convention offered to report my name again, which would have secured my nomination; but I declined, and secured the nomination of L. J. Farwell, and we elected him. In 1852 I had the affairs of the Phalanx closed up, paying every debt on the stock and three dividends on the stock after it was all paid from the surplus property and sales which belonged to it. In this year the National Convention of the "Free Soil" party was called to meet in Pittsburgh, Pa., and I was sent by the State at large as a delegate and chosen one of its vice-presidents, Henry Wilson being president. I was also selected to make the last of four speeches before the convention after we had nominated John P. Hale and J. W. Julian, — Joshua R. Giddings making the first, Gerrit Smith the second, Fred Douglass the third, and I the last, the evening before the adjournment. I was also on the electoral ticket of Wisconsin for this nomination, and strangely enough ran ahead of my ticket. On the way to and from this convention I stopped and lectured on Spiritualism, as I did in Pittsburgh after its close, and as I often did while canvassing for the fall election. I was never aware of losing popularity by this course, except with a few bigoted Christians under the influence of a scapegrace preacher, named Henry Drew, who pretended to be a Methodist, but who, if known as he was, would have been at once rejected by that denomination and all others. During the years of 1852 and 1853 I spent most of my time lecturing on spiritual intercourse and other reform subjects. In January, 1853, while attending the United States District Court as a juror in Milwaukee, I gave a course of lectures there and wrote some severe criticisms on Judge Miller and his court, as I could not let politics alone, although my life was consecrated to the new gospel and I was getting out of politics. When the legislature was about to erect a United States senator, I was told that a paper had been circulated and signed with pledges to vote for me if a sufficient number of names could be got to elect me on the first ballot, and that the paper only lacked five, which I could secure by personal effort and pledges; but I utterly refused to make any concessions or promises, and my esteemed friend and a believer in spirit intercourse, Charles Durkee, was elected, and he told me himself that I ought to have had his place; but I did not want it, and have never regretted my course or choice of occupation.

In 1853 I was elected an officer of the State Agricultural Society, and declined an invitation to deliver its annual address; but lectured in the assembly hall of the capitol, on Spiritualism, in response to an invitation by resolution of members. Took an active part in the Free Soil State convention, but declined all honors. In this year I received the last of my popular and political honors from Wisconsin as commissioner of the State to the grand and world-renowned Crystal Palace exhibition in New York City, and attended it, taking notes and reporting for the State, but was constantly lecturing on my subject of Spiritualism. During 1854 I travelled all the time, and lectured mostly out of Wisconsin, and in 1855 took my family out of Wisconsin to a new home five miles from the village of Battle Creek, Mich., where there was a liberal academy in which I could educate my children more to my liking, and where Spiritualism was not ignored or ridiculed as it was, and is, in the college at Ripon, which I helped to get up, and where I made the speech at the laying of the corner stone. In Michigan I took no part in politics, but had my home there till after the publication of my autobiography, which reaches up to 1857, since which the record is by sketches. I took little part in politics till 1860, and in the election of Lincoln, in which I did all I could for his election, and on the breaking out of the war, and during its continuance I made speeches continually in many parts of the country in support of the union of the States and the army that was endeavoring to maintain it. I, during that period, published my third book, "The American Crisis; or, Trial and Triumph of Democracy," a purely political work, which was very popular, but which, being confined principally to the contest and the miscegenation of the races, was allowed to go out of print after the close of the war. I had a personal acquaintance with President Lincoln and Senators Wilson, Wade, Howard, Howe, and many other popular leaders of the Republican party during the war, and knew the above named except Howe were Spiritualists as I was; but my life was devoted to Spiritualism, and theirs to politics and our common country, the interests of which were also sacred to me, and never neglected when I felt that my services were needed. My oldest son was in the army, going voluntarily from college to the ranks as a soldier, but was soon promoted to assistant-surgeon. He was with his regiment at the capture of New Orleans, and returned safely after his three years' service, making his father's and mother's hearts glad, and thankful that his good habits of life had not been tarnished by college or army associations.

At the first election of Grant after the war I voted for him in New York City, where I was then doing business. I did this, not because I considered him the right man, but because I could not vote for Seymour, on account of his war record as governor of New York. At the next election of Grant I took an active part in the Liberal Republican rebellion and its nomination. As I was then in St. Louis lecturing and selling liberal books, and in the 4th Congressional District, I was put on the electoral ticket; and canvassing with Carl Schurz, we carried the State of Missouri for Greeley by a large majority. I was elected presidential elector with fourteen others. As Greeley died after the election and before the meeting of the electors, I, with six others, voted for Governor B. Gratz Brown; some others, for Hendricks; and one, for another. I was not nominated by the Democrats, but accepted by them as a Liberal Republican. Since that I have been a Greenbacker, and not in either of the old parties. In another chapter will be found the social line of my life, as this is of the political line only. In 1877 I was living with my second and present wife in Santa Barbara, California, editing a Greenback paper and lecturing on Spiritualism Sundays. A constitutional convention had been ordered, and my friends knowing that I had been a member of two and of a senate, induced me to run as a candidate; but the monopolists feared such radical minds, and induced the circuit judge to run against me, as they said he was the only man that could beat me, and I being but little known out of the city, and had been in it less than a year. This was before I had taken charge of the paper. At the court house precinct near which we both lived, I beat him; but in the county he was elected, though really not eligible, as he was still circuit judge, and only by a strong legal support secured his seat, and his pay for both offices. He soon after died. The liberal element prevailed in the convention, and a good constitution was the result, though a desperate effort to defeat it was made by monopolists and in the Catholic and some other churches, because it had a provision for taxing all church property. In this fight the opponents had 140 papers opposing it, and many able and paid speakers and writers, and we had only forty-two, one of which I edited, and also made many speeches, and we carried it against these odds by about 12,000 majority.

My share and interest in this fight gave me the nomination and election to the State Senate in 1879, for the fractional term of three years,— 1880-81-82,— during which time we had three sessions. My district consisted of Santa Barbara, Ventura, and San Luis Obispo counties. My popular Republican opponent was in the same county with me. He had been a senator and a judge, and was the most popular man in the county, if not in the district. He beat me in our county, but in the district I was 339 votes ahead of him, to his surprise as well as to that of his friends.

An effort was made by my Republican opponents to have me unseated, because I had not been in the State three years when elected; but the Republican senators who could do it would not, as I was elected by law under the old constitution, which did not require that term of residence. My first contest in the Senate was to prevent the election of a chaplain, and I succeeded, with the aid of Catholic and Liberal votes and three of us Spiritualists; and we had none in either of the three sessions I was in. I tried to get a land-limitation bill through, and did get it passed; but the monopolists got two men elected by workingmen to change their votes, reconsider, and defeat it. Other reform measures presented by me met a like fate. As monopolists controlled the Legislature, and I saw no chance to do good there, at the end of my term I decided to return to the East, and confine myself to my favorite business of lecturing, which I had not neglected during the sessions. In the Greenback (State) convention in 1882 I was nominated for Congress, to represent the State at large; and, as I could not be elected, accepted it, and, by the aid of a few friends, made quite an extensive canvass for our party ticket. In the following March I returned East, and was sent as delegate for the State in the National Greenback Convention, held in Indianapolis, and, in that convention, nominated Gen. B. F. Butler, for California; and he was our candidate that fall for President. This ended my political career, as I am now a citizen of Massachusetts, where there are candidates enough without me. As it was some time before he fully accepted our nomination, and somewhat uncertain how far he would act with and for us, I did not make many speeches for Butler. As I had not sufficiently located to have a vote, I dropped out of the political arena almost entirely. The following brief notice of me, published in a volume of "Pen Pictures of the Representative Men of California," in the year 1880, may suffice to wind up this sketch of my political life:—

"HON. WARREN CHASE.

"There are few men who have ever sat in the legislative halls of California who can look back with more pride to a larger, more honored, or more useful career than can Senator Chase. Looking down the long vista of sixty-seven years, when his infant eyes opened for the first time upon this world, in Pittsfield, N.H., and following up his infant footsteps until the time when the down upon his cheek heralded his approaching manhood, with all its bright hopes and high ambitions, until the present era, now that the snows of many winters and warm summers of a well-spent and active life have silvered his hair, — he can assuredly find nothing to regret in the least except that it is passed; while he has ample cause for congratulation that the sun of the present shines upon a character untarnished by the storms which he has battled so long and so well, and that his future opens before him full of the ripened glory of a life of usefulness and of honor. Senator Chase represents the counties of Santa Barbara, San Luis Obispo, and Ventura.

"In 1835 he removed to Michigan, then a Territory; and in 1838, to Wisconsin, and settled in Southport. In 1844 he removed to Fond du Lac County and settled with a colony what is now the city of Ripon, where he first gave evidence of his eminent fitness for public life, as a delegate to the first constitutional convention, in which body he took a prominent part. It was here, also, that he announced those sentiments of equality and of sympathy for the downtrodden, which should endear him to the heart of every true patriot. He was the mover in that convention of measures which declare the God-sent truth, that no person should be debarred civil or political rights on account of color or sex; and at a time, too, when in the majority of the States of the Union such doctrines were held to be political heresies, and the author of them to be an outlaw in the popular estimation. He also defended the measure allowing married women to hold and control their own property, which defeated that instrument, and also one to prohibit land monopoly. These opinions, expressed while a member of that convention, showed that as a legislator and as a man he was a fearless advocate of the right. Such, however, was the power of bigotry and prejudice in those days, that the measures and constitution were defeated; but in spite of the machinations of his enemies, and the enemies of the people as well, Senator Chase was elected to a second convention, in which he took a very active part, leaving more reference to him in the journal than to any other member; and on the adoption of this constitution, he was elected to the State Senate by the counties of Winnebago and Fond du Lac, which he represented in the first two sessions of the State, taking an active part, — and in the second session, as one of the judiciary of three, — which session revised and adopted the statutes of the State.

"In 1849 he was the Free Soil candidate for governor,

receiving a large minority vote; and in 1852 was a delegate in the National Convention held at Pittsburgh, Penn., which nominated Hale and Julian; and made one of the four set speeches of that convention, with Gerrit Smith, Joshua R. Giddings, and Fred Douglass. In 1872 he was a citizen of St. Louis, and nominated by the Third Congressional District for presidential elector; and on the State ticket elected, and held an electoral vote for Horace Greeley when he died. In 1876 he came to California, residing a short time in San Francisco and San Jose, and early in 1878 removed to Santa Barbara. He has displayed a great deal of fire and ability in the journalistic field, as editor of the *Santa Barbara Independent*, one of the most lively and progressive country journals on the coast.

"The senator is a Greenbacker in politics, and a married man. He is a hard-working and useful member of the committees on city and county and municipal governments, enrollments, public morals, and labor and capital. He was elected to the present Legislature by the Workingmen's party."

Since my return to the East from California I have not voted; but I am in sympathy with the Knights of Labor and the workingmen's organizations, and hope they will all unite and adopt Henry George's reform measures, and correct anarchy by the ballot, as I have no sympathy with dynamite.

CHAPTER VI.

THE LIFE LINE OF DOMESTIC LIFE CONTINUED.

"Through and through the woof of ill
There runs a thread of goodness.
Winds that shake the wingéd·mill
Feed us with their rudeness.
Frosts that autumn blossoms kill
Ope the nut burs on the hill.
Griefs that settled heart swards tear,
Fit for greener blessings there."

THREADING HIS WAY.

"He wires in and wires out, and leaves the country still in doubt
Whether the hound that's on his track is going south or coming back."

AT the time my "Life Line" was published, in 1857, I was living in a little cottage I built mostly with my own hands and those of my son, in Harmonia, in the town of Battle Creek, Mich., five miles from the station and city, where I often got off the cars as I returned from lecturing, and walked home five miles, carrying much luggage. Here we had improved and cultivated our one acre in the best manner we could, and with my pay for lectures, always small, and the most rigid economy of one of the best of wives and mothers, we sustained the family of five and kept three in the academy across the street from our house, till the oldest son was prepared to enter the University at Ann Arbor, where he graduated from the medical department during the early stages of the war, and leaving there enlisted in the Michigan Sixth Regiment, at Kalamazoo, soon rising to the position of assistant-surgeon. He went with the forces to New Orleans and was there at the capture of the city. He did surgeon's duty in that city nearly two years, and came home safe and sound near the close of the war.

While I lived there, the election of Abraham Lincoln, in which I took as active a part as I could, brought on the war, and in that my tongue and pen were both active most of the time. The time South Carolina adopted the snake and palm flag I wrote the only poem of any note I ever wrote, and had two thousand copies printed and distributed, of which only one is to be found in our family, and that in my scrap-book. Soon after this, I issued " The American Crisis ; or, Trial and Triumph of Democracy," which had a rapid sale, but after the war soon went out of print. Until near the close of the war, there was seldom a week, and in some periods not a day in many consecutive weeks, that I did not make one or more public speeches in favor of sustaining the national union at all hazards ; but on Sunday I almost invariably spoke on Spiritualism, which deprived me of the reputation and glory I should have won had I been a Christian, but which I then and ever scorned to seek at the cost of honest convictions and the knowledge I had that spirit intercourse was a fact. By my old diary, I see that on Sunday, Jan. 1, 1860, I was in Hartford, Conn., and gave two lectures on our philosophy to good houses, and during the week spoke in Winsted three evenings, closing on my forty-seventh birthday, Jan. 5th, and reached New York City Saturday, where on Sunday, the 8th, I spoke twice in Dodworth's Hall to large audiences. Jan. 12th I was shocked with the news of the terrible fall of the factory in Lawrence, Mass., and loss of life. I lectured again the 15th in Dodworth's, and during the week went to Bridgeport and gave three lectures, then back to New York and gave three on the 22d. So my time ran, and had run, since the publication of "Life Line" to this date, and continued, of which only a few notes are necessary to keep the thread running in the web of life I was weaving. Jan. 27th my diary says I had grand circle and visit at the home of the elder of the Fox sisters, now Mrs. Underhill, and spent the night there; remarkable manifestations, etc.; 29th, Sunday, lectured in Newark, N.J.; Monday visited the North Orange home of A. J. Davis; and 31st, listened, in New York, to the eloquent bugle peals of Wendell Phillips, who even then felt the war-cloud coming; also heard H. W. Beecher, in whose mind were also premonitions of the coming storm. During February I lectured in Sansom St. Hall, Philadelphia, and in Baltimore in March, when the political pot was boiling with great fury, and had many talks with Brother Wash. Danskin, whose wife was and is a good medium, and he is in the spirit sphere. He was deeply in sympathy with the South and slavery at that time. I remained there only two Sundays, and then ran back to New York and up to West Winfield, where I spoke several times, and then in Rome, N.Y.; visited the Oneida Community, lectured in Syracuse, as I often had before, and received poor pay, and felt sad and sorry, as I often had, from the abuse of these who ought to be my friends, as I was theirs; and also for the low state of my finances, which were ever scattered where I felt they were needed and deserved, making the home demands most imperative. Lectured in Oswego and Mexico, N.Y., and crowded in lectures between the Sundays.

In May, 1860, I worked westward, lecturing along the route in Western New York, Ohio, at Conneaut, Geneva, Cleveland, and other places. Visit Dayton, O., and Richmond, Ind., and Terre Haute, lecturing in all, and in other places. Spent most of June in St. Louis and other localities near the city, and lectured three or four times each week. Spent July chiefly in Iowa, Wisconsin, and in Minnesota, at Lake City, where I had a lively discussion with a clergyman in his church. In August I reached home, at Harmonia, lectured *en route*, and visited the old Ceresco home. In September, while lecturing in Chicago, the steamer *Lady Elgin* sunk, and three hundred persons lost their lives in the night. The sad event was the subject of one lecture. The Prince of Wales was in the city, and I would not go across the street to see him. October spent in lecturing in Indiana and Michigan, busy all the time. November, visited my son Milton, who was then in the University of Michigan, and heard the dean of the medical department, in a lecture to the graduating class, on authority, say he took no authority except on the subject of religion; "on that," he said, "I shut my eyes and go it blind"; and I thought so, as he was an Episcopalian, if anything. I also lectured in Detroit, in November, and on the 5th went home; and Nov. 6th voted for Lincoln for President in our precinct, and was ridiculed by Democrats and Whigs as a Spiritualist and fanatic. Very busy during the month of November, ending it in Central Illinois, at Brother Blanchard's, whose wife I had cured by magnetism when other remedies failed. December I was busy all the time in Illinois and Ohio, and closed out the year at Toledo, at which time the air was filled with the rebellious sentiments of the South over the election of Lincoln; but the North was as slow and quiet as it could be under the lashing it had. My diary for 1860 says, 184 lectures in thirteen States, of which two, Maryland and Missouri, were slave States. Received for them and the sale of books, which I always carried with me, $795.50, and paid for my books and my expenses out of it, leaving a meagre support for my family.

1861. "Threading my way." Opened the year in Cleveland, and, on the 5th of January, my forty-eighth birthday, was in Baltimore, Md., listening to the reckless utterances of rebellious citizens hanging around the saloons. Sunday, the 6th, opened my course of lectures to large audiences. Strong union sentiments expressed, and yet the rebel element controlled the marshal and city officers. Lecture four Sundays of January on Spiritualism, and several week evenings on that and other subjects in that city and its vicinity. Excitement increasing all the time. Lecture four Sundays of February in Philadelphia, and some evenings in the vicinity. Strong union sentiment here. Lecture in Trenton, N.J., Feb. 25th, Monday evening, to small and poor audience, gotten up by David Lukens, father of my present wife, and one of the earliest, honestest, and most devoted believers, a prominent antislavery advocate, who came out of the Society of Friends, from Orthodox to Hicksite, and Hicksite to Friends of Progress and Spiritualism. All of the Sundays of March I lectured in Oswego, N.Y., and evenings in Penn Yan and Mexico, and held a discussion two evenings with Professor Grimes, he opposing, and I defending, spirit life and intercourse. At the close he said to me, "I have got the money, and you the glory, and I am satisfied, and suppose you are." During this month the events at Washington were thrilling the whole country, and of course I was in it. First Sunday in April I lectured in Utica, N.Y., and during that week, April 12th, the fire began to fly at Charleston, S.C., and the fever began to rise in the North. I was at a quiet town on Long Island, but felt the shock, and began at once to take active part with my tongue and pen — the only weapons I could use. Sunday, spoke in Troy, and spent the week in a convention in Worcester, Mass., with Mrs. Spence, Sister Barney and others, and we all made speeches for the Union. Next two Sundays in Providence. Troops left while I was there, and war fairly began; fever ran high. On the Sundays of May I lectured in Putnam, Conn., and several evenings on the national conflict and its issues. In June lectured in four or five places in Connecticut, and in several in Massachusetts and Vermont, filling all the Sundays on Spiritualism, and evenings on the war, which was now fairly opened. Scandalous letters were constantly sent round ahead of me to defeat my work in Spiritualism and stop me, as such lies had stopped and sometimes killed others more sensitive and with less firmness and perseverance. Spent all of July in Vermont, and lectured constantly, in Stowe, Hardwick, and other places. Spent most of the month at South Hardwick, in Samuel and Susan Tuttle's pleasant and beautiful home, and wrote my second book there, "The Fugitive Wife," long since out of print. Met in Vermont "Sleeping Lucy Cook," and other early mediums, among them Mrs. Blair, the painting medium, who to this day is one of the most remarkable and convincing mediums this country has yet produced. In August my son received his diploma at Ann Arbor, went home, and enlisted in the Michigan 6th Regiment at Kalamazoo, and wrote me an excellent letter, giving as his reasons for doing so that being in good health, of right age and no family, he felt it to be his duty. This month, also, my first grandchild was born, Henry Whelpley, now a professor in the St. Louis College of Pharmacy. Spent all of August lecturing every Sunday and many evenings, in Vermont and New Hampshire, closing at Newport, N.H., the home of my wife. Spent September in Massachusetts and New Hampshire, speaking in Lowell, Boston, and Manchester to good audiences, and often on the war. Lectured all of October in Massachusetts, Vermont, and New Hampshire, busy all the time Contracted with Bela Marsh of Boston, to publish my new book, "The Fugitive Wife." November was spent in Massachusetts, mostly in Boston and Quincy, with a visit to Providence, and all the time busy with tongue and pen, writing for papers, and carrying on a large private correspondence, largely on reforms. Spent December in Massachusetts, and had at its close lectured every Sunday of the year 1861, and many week evenings, giving in all 170 lectures, receiving on an average for each lecture $3.52. Closed the year in Boston, Mass.

1862. Found me as the old year left me, with the harness on and ready to begin a new year and continue the old work. Began in Providence, R.I., first week in January; second Sunday in Boston, third Sunday also; fourth in Foxboro and back to Providence again. During these trips and lectures many incidents transpired that were important and worthy of notice, but they have passed from memory, and cannot be recalled sufficiently to be recorded. Opened February in Philadelphia, and Laura De Force Gordon, now an attorney in the Supreme Court of California and the United States Supreme Court, spoke on the same day. I had known her since her starting as Laura Force, who lived with her parents of that name in La Crosse, Wis., a remarkable girl and good medium. In those years of '61–2 I often, in my visits to New York, went down to Modern Times, L.I., where T. L. Nichols and Mary Gove Nichols had started with others a settlement, and effort at social reforms, as I had friends there, and there I first became acquainted with Emma Hardinge, now Emma Hardinge Britten, one of our most active and efficient workers in England, and well known in our country. She and her mother were quietly living there then, or about that time, and she was developing into mediumship, and soon after went upon the rostrum. In Philadelphia I found my home with Dr. H. T. Childs and Dr. Chase. My son Milton, and the Michigan 6th Regiment, to which he belonged and of which he was now hospital steward, were in Baltimore, and I visited him and them and lectured in Baltimore in the midst of the rebel elements. Feb. 9 being Sunday, spent a week in camp, mostly with my son. Also visited Brother and Sister McCombs at Jarretsville, Md., and the third Sunday in February I lectured in Cincinnati, O. The war was now raging terribly, and I used week evenings often in speaking for the National Government and its armies, but Sundays always for Spiritualism. From Cincinnati I went to Centralia, Ill., to visit a patient I had often and successfully treated before, and there begun, and soon after completed, my third book, "The American Crisis," which Bela Marsh published for me in Boston — a purely political work on the war and slavery and the results. Lectured at Sandoval and other places on the issues of the war, etc.

In March I visited South Pass, Ill., now Cobden, where G. H. Baker, and others of our old Phalanx members, had settled for favorable climate and soil for fruit-raising, and I was looking up a place for the same purpose for my family home. Visited and lectured in Carbondale, where I had old friends living. April, lectured in Decatur several times, also in Milwaukee, Wis. Diary says, went to Fond du Lac, and could not get place to lecture; went on to Nenah, and walked in rain and mud five miles, carrying baggage, and got wet, tired, and discouraged, but found good hearts in a poor home, and rested as well cared for as their circumstances would permit. Went out there on business for a friend, but it was a failure, and one of the many hard times I had to pass through as a part of my lessons in this life. Back to Milwaukee, and lectured there again, April 15, to good audiences, also in Waukesha and other places during April. I crossed the lake to Grand Haven, and lectured there; also in Grand Rapids, April 27. If this was not a tramp life, I do not know what could be. In all those journeys I did not get more than expenses, except an experience in colds. Reached home at Battle Creek, April 28, tired, sad, sorry, and poor, as usual, and yet confident of the value of the cause in which I was engaged. Spent most of May at home, but lectured at Battle Creek and Sturgis, Mich., and first Sunday in June, also in Sturgis; after that in Adrian and Toledo, Cleveland, Chagrin Falls, and Braceville, O. Lectured nearly every evening on the war issues, and closed June at Chardon, with Lucia Cowles, a good lecturer and excellent woman, developed through great tribulation and a social hell. Saturday, June 5, lectured in a church in Clyde, O., on the war, and Sunday, 6th, on Spiritualism, in a barn out of town, as no place in town could be got for that subject. Stayed at Brother A. B. French's, as I had before, as he was a younger worker in the same cause, and a good one. July opened in Syracuse and Hastings, N.Y., and Colosse and Mexico and several other places; during July at Watertown, N.Y. August opened at Stowe, Vt., with good meetings; went to South Hardwick with Samuel and Susan K. Tuttle, two of the best friends and best Spiritualists I had ever found, and where I often visited and wrote much of my books. Lectured all of August in Vermont, north and west of Montpelier, and closed August at Bethel. September was a stormy month in war news, and I lectured many times on it week evenings, and Sundays as usual, mostly in Vermont, about Gaysville and Hardwick and Bethel and Barnard, and closed the month at Lebanon, N.H., and Meriden, lecturing in both places. Oct. 1, was at the old home of my wife in Newport on a short visit. Lectured there in the town hall on the war; but my pious brother-in-law, Nathan White, now in spirit life, would not come to hear me because I was a Spiritualist and he a Baptist, yet a zealous advocate of my views on the war. Lectured all of October in New Hampshire and Massachusetts. Sundays, mostly in Lowell, to good audiences, much better than can be secured there in 1887, since Catholicism has got control of the city, and shrouded it in sectarian darkness, as it does every place it controls. In November Bela Marsh got out my book, "American Crisis." I lectured in Quincy and other places in Massachusetts; the last Sunday of November, in Lewiston, Me. Spent much time in Boston. When in Quincy I went home one day for tea with a friend to Neponset, whose daughter was controlled by an Indian chief, who named all the speakers and mediums he brought home, or who came there; and he was anxious to get my name. Soon after our arrival the Indian came and greeted me as "North Star," and the old gentleman asked why he gave me that name, and he replied, "Because the mariners set their compass by him." It was curious, but quite a compliment. December, lectured in Brunswick and Yarmouth, Me., and Taunton, Mass., and visited Providence, Boston, Lowell, and several other places; gathered war news, which was exciting and varying in results of battles. Closed the year in Boston — a very busy year. My son was with Gen. B. F. Butler's division in New Orleans, and assistant-surgeon of Michigan 6th Regiment, and well. I had delivered 136 lectures this year, and in eleven of the States, thirty-one on the war, and 105 on Spiritualism, for all of which I received $449, which would not much more than pay my travelling expenses, on which I could not have met my expenses had I not carried and sold books, which assisted me, and which, with my satchel and clothes, I often carried long distances from the cars to the friends with whom I stopped. This was one of my hardest years, and yet with good health and the frequent encouraging messages from spirit friends, I did not falter, as I had taken hold of the plough not to turn back, even to the political flesh pots.

Jan. 1, 1863. In Boston with my old and dear friends, Samuel and Susan Tuttle and Fannie Remick, late Mrs. Allen Putnam, all now in spirit life, and still good friends and interested now as then. We parted, Samuel and Susan for their Vermont home, and I for my work, which opened in Providence with three lectures, the first Sunday of the year. Lectured in Woonsocket and visited with one of our old pioneers, Seth Vose, and others; also in Pawtucket evenings, and 2d, 3d, and 4th Sundays in Providence, where we had full houses at five cents admission. I had the receipts for pay, and got well paid, as I thought, when compared with receipts in many places where I was employed. First Sunday in February spoke in Philadelphia; second, in Foxboro, Mass., and in New York and Philadelphia. Third Sunday in Plymouth, on old Puritan landing ground, and now saturated with this heresy which would have been crushed out in the first half-century after the settlement. Next in Kingston, where I found a quite liberal sentiment. Visited Milford, N.H., once the home of the celebrated Hutchinson family, which had greatly liberalized the mind there, as elsewhere, with their inimitable songs of freedom and justice. Lectured there, and returned to Foxboro to close the month of February, during which I had been on the run, lectured in five States, and opened March in Foxboro, but passed most of the month in Maine, Brunswick, Lewiston, Yarmouth, Kennebunk, and Portland, and in Massachusetts at Marblehead and Salem, on old witch ground, where they once crushed out mediumship with the cruel death of mediums under the Christian's cruel mercy.

My diary records this month as one of sorrow, sadness, and discouragement, and yet I kept on my work, almost heartbroken sometimes, and often out of the reach of the spirit guides, who could only comfort me when the conditions were right in me; but I had scarcely then learned that the impress of sorrow and suffering were necessary to bring up and out the finer expressions of thought and feeling. First half of April was spent in Vermont, mostly at Brookfield, and South Hardwick, at Brother Tuttle's; plenty of snow, a good place for sugar, but poor for lectures. Last half of April was spent in Northeastern New York, at Potsdam, Watertown, and other places, where I lectured and got little pay, but found the best of friends, among them Dr. E. A. Holbrook, of Watertown, quite a poet and an early Spiritualist and of the Universalist church, which was not the Nazareth out of which no good thing could come. Spent all of May in State of New York, lecturing in central part, and closing at Brighton, but spent two pleasant weeks at Colosse and Hastings with my old friends the Cones and Chutes, faithful and efficient Spiritualists of that time and since. During this month the war news was very exciting, and generally good on the whole — especially to me from my son in New Orleans. June I spent in New York and Ohio mostly, and lectured in Rochester, Buffalo, Lockport, and Pekin, and the 16th in Ohio, at Painesville and Chardon, at the home of Lucia Cowles, one of our best lecturers, and now in spirit life, and closed the month with a grove meeting at Newbury with Brother and Sister Allen, two radical and thorough reform workers, and still at it in 1887. During July I lectured many times in Ohio, about Seville, Westfield, New London, and other places, much with Mr. Farnum and his family, best of people and thorough Spiritualists. 21st, I visited Angola, Indiana, and Waterloo, and lectured there several times, and closing July at Adrian, Mich., where I had lectured many times, and had good friends but small pay, as in most places. August opened with my lectures in Adrian, and my daughter Lottie came to meet me, and we visited her uncle, William White, at Monroe, and then went home to Battle Creek and spent one quiet Sunday. Aug. 9th had long journey and great variety of incidents, but little pay over expenses, yet sent home all I could. Aug. 16th lectured in Albion, Mich., and as usual had good audiences, as it was before the free love scare had its effect in keeping away many, as it did in later years; but most persons came from curiosity, and not as converts. Returned home 17th, and diary says, cold hearts there except in our home circle;' but had good audiences Sunday, 24th, and closed August with grove meeting at Evansville, Wis., with Mrs. Kate Stowe and other speakers to help me, and retired to Janesville with the Stowes.

September I lectured in Janesville and Fond du Lac, Oshkosh, and Milwaukee, and visited my old home in Ripon, once Ceresco, but now given up to whiskey and religion, which divide the place between them; hence there is no sale of my old home in the valley, so beautiful when no liquor was sold or kept there, and no preachers, lawyers, or doctors were needed. Close the month with lectures in Broadhead, Wis. October spent in Chicago, Ill., Elkhart, and Goshen, Ind., and other places, and closed the month in Bloomington, Ill. Diary records last two months as among the saddest, most discouraging of my life. I was almost compelled to give up all and retire to obscure life. November, a little better. Lectured many times in Bloomington, Clinton, and Decatur, and visited General (now Governor) Oglesby, then a Spiritualist, and for aught I know, one still. Lectured in Sandoval, Salem, and Centralia, and got about enough to pay travelling expenses. Looking up a place for a home farther south than Michigan, visited Carbondale and Cobden, Ill., and closed the month at Cobden with friends G. H. Baker, E. A. Blanchard, and their families, and in looking up a place to locate. December lectured in Cairo and Cobden, and selected lot and purchased the improvements of Captain Philips' railroad land in village of Cobden, and which has ever since been my only home, with my son-in-law, J. T. Whelpley and family, and my beloved daughter, ever endeared to me, and I to her, and her excellent family of six children.

I took thirty, and Mr. Baker ten acres of the forty, his adjoining his farm across the road. Having closed this trade I moved north and lectured in Du Quain, Centralia, and Sandoval, and visited Brother and Sister Wilson. Lectured in Decatur, and closed the year 1863 at Clinton, Ill., at the home of Brother Lintner, who afterward backslid, as Christians often, and Spiritualists seldom do. Diary says this had been a year of joy and sorrow,— latter largely in the ascendant,— of severe trials and poor financial prospects; yet there came good out of it ultimately, and the great causes of suffering gradually wore away and were overcome. Delivered 170 lectures during the year and received $582, and paid travelling expenses $357, leaving $225 for support of family and life insurance and interest on note given for money to build the home at Battle Creek. These lectures were given in twelve States of the Union,— many of them week evenings,— on the war, which that year took up most of the public attention. Diary says I wrote over one thousand letters that year, many of them published.

Jan. 1, 1864, found me in Clinton, Ill., in a severe snow-storm, and the mercury at 23 below zero. Too cold for lectures, and I pass over Sunday and go to Decatur, to find a hall closed after it had been engaged for my lecture in the evening; but Sunday we had the courthouse. As the Christians had got the hall closed against us, the two Smiths, E. O. and T. O., both worthy citizens and Spiritualists, got the court-house for me. I return and lecture in Clinton the 16th and 17th. Return to Decatur, and, finding Von Vleck advertised to lecture against me, I lectured on him, his history and mediumship, and treachery, as I had known him from boyhood, and he gives it up and departs. Gave several lectures in Springfield, and close the month at Bloomington, — a hard month, — and feel very poor and discouraged. The war was raging, and so was our war with the churches. Like our officers in the Revolution, I often get down-hearted, but never gave up. Spent February in and about Chicago, and lectured often to good houses and for very small pay. March was also spent about Chicago and Milwaukee and at my home in Battle Creek, where my eldest granddaughter, Ada Whelpley, was born, March 22, at 3 A.M. Her uncle Milton, M.D., arrived from New Orleans on a furlough the same night at 12 M., and I at 1 P.M., and we all talked over our prospective removal to Southern Illinois, then called Egypt for its moral, social, and political darkness, but not for its religious, for it had several preachers who could not read any printed language, but could preach "Christ and him crucified," as they had heard of it, and could save souls with the story.

I sold the Battle Creek home for $700, a small part of what was needed to pay for a fit-up in the new one at Cobden, but hoped in vain to sell the old one at Ceresco. That hope was like the Christian's hope — a failure of realization, at least, when it depends on a bodily resurrection or a reception by Christ in the next stage of life. April was a busy month with me; lectured at several places in Illinois, and visited Cobden, and myself and son-in-law, J. T. Whelpley, begin work on our new place, root the old sucker out of his den, and get possession. J. T. W. remained there, and I returned to Michigan home, and parted with Milton, whose furlough ended, and he returned to New Orleans to his post in army as assistant-surgeon. I moved out of the little cottage I sold, into the next house, and packed up goods for final move. Scattered some lectures on my journeys, and closed April in Chicago, where I commenced May with two lectures on the 1st in Wetonsky Hall, to good audiences. I visited Wisconsin and my old home, to try to sell, but sadly returned to work; no sale, and discouraged, but pursue my calling in spiritual work faithfully, and hear heaps of abuse for my itineracy in a work so terribly heretical. Of course I was as bad morally as I was religiously to bigots and hypocrites and the self-righteous. Lectured again in Chicago, Ill., Davenport, Iowa, and Geneseo, Ill., and closed the month in Galesburg; a busy month, but expenses use up nearly all receipts for lectures. During June I lectured in La Harpe, Ill., where I was sick, and for a week not able to swallow food except liquid, and yet gave six lectures. Such was the pressing necessity with me for the mere pittance of pay, as it had been all my life in every one of my fields of labor. Speak also in Carthage and Galena, and attend convention at Geneseo, and find many good friends there, among the speakers, Dr. Samuel Underhill, one of our oldest and ablest defenders; and also Mr. Allen, a resident, and once a clergyman. Gave a course also in New London, and closed the month in Aurora, Ill.

July opened with a convention at St. Charles, Ill., at which were Leo Miller, then an able advocate, and Benjamin Todd, another, and also one of our best in the field, Dr. Juliette H. Severance, now of Milwaukee, and also Prof. A. B. Severance; closed the 5th. Went to our new home in Cobden, and worked on lot, and got lumber for single board additions to old log-house. I leave Mr. Whelpley to fit it up, and return north, and lecture in Odin, Sandoval, Bloomington, Jolliet, and Chicago, Ill. Close July at Whitewater, Wis., at the Severance home. August lectures commenced in Milwaukee. On the 9th we open our national convention of Spiritualists in Chicago ; and as the war was raging, its spirit got in our convention, and a bitter spirit was engendered on political questions which marred its harmony and usefulness, and we closed it the 14th without accomplishing much besides talk ; but most of us speakers said our say, and stirred the subject. From there I went to Morrison, Prophetstown, Freeport, and Rockford, and closed the busy month at Belvidere, Ill. ; a hard and busy one, and much sorrow in it and its trials. Opened September with a grove meeting at Belvidere, and had a good time, but some scandalmonger wrote a scandalous report of it for A. J. Davis' paper in New York, and lied about us for the glory of God and scandal of Spiritualists. Sept. 8th I reached my old Michigan home ; lectured there for the last time, and packed once more for a move in life to another new home, as rude as the others had been, for my work in this unpopular cause had not enabled me to get a better home than my work in the sawmills had. On the 15th we all started for our new home in Illinois, — self, wife Mary, and daughter and her two children, and son Albert, of all of whom, and the rest of my descendants, I am very proud, and have good cause to be.

We all arrived safely, and I lectured on Sunday at my new home, and worked on house, and we all boarded till it was fitted. Milton had resigned his commission in the army, and come home to help us ; and we soon got into the rude shanty, all of which had given way to better rooms except the old log part. Went to Cairo, and lectured, and closed out the month of September, and began October by transferring Wisconsin property to Milton for sale, and he went to dispose of it as best he could. Closed the month with hard work and moving in new house, and Oct. 4 started north on lecturing tour again, and commenced in Decatur. I was now a citizen of Illinois, it being the fourth State I had been a citizen of, and twice of Michigan, within sixteen years, during which time I had gained the reputation of being one of the fathers of Wisconsin. Lectured in Princeton, Galena, and several other places on my way north, and also in South Bend, Elkhart, and Goshen, Ind., and closed October at Elkhart. Eventful month, and mostly pay out, and not in, pocket. Opened November at Sturgis, Mich., where we had and have a church belonging to the Spiritualists, but run into a sort of conservative Christian Spiritualism of late years. Lectured most of this month in Ohio, including several lectures in the Mormon temple at Kirtland; spoke at Chardon and Burton, and closed November at Meadville, Pa. December, visit Meadville, Corry, and Erie, Pa., and reach Syracuse and lecture there the 4th, and visit Dr. Butterfield, a very successful healing medium. Spent a week at Colosse, and returned to Syracuse and gave three more lectures, and then to Binghamton, where I had some of the best friends and good lectures, but light pay, as usual. Visited the Oneida Community. Good visit; but its theological founder, Noyes, does not like me, yet the others do. I have often written them up for our papers, and will not do it here. Returned and lectured again at Syracuse. Spent Christmas there, and over a crooked route via Pennsylvania to Maryland, to lecture at Sarah Furnace, Md. Closed the month and year in Washington, D.C., at the home of Major Chorpening, and with a visit to President Lincoln. During the year 1864 I gave 158 lectures in eight of the States, but most of them in Illinois; and fifty-five were on the war, and the others on Spiritualism. For all I received $643, and paid in my personal expenses $418, leaving for family and moving expenses $225. The books I carried and sold paid a little over cost and expressage. This was a hard year, and one in which I had many sad hours and sore afflictions, and some very happy ones with dear friends I cannot forget, although I see them no more.

Sunday, Jan. 1, 1865, lectured in Washington, D.C., to good audiences and with success. Met many friends in Washington, among them several mediums, who were giving private sittings to President Lincoln, especially Nettie Colburn, now Mrs. Maynard, formerly of White Plains, near New York City, and Colchester, now in spirit life, but then a good test medium. I mention this because many prejudiced people deny that Lincoln was a Spiritualist, and I know he was, as also were Senators B. F. Wade, Henry Wilson, Senator Howard of Michigan, and many others of our prominent public men of that time. Lectured to good houses the five Sundays of January; visited the White House and halls of Congress. I had good success in our cause, and the war drawing to a close, with the triumph of freedom and the union of States. In February I retired to Brother McCombe's, at Sarah Furnace, Md., and wrote out my five lectures given in Washington, under the title of "The Gist of Spiritualism," which now, in its sixth edition, is published and sold by Colby & Rich. During the last half of February I gave ten lectures in Philadelphia and three in Vineland, N.J., which was then a promising new settlement for reformers, but soon got under a theological control that blasted the hopes of progressionists. During March I gave a number of lectures in Vineland, and joined Dr. George Haskell and Mr. John Gage in an effort to start an industrial college at Vineland. We organized, and they bought the ground for it; but it failed for want of sufficient interest and financial aid and from religious prejudice against us. Closed March at Syracuse, N.Y., where we received the news of capture of Richmond and Petersburg.

In April, while I was visiting and lecturing in Syracuse, N.Y., the news reached us of the close of the war; and that of the murder of President Lincoln, Friday evening, April 14, caused the whole country to be shocked and draped in mourning; all parties and persons seemed sad and to deeply regret the event. Sunday, the 16th, I delivered a eulogy on Lincoln's life and tragic death. Lectured in Syracuse four Sundays, gave eight lectures, and received $20 for the month; but gave some evening lectures in vicinity on the tragedy. and duties of all in the hour of trial, suffering, and triumph. May 7th, gave two Sunday lectures at Hastings and got $1.75 and rode six miles to deliver them; even this was better than I was paid many times, and yet I never faltered or neglected an opportunity to tell the few that would come to hear me what I could about our philosophy and our facts. May 14th, lectured in La Fargeville, N.Y., and return to Watertown, where I was visiting Dr. E. H. Holbrook, one of our active workers with his poetical pen. Lectured there and in several other places. Closed the month with course of lectures in Potsdam, and visited that greatest of sufferers I ever saw, Austin Kent, whose release from his mortal body some years ago gladdened me, as it must have done him, for his mind was clear and strong in his trials. During June I lectured in Vermont, — a month in South Hardwick, — and wrote a large part of my book, "Essence and Substance," which was not published till 1886. July was also spent at Hardwick, at the pleasant home of Samuel and Susan Tuttle. August, lectured in Glover, Derby, and Charleston, Vt.; also at Gayville, and attend the Vermont State Convention at Ludlow and do good share of speaking, and closed the month with lectures at St. Albans, Vt. September, lectured in St. Albans, Brookfield, Williston, Bethel, Rutland, and Milton, Vt., and Granville, N.Y. Visited Saratoga and closed

September at Syracuse. Oct. 1 and 8, lectured in Syracuse, where the cause lags and never was strong. Lectured in Rochester, where the cause is better, as it was the cradle in which the " knockings " were rocked in their infancy. Oct. 16, attended Spiritualists' national convention in Philadelphia, with John Pierpont, president, whose old pious friends try to prove he was not a Spiritualist, since he is not here to dispute them or to defend Spiritualism, as he ably did when visibly present with us. The convention held five days, during which much discussion was engaged in and business transacted, but its results are all gone now, as they possessed no permanency. Oct. 22, lectured in Wilmington, Del., on Spiritualism, and stopped with that well-known philanthropist, Thomas Garrett; also lectured there the 29th, and closed the month in Philadelphia at the home of Dr. Chase. Lectured all of November in Vineland, N.J., to good houses, — great free-love excitement, but it was all "much ado about nothing." I was not in the tempest at this time, but had often been a target for the shots of a vulgar rabble of impure puritans in social matters; but it never hurt me or my influence, as it always run off like water from a duck's back. December, lectured in New York City, and Newark, N.J. Met and visited with Professor Upham, of Bowdoin College, a confirmed Spiritualist when not at home with his Episcopal wife. Lectured in Bridgeport, Conn. Visited the socialist community at Wallingford and saw — as I had at Oneida — where they had made a fatal mistake in their organic effort, as we did at Ceresco. Spoke at the funeral of a boy, — Parker, — in New Haven, and found some good friends. An accident, not from any cause of mine, threw me out of an engagement for this month in New York, which I greatly deplored, for I was sadly in need of money for our new home in Illinois, where nothing had been raised to support the families. Closed the month and the year at Newark, N.J., with course of lectures. During the year I delivered 121 lectures in six States, and Washington, D.C.—one hundred on Spiritualism, twenty-one on other subjects. Received for all $424, and paid out for my expenses $263, leaving $161—a meagre amount for the support of my family; had to hire money and worry all the time, but never gave up the cause nor my work in it. This was one of my hardest years, as we were starting our new home in Southern Illinois.

1866. Spent January in Washington. Lectured the four Sundays and several evenings, and had my home with Judge Tabor, of Iowa, then an auditor in the Treasury. February, lectured in Wilmington, Vineland, and Newark, and in Westfield, Mass., and Poquanock, Conn. March 1st found me lecturing in New Haven; the 2d, in Newark, N.J.; and 4th, in Philadelphia. I cite these to show how rapidly I moved about to find work, though it barely paid expenses. Spent most of the month in Philadelphia, but closed it with lecture in Syracuse.

Lectured in several places in New York during April, and closed the month with lectures in Painesville, O. May, lectured in Cleveland, Akron, and other places. Reached my new home in Illinois the 15th, and lectured there, October, Sunday, the 20th, at Villa Ridge; 27th of June, commenced lectures at Decatur, then gave a course at Clinton, and closed the month at Rockford, Ill., in a three days' convention of Spiritualists. In July I visited Chicago and made payment on land, and lectured July 4th in Tippecanoe, Ind., then back to Cleveland, where I heard of the death of Susan K. Tuttle of South Hardwick, Vt., whose house had so often been my resting-place, and where I wrote much for my books. She died, and her mortal remains were buried at Syracuse while she and her husband were visiting there: hers was the first materialized face I ever saw that I knew in life. This was not long after her transition, and was in Western New York. I saw plainly a scar she had on her under lip, and did not think of it till I saw it as I kissed her, but knew the face as soon as I saw it, though not thinking of her. Lectured in Cleveland the 8th, visited that best of reformer's homes, D. and S. Allen's, in South Newbury, O., and lectured at Chagrin Falls; visited River Styx and attended the funeral of Mrs. David Wilson, and closed the month with lectures in Cleveland. In these years of my itineracy we had occasional conventions and grove meetings, but that was before we had inaugurated our camp meetings. I was as busy in summer as in winter. August, lectured in Geneva, O., and had a sick turn from weariness, and discouragements financially, but not from any fear of failure in our cause. Attended a grove meeting in Windsor, on the 12th; long journey and poor pay when funds were most needed. Aug. 21st we met in stormy convention in Providence, R.I., Mr. Toohey, Lizzie Doten, and others; never a storm but a calm follows, and all at last were satisfied but Toohey, my diary says. Lectured again in Windsor, and closed the month in Boston, visiting Samuel Tuttle and others. September opened with lectures in Foxboro, Mass. Sunday, the 2d, and on the 7th I was at the State convention in Montpelier, Vt., where we had, as usual in that State, a good and profitable session. Return, and lecture in Massachusetts and Providence, and closed the month at Painesville, O., with lecture on Sunday, the 30th. On the Sundays of October I lectured in Chicago and several evenings in Wisconsin. November opened in Davenport, Iowa, for Sundays, and in Iowa City and other places, evenings. Closed the month at Rock Island, and lectured there Dec. 2d, 9th, and 16th, and in Vermont, Illinois, and several other places, and reached my new home in Cobden the 25th. Lectured the 30th in Cleveland, and closed the month and year in cars on my way to New York City. This was another hard year, one of the worst for labor I ever had, poor pay and long journeys, and troubles of various kinds. Gave 147 lectures in twelve States, and Washington, D.C., all but eight on Spiritualism, and received for them $982, and paid in personal expenses $587, leaving $395 for family and home expenses, where much more was needed, as I had life insurance, taxes and payments on home land to meet, and had to hire money to meet them.

Jan. 1, 1867, reached New York City over Pennsylvania Central Railroad and took charge of the bookstore and business which Colby & Rich had bought of A. J. Davis & Co., at 544 Broadway, which business I had the care of as long as Colby & Rich continued the branch office in that city, to their satisfaction, but not at a profit to them after paying my salary, which was the highest and best pay I ever had. The business did not prevent my lecturing most of the Sundays in the vicinity of New York, and many evenings. I had also a New York column in the *Banner of Light*, with an editorial heading, over which Brother Colby had supervision and control as sole editor, which position he has ably held many years. In June of this year an incident occurred never to be forgotten by me. A friend by the name of Hopkins gave me $150, to pay debts which I had incurred before I came to the store — a free and voluntary gift from him after asking me how much I was in debt. It was not the last donation from that best of friends, but the largest. During this first year in the store I gave seventy-five lectures on Sundays and kept up a large correspondence. I was engaged in the store during all of 1868; lectured about the same as the year before, and kept up my regular correspondence in the *Banner of Light*.

The opening of 1869 found me still in the store at 544 Broadway, New York, and on my fifty-sixth birthday, being January 5. The 1st of May this year was fixed as the time to close up the business of the New York branch of Colby & Rich; and the last of April I packed the books, selecting, under Mr. Rich's direction, an assortment for the American News Company as their New York agents, and we gave up the office April 30, which many New York friends greatly regretted, as it had been a favorite headquarters for Spiritualists. I had lectured most of the Sundays, whether I got pay or not, though I usually received small sums; but my salary supported me and enabled me to pay for the place in Illinois, which made my family a home wherein they could by hard work and strict economy get a subsistence. I was retained at a small salary on the *Banner* corps of correspondents, for that year. After closing up the store I travelled and lectured, visiting our home in Illinois, and, returning East, took in two partners, and we each invested $500 in liberal and Spiritual books and stationery. I selected this stock in Boston in August, shipped it to St. Louis, and opened a store there, with the sign of "Liberal and Spiritual Literature. Warren Chase & Co." Soon as I got settled, with my two lady partners to take charge of the store, I lectured Sundays, and often evenings; hired a hall myself, and had a legally organized society, and was legally ordained its pastor, which authorized me to lawfully perform the marriage ceremony, and has ever since, I being also legally authorized by a society in Illinois and in Iowa. My diary for this year is incomplete, and I do not know the number of lectures; but they did not fall much short of previous itinerant years. I remained in this business and lectured until January, 1873. I paid back their investments to my partners, and sunk the whole capital in the enterprise, but by my lectures and salary from the *Banner* paid all up in two years after closing out; and I came out as poor as a church mouse.

In 1872 my name was on the presidential electoral ticket for Horace Greeley, and as our ticket was elected, I received pay enough to get a suit of clothes. I had made a trip to Denver on a railroad pass, and gave a course of lectures there; visited many places in Missouri, Kansas, Illinois, and Iowa, and did not slacken my labors in the work to which my life was consecrated. I sold out the stock, or what I could of it, and lost $150 more in that trade by the failure of the person to whom I sold; and I gave him up his note and never asked him for anything for it, even though he is still in St. Louis, but poor. I owed the amount to the *Banner* office, but soon paid it up. Then we closed my salary at the office as one of the paid contributors. It was the first and the last pay I have received for correspondence, although I have constantly written for the Spiritual papers, and expect to as long as I can write and read. As my diaries are lost, — if they were kept during my time spent at St. Louis, — and only fragments remain of 1873, I can only guess at the lectures and pay, and will not insert a guess in this book on the subject.

In August of 1873 I took active part in the great camp meeting at Silver Lake, Mass., gotten up by Dr. Gardner and Dr. Richardson, and in which Horace Seaver, editor of the Boston *Investigator*, and Victoria C. Woodhull, the greatest social agitator this country has produced, took part; and it was a camp meeting never to this day excelled by any of the hundreds held since, and none ever better managed. Reporters estimated 15,000 people there at one time, — the day Mrs. Woodhull spoke, Horace Seaver and I and Lizzie Doten spoke. That year I lectured in many places, including Leominster and Clinton, Mass., Saratoga and Syracuse, N.Y. I also attended the celebrated Hemlock Hall meeting in Collins, N.Y.; and there, Mrs. White being the medium, saw materialized faces, among them those of Mrs. Susan K. Tuttle and William White, of the *Banner of Light*, who suddenly passed on to higher life April 28. Both gave me evidence of identity by the intelligence they manifested, as well as their features. Lectured in Pittsburgh, Penn., and Wooster, O., and in September attended the Liberal convention of Mrs. Woodhull and her sister, and in the social contest took sides and active part with her, which greatly prejudiced some of my friends, among them S. S. Jones, editor of the *R. P. Journal* of Chicago, who never got over it till he was shot and killed by a jealous husband, who was never punished for the murder; but this friend's eyes were opened soon after his transition, and he saw himself as others saw him; but his active mind has outgrown it and atoned for it since. I lectured in Chicago that month to large audiences, which were not diminished by my course in the convention. In October attended the Iowa State convention at Des Moines; it was a grand success. I also attended the Kansas State convention at Leavenworth, and did most of the speaking. Visited Lawrence, Kan., lectured in St. Louis, and reached our home in Cobden, October 27. That night, at 12.30, my daughter's fourth son, Warren Chase Whelpley, was born, with the peculiar and fabled old mystery of a veil over his face, from which occurrence we have seen nothing remarkable as yet. Spent the remainder of 1873 in lecturing in Illinois, from Cairo to Chicago, and from Dakota to Wisconsin, and in Iowa, and closed the year at Council Bluffs.

In 1874 I commenced lectures in Des Moines, Iowa. July 4th I delivered an oration at Colfax, Iowa, to 2000 people, which, with many more on the political situation and the Greenback party given in that congressional district and the adjoining one, stirred up the people to such an extent that J. B. Weaver was elected to Congress, and drawn into the position that made him the Greenback candidate for President. The other district also elected a Greenbacker, Gillette, with the State capital in that district, and where I had lectured even in the state-house and court-house on this subject. Visited Canada, and gave twelve lectures there on Spiritualism, and in other places during September. On the 16th of September I attended a convention in Boston, reaching there, via Montreal, sick with ague chills which Dr. H. B. Storer cured at once. In October attended an Iowa State convention at Des Moines. My diary records 167 lectures this year in seven States and Canada. Married several couples and attended funerals, as I always have, when called upon, in my itineracy. Made several visits to my son's home in Otsego, Mich., where my wife spent this year and also part of next, while I had an addition to the old house built for ourselves, when we could be there. My pay this year was but little over living expenses, and not what was needed at our new home; but my heart never faltered in the work. During this year and the next I distributed a large amount of our literature, more than any previous year in St. Louis, if not in New York, as I took out a large part of the stock from the store in St. Louis, and increased it so as to include nearly everything of value in that line from the *Banner* and *Investigator* offices in Boston, locating the stock in Colfax, Iowa, and taking portions of it round where I lectured, and at conventions, until I ran the stock out.

1875. Jan. 1, I was in Colfax, Iowa, where I kept my supply of books, and commenced lectures Sunday, the 3d, in Des Moines, which at that time was quite prominent as a place for Spiritual meetings, and had Mrs. Woodhull there to lecture on the social question, which was her hobby, while she endorsed spirit intercourse and was a medium. Jan. 5, the diary says, sixty-two years old and thirty-eight years married to-day. Gave twelve lectures this very cold month in Iowa. In February drifted in at Independence, Iowa, and walked a mile where the thermometer was thirty-three degrees below zero, and nearly froze, but reached a good home at Charles Patricks'. Worked in Iowa till April, and then visited Illinois home; built another addition to our house, and in June visited my son in Michigan, where my wife Mary was still visiting, but lectured at every opportunity I had to get an audience. In July attended Vermont State convention at Plymouth; also lectured in Paine Hall, Boston, and attended the Cape Cod camp meeting; also visited Saratoga and the Eddy's old home in Chittenden, Vt., where they were giving very satisfactory séances and materializations. Attended the Iowa State convention, at Iowa Falls, in October. Nov. 16, my wife reached our home in Illinois, from our son's home in Michigan. I was there, and our son Albert, and we all had our last family Thanksgiving meeting with all but the doctor, our oldest son, at our turkey dinner. I had been finishing up the work on the kitchen addition, and on the 18th left for Iowa, parting with Mary, the last time I saw her in the flesh, and with no thought of its being the last; but I have since seen a materialized form resembling hers several times when the intelligence that came through it removed every doubt of its being controlled by her spirit. Nov. 24, I was at Colfax, Iowa, and had had dreams and signs of death, but had no idea of the cause until I reached Anita, in Cass County, where I was to lecture Sunday, the 27th. On reaching there late Saturday eve, I found the telegram telling me of Mary's transition at 12.30 A.M., the 26th. They knew of my Sunday engagement there, as they usually did, but did not know where else to address me. It was as sudden to all at home as to me, for she was about the house the day she passed over at midnight. I could not get home to the funeral, and beside, had no money to go with, having just come from there and used up all I had. I kept on my course to earn the money to pay the expenses, but I had good messages from her before she had been five days in spirit life, assuring me that all was well, and urging me on in my work, as she has many times since, always assuring me of her interest in the cause which was dear to her for many years before she passed to spirit life. I changed my route as soon as I could do so, and get employment so as to reach home as soon as possible and have the expenses paid, as everything was done in the manner she would have had it. Mrs. Dr. Cutler gave the funeral address, and we had it published in the *Banner of Light*. It was worthy the author and the subject.

Sunday, 28th, in sadness, I lectured in Anita on death, taking in the recent one, the effect it had on her and us, and closed up the year at Council Bluffs, Iowa, after a visit and many lectures in Kansas. Diary reports 148 lectures this year, pay not varying much from other years, but larger book sales, the receipts from which were always mixed with those for lectures. The actual receipts for lectures were less than $700, more than half of which must have been used for travel and personal expenses, and the profits on the books were small.

Centennial year, 1876, began lectures in Omaha Jan. 2, and continued to lecture in Iowa, Illinois, and Ohio, till June 12, when I went from Alliance, O., to Centennial, and spent two weeks in that place, lecturing three times each Sunday, and thereby paying expenses. Returning to Alliance and my work, I spent most of September at our home in Illinois, and Dec. 1, started from Omaha for California. Stopped in Columbus, Neb., and gave four lectures, also stopped and gave a course of lectures in Salt Lake City, to large and appreciative audiences of Gentiles, but few Mormons. I reached San Francisco Dec. 30, at 11 P.M., having closed the year, an eventful one, with the Centennial in it and the transition of many friends following that of my wife to the spirit world, and many trials and perplexities, as in previous years. Diary reports 158 lectures, six in Salt Lake City.

1877 was an eventful year for me and my work. Rachel Lukens, daughter of David Lukens of Morrisville, Penn., across the Delaware River from Trenton, N.J., for many years a well-known medium who had given tests in Philadelphia, New York, Chicago, St. Louis, Denver, and San Francisco, and well known to me and my family, and who had been two years in California, gladly received and welcomed me, and we were married in January. The society had a speaker engaged for January, and I waited and commenced my work in California in February, which was successful in the State, and continued to be so during my stay in California: in Sunday lectures on Spiritualism in whatever public capacity I was engaged, while editing the Santa Barbara *Independent and Pacific Greenbacker*, during my three sessions in the State Senate, and while canvassing for that office and as a candidate for the constitutional convention of Santa Barbara County, and for member of Congress for the State at large for the Greenback party, which, of course, could not elect me. I lectured in many parts of the State and many times in the large cities and towns, sometimes taking my wife with me when she was able to give tests. Diary for Jan. 5 says, sixty-four years old to-day, married forty years ago to-day to Mary P. White, and lived with her nearly thirty-nine years, and she passed over to the spirit life Nov. 28, 1875, the first break in our family since the little boys passed over in 1843. Diary reports 132 lectures first year in the

State of California; in many places, but chiefly in San Francisco, San José, Santa Barbara, and more each succeeding year in the State. Spiritualism at that time was as popular in California as in any part of the Union. Its meetings were treated with as much respect as those of any church by the people generally, as was evinced by my election to the State Senate and my popularity in that body, which was not affected disadvantageously by it, as I was the recognized leader in that body in the cause of temperance and woman's suffrage, as well as other reform measures, and I succeeded in defeating the election of a chaplain to be paid out of the State treasury, — a shameful proceeding of other States, and of that also in previous years.

1878. After residing a short time in San José, and lecturing there and in San Francisco and Sacramento, early in February we moved to Santa Barbara, and into a little cottage, which was our home as long as we remained in the State. I lectured there constantly till I went to the Legislature, and as editor had too much on my hands for a short time, but still never failed to fill all engagements I could get, as I ever have, up to this time of writing, *never* failing from a personal cause. In July of this year I started and edited the Santa Barbara *Independent*, after having departed for the constitutional convention, and continued to edit it until my second session in the Senate, where my duties were such I released myself from the paper, and it was soon after sold to the Democrats, who had no paper at the county seat. 1879 was a very busy year with me; but my work was largely local, advocating the adoption of the new constitution with tongue and pen, mainly because it required the taxing of all church property and unimproved lands to their actual value. Our success in carrying this measure in our senatorial district put me in the Senate at the first election under it. I also took an active part in the Greenback political party and in its conventions; but my Sundays were sacred to Spiritualism. With the help of a few friends, especially Mrs. H. F. M. Brown, who was stopping in Santa Barbara, preparing for her transition, which she knew was near, we kept up a lyceum for about two years. Closed the year in San Francisco. During this year I had seen the cause of Spiritualism growing rapidly, and I had not failed to do my part towards its advancement. 1880, Jan. 1, I reached the capitol at Sacramento, where the Legislature met. Jan. 5 was my birthday, — sixty-seven years old, — and the oldest member of the Legislature. I was soon invited to lecture for the Spiritualists Sunday evenings. I of course accepted, and had the governor and his wife at my second lecture. I continued to edit my paper during this session of one hundred days. Returned home April 24, stopping to lecture in San Francisco. I supported J. B. Weaver for President, with tongue and pen, through the campaign. When we started our paper, there were three in the city; and in July, my diary says, ours was the only one in the city. One of the others had been bought out by our publisher, and the other suspended before its new editor came and was shot and killed — a good man and a Spiritualist, known to me in the East. The murderer, after three trials, got legally cleared, but not morally or spiritually. Diary of Sept. 25 says, Theodore Glancy, editor of *Press*, shot by Clarence Gray, under influence of liquor, died next day. I spoke words of comfort and consolation to the mourners at several funerals during this and preceding and subsequent years. Closed the year at Sacramento, ready to meet in Senate session for January, 1881. Sunday, Jan. 2, lectured for Spiritualists, and spoke at the Irish League meeting; and Monday, 3d, Senate met, and I was in my seat, which my enemies had tried in vain to have vacated, because, as they said, falsely, I had not been in the State long enough when elected, and they depended on the party vote to rule me out because I was not a Republican nor a Democrat; but failed, as I was popular with both parties, and the chairman of the committee told me they should keep me and needed more like me. Lectured Sundays during the sixty days' session, and attended and spoke at funeral of the landlady where I boarded during the first session, Mrs. Julia Hancock, her family Spiritualists, and many more in Sacramento. Disconnected myself from the *Independent* at opening of this session and wrote for Santa Barbara *Press* occasionally after my return in March. The governor called an extra session for April, because important business had been neglected by party wrangling and squandering away the time of the sixty days' session; and in April we met again, but to no useful purpose, as party strife defeated every effort to get the required measures passed. On the whole, it was a disgrace to the State and the Legislature, and I was glad my time was out with the session, and that it was the last I should take part in. After all efforts of the honest members failed, we adjourned May 13, and I then took the cars for the East, via Utah. I stopped over at Salt Lake City and Ogden and gave a course of lectures in each place. I reached Anita, Iowa, May 25, going to the home of Brother Edwin Cates, where I had once received the notice of the death of my wife. June 1, I spoke in the Greenback State convention in Marshal, Iowa, and met my daughter in St. Louis; we spent a week there, lectured, and then went home to Cobden with her for a rest and visit, which I greatly needed and greatly enjoyed, as all who participated did. June 14 was at my son's, the doctor, in Otsego, Mich., and lectured in Allegan Sunday. I could not rest easy on a Sunday if I did not have an audience to address on our glorious truths. June 28, I attended a Greenback camp meeting at Lansing, Mich., and took an active part with old friends, Jesse Harper, Solon Chase, J. B. Weaver, D. La Mater, Gillette, and others, many of whom were Spiritualists, especially Brother Potter, who got up the camp meeting and conducted it successfully through the 4th of July. After lecturing in several places in Ohio I reached Cassadaga, N.Y., camp meeting, Aug. 5, and said my say as usual there for several days. Aug. 14 and 15 attended the Lake Pleasant camp meeting and spoke there on politics Monday, 15th; I also visited Onset and spoke there Sundays, the 21st and 28th. Opened the camp meeting at Harwich; returned to Boston Sept. 1, and lectured in Paine Hall Sunday, Sept. 4. Closed the grove meetings for the season, Sept. 11, at Shawsheen grove, with Dr. Richardson's picnic. I was engaged the remainder of the year busily lecturing all of the Sundays and many evenings in Massachusetts, New York, New Jersey, and closed it at Trenton, N.J., at the home of my present wife's mother and sisters, visiting them. Trenton is to this day one of the most aristocratic, orthodox places I have ever visited, and far behind most other cities of its size and population in intellectual, advanced thought, yet is steadily outgrowing its old fogy formalities. January, lectured in New Jersey, Pennsylvania, and Maryland, and on the 20th was in the Woman's Rights National Convention in Washington, D.C., but not called to the platform or introduced by the leaders, though one of the oldest and boldest public advocates of equal rights between the sexes in the country, and one who had introduced woman's suffrage into a legislative body in 1846, so far as I know, the first instance of the kind. But I was not orthodox, and it was clergymen and members of Congress they were seeking for indorsers. They had Congressman Orth, a Spiritualist, on the platform to speak, but none of the leaders and but few of the audience knew he was a Spiritualist; but I did, and all knew I was, and that excluded me from the leaders to whom I was well known as older in the cause as a public advocate than any of them. Had a pleasant visit with my old friend, Col. R. G. Ingersoll, and my old political friend, Postmaster-General Howe of Wisconsin; also Senator Miller of California, and through his politeness was introduced to President Arthur. I had also many personal friends in Congress, among them both senators from Missouri, who were on the Presidential electoral ticket of Missouri with me in 1872; and yet the woman suffragists snubbed me, partly, perhaps, because I was a personal friend of Victoria C. Woodhull, who did more for the cause in her three years' work than any one of them had done in any six years, and more than most of them have done in their lives, in directing public attention to the injustices done women by unequal laws. I delivered the address on Thomas Paine's birthday to a large audience, and lectured on California and on Spiritualism during my stay in Washington.

Spent two months in Washington; returned, and lectured in Philadelphia in March, and also in Worcester, Mass., where we celebrated the thirty-fourth anniversary of the spirit rappings at Hydesville and the good work of the Fox girls. In April I started West, stopping to lecture in Binghamton, N.Y., and Alliance, O., Cleveland, Clyde, and Toledo. May 24, with the National Greenback Committee in St. Louis, and visiting my son Albert, who was then and is now a police officer in that city. Lectured there and visited Cobden home, and lectured in Kirksville, Mo. Reached Ottumwa, Iowa, in time to see the clouds in the distance that carried destruction in a cyclone to Grinnell. Saturday eve, June 17, 1882. Sunday, 18th, lectured in Ottumwa, and the 25th, in Council

Bluffs ; great excitement about the cyclone. On the 27th took emigrant train for San Francisco, and had good fare and pleasanter time than on the express, by which I had travelled over the route, and should prefer the former again at the same price for each, as I belong with the poor and laboring classes. Reached San Francisco July 5, home the 6th, and had no incident *en route* worth recording, unless I write a novel about it and the sand storms of the desert. Remained about home at Santa Barbara till the Greenback convention nominated me for Congress for the State at large, and a few friends furnished me travelling expenses, without which I could not go out to canvass ; and then I started and made political speeches week days, and lectured on Spiritualism Sundays, as for no cause would I ever give up that work, and all knew my views on that subject. Visited many places and made many speeches, sometimes accompanied by others, among them Mrs. Marion Todd, attorney-at-law, who was also on the State ticket. Of course, none of us expected to be elected ; but in accordance with my past record I ran ahead of most of those on tickets with me, which went to show that my religious belief and social character did not injure me with the people, although plenty of lies had been told about me. In San Francisco election day, and of course I could not vote, but stayed and lectured there and in other places, and closed the year in the city. I passed January 5, 1883, my seventieth birthday, in San Francisco, where the Spiritualists and my political friends got up a reception in Ixora Hall, and about 500 people called during the evening and made many speeches and read poems ; some of the latter may be found in the poetical chapter of this book ; but the speeches were not reported, which I have ever regretted. Received also many presents and over $50 in money, and enjoyed the grandest time of my life ; for my labors and motives seemed to be appreciated by so many personal friends. Lectured in San Francisco and Sacramento till Feb. 26, when I went home to sell and close out at Santa Barbara, prepare to move East with my family, and leave California till I could visit it as a spirit without an earthly body. Closed my lectures in Santa Barbara Sunday, March 11, and sold house lot, with all the furniture, etc., for $675. Started East on the Southern Pacific Railroad, and reached St. Louis the 22d, where we met my son Albert, and grandson H. M. Whelpley, of the College of Pharmacy. Spent a week and lectured there, and then Rachel and Ida moved on to Trenton, N.J., to board with sisters and mother. I left the train, and lectured in Terre Haute, Toledo, Clyde, and other places on my route via Corry, Penn.; also at Jamestown. All along my line of travel I found interest in our cause, and lectured continually, as I had done for so many years. At Erie, Penn., met Moses and Mattie Hull, two old, able, and faithful workers in the cause; also visited my friend Anna D. Weaver, author of "Richard's Crown," and a contributor to several reform papers. Lectured in the large house of Oliver G. Chase, in Jamestown, N.Y., because we could not get a hall except at an extra and exorbitant price. Oliver and his family had long been among the pioneer workers. Reached Trenton June 28, where we have plenty of friends, but no home, and where I never want one, as the atmosphere is too blue for me; but I lectured there to a few, most of them as much Christians as Spiritualists, and who did not dare to get far from the Bible and the creeds founded on it. July 5, self and wife went to Boston on first trip of steamer *Pilgrim*, the finest boat on the line at the time. From Boston we went to Onset camp-ground, and also attended the Cape Cod camp meeting, taking part as usual in the exercises of both. Rachel returned to Trenton, and I went from Boston on steamer to Bucksport, Me., and attended camp meeting there. From there I went to the pleasant home of Dr. Samuel Emery's family, at Glenburne, Me., and with them to Ætna camp meeting, and returned to Boston at the close via coast steamer, and lectured in Worcester during September and October to large audiences. Continued to lecture every Sunday and many evenings in New York till last of November, when I went to Trenton, and lectured in Vineland and other places till the end of the year, Dec. 31.

1884 was a busy year, opening my lectures in Washington, D.C., where I hired the hall myself for two months, and kept up my meetings, stopping with my excellent friends, Mr. and Mrs. George Roberts, who got up a very pleasant social party on my seventy-first birthday, at their house. Mrs. Roberts has since gone to spirit life, now followed by her husband. Few better women or men have passed on from our ranks. During March and April I lectured in Indianapolis, and had large and intelligent audiences in the old Plymouth church. May and June I spent in Ohio and Western New York, taking in Mayville and Jamestown. Returning to New England, I was engaged all of the time and in many places, closing the year with excellent audiences in Norwich, Conn., and at the home of one of our best and ablest workers, Byron Boardman, who has since prematurely gone to spirit life, from his body being overworked. During the year I attended the camp meeting at Onset, and four in Maine, and lectured in Portland, where I had not lectured for thirty years; also in Newburyport and Amesbury, and many other places.

1885. Opened in Worcester, and had a good public reception on my seventy-second birthday, Jan. 5, in the hall where I was lecturing. February, lectured in Norwich; and the eleventh of the month our daughter Ida was married in Trenton, to Charles W. Bergen — a very satisfactory match to us all. Lectured in Cincinnati, O., the five Sundays of March, and gave the cause a new impulse there, that continued to increase for several years, and continues at the time of writing this. Caught a severe cold that laid me up half of April in Toledo. Visited son's family in Otsego, Mich., in April; lectured there and in Grand Rapids and several other places. Crossed the lake to Milwaukee, and had a pleasant home while in the city with those noble workers in our cause, A. B. and Dr. Juliette H. Severance. Visited and lectured at my old home, once Ceresco, now Ripon, Wis., and in the substantial hall of the Spiritualists in Omro — a place where I planted the first seeds of our philosophy. Had grand visits with old friends, Phillips, Lockwood, Woodruff, Mason, and others, where the cause has never languished since we first started it in that part of the State, though strenuous efforts have ever been made by the churches to put it down and out. Lectured in Detroit on return East. Many years since I had lectured there, and on this visit found it about the same as formerly, — too much church aristocracy, but religion at low ebb. Lectured in the Universalist church at Clyde, and in our church at Geneva, O. Lectured in Saratoga on the Sundays of August, and had good audiences, except on the 16th, when I spoke in Onset, Mass., on camp grounds. September, at Queen City Park camp meeting; spoke also in Leicester, Stowe, and Bellows Falls, in a church at each place. I found the Universalists in Vermont more liberal than in Massachusetts or New York. Spoke in Boston and other places in Massachusetts, New Hampshire, and Rhode Island. November, in Norwich, Conn., and Willimantic, in our church. December, lectured in Worcester, and closed the year there. Diary says, very busy year, and barely paid expenses of self and family.

Jan. 1, 1886. Opened lectures in Springfield, Mass.;

and Jan. 5, had a very pleasant and large party at Mr. J. M. Johnson's, to celebrate my seventy-third birthday. Lectured in Massachusetts, Connecticut, and New York till last of February, and then went via Trenton, N.J., and Cincinnati to Louisville, Ky., where I lectured two months, during which time we had the great Southern Convention of eight days in that city, — a grand time and good results.

May, I spoke in Evansville, Ind., Cairo, and other places in Illinois, and spent most of the month at my home in Cobden, with the pleasant and happy grandchildren and their parents. In June, lectured in Springfield, Mo., and in Liberal, Mo., where we had a grand three days' meeting, closing July 4 — being Sunday. We had no prayers in our meetings and very large attendance; no liquor, nor drunkenness, nor quarrelling, and hence needed no priest or magistrate. Lectured in Warsaw, Ind., and Clyde and Geneva, O., and reached Saratoga Springs Aug. 6. Lectured there during August to good audiences. September, lectured in Massachusetts and New Hampshire, at Keene, and Lunenburg, and Princeton. All of October I lectured in Springfield, Mass., and made arrangements for a temporary home in Worcester, where I am writing this book. My wife joined me in this new home Oct. 26. On the 31st I closed my lectures in Springfield and spoke at the funeral of Mrs. Robinson the same day. In November I lectured in Vermont and New Hampshire, and visited the old home of my first wife in Newport, N.H., and the farms on which I labored from my fifteenth to twenty-first years, in Pittsfield, N.H., my native town; and also the spot where once stood the old rotten log-house where I was born; and the cellar (all that is left) of the house where my mother died. Saw the twelve graves where her earthly remains and those of her parents and the rest of the family were buried in the old orchard, with rude granite stones to mark the spots. Deep reflections on my long and varied career of life, which I never want to pass through again by re-incarnation; so please let me pass on, never to be clothed again with an earthly body. In December I lectured in Haverhill, Mass., and Troy, N.Y., and closed the year at our temporary home in Worcester; a remarkable year and a busy one for me, with many incidents in it not soon to be forgotten, but like all of my past years I left it without debts, but with nothing saved for old age or sickness; yet spirit friends assure me I shall be provided for — as I know I shall when I get over there, where I have so many friends that have labored with me here, and many who have suffered with me here, for taking part in this great work.

1887. The fortieth year of my labors in the cause of our new gospel was opened in Worcester, at our temporary home; it closes the running years of this narrative, and I will leave the rest for more interesting and more valuable matter for the readers. Had grand public reception on my seventy-fourth birthday, Jan. 5, in Worcester, and during January lectured in Woonsocket, Providence, and Lynn, and spent remainder of time at home on this book. In February, tried to get up lecture in Lawrence, but found the place was so nearly given over to Catholicism that it was a failure, leaving only a call for mediums and phenomena, which in time will save the cause, after which it must educate the people on the philosophy. Lost the month, and fell behind my expenses largely, and felt quite badly, because I had scarcely any reserve after nearly forty years' labor, as faithfully done as I was able to do it. March was a busy month in Troy and Albany, N.Y., and in Haverhill, Mass., and partly repaid me for the loss I sustained in February. No person has more fully realized that time was his estate than I have, and do to the time of this writing. Sunday is my harvest day, and when that fails, I am short of funds. April was also a busy month in Massachusetts. In May, five Sundays were filled in Bridgeport, Conn., where I had not lectured for over twenty years. June, lectured one Sunday in Worcester and one in Lunenburg, and then lost the rest of the time on which I so much depend.

July 8, self and wife repaired to Onset camp meeting, rooming in Mrs. M. S. Wood's sub-let cottage nicely for three weeks, during which time I did my share of the talking, and sold a large number of my books. At the close of the three weeks I went to Hanson, and had good audiences on Sunday, July 31. After a few days at home in Worcester, I went to the Sunapee Lake camp, Newbury, N.H., where three thousand people gathered. On the Sunday I gave two lectures to good acceptance. We had a grand success there; and after a short visit to the old home of my first wife, in Newport, N.H., among the descendants of her parents, I spent a few days at home. At Onset met my esteemed friend Darius Lyman, who had for twenty-four years held a responsible position in the United States Treasury, and had just resigned. He had been an active Spiritualist all these years, often using his pen in defence of Spiritualism. He was the teacher of an academy in Michigan before the war, and a Spiritualist then, and my children and my son-in-law attended his school at Harmonia, Mich. He is one of our ablest defenders of mediums and mediumship.

Returning from Sunapee, I visited Lake Pleasant without invitation as a speaker. There I remained during the two closing days of the session, in the midst of a large, enthusiastic, and a quite harmonious gathering, considering the many stories told about wrangles there. They had some of our best speakers and mediums in attendance; among the former, J. Frank Baxter and C.

Fanny Allyn; and among the latter, Margaret Fox Kane, one of the three celebrated Fox girls, in whose presence phenomena occurred about forty years ago, that attracted world-wide attention, and made for themselves a reputation that will endure for many centuries. Margaret assured me that she was but five years old at the time they began talking with the invisibles that made the raps in Hydesville, and that her sister Katie, who was the first cause of them, was only three, and thus, of course, both were incapable of being engaged in such nefarious work as has been charged to them by thousands of dishonest Christian professors and preachers of sectarian Christianity. These three sisters have been tested to this day, hundreds of times, by the most critical and sceptical persons, and have *never* been detected in any effort to deceive, for they never had a necessity or disposition to do so.

Under the presidency of our oldest camp-meeting preacher yet living, Dr. Richardson, I addressed the largest audience one Sunday, at Sunapee, I had addressed this season; and a more attentive outdoor audience I had never met. The grounds were rough, rude, natural; the scenery romantic; the entire place a delightful retreat for a Spiritual camp meeting. Here I met one sister of my first wife, and several families of later generations from the old stock intermarried with congenial companions, and all interested in our philosophy; and I visited some of them at their Newport, N.H., homes, and enjoyed the visits as in olden times, reviving pleasant memories of former years. This visit to New Hampshire and its camping-grounds will be remembered long after I go to the new camping-grounds on the other side of the River Styx.

By engagement I spent the last two weeks of camping season at Queen City Park camp-grounds, in Vermont, on the shore of Shelburne Bay, near its entrance into Lake Champlain, two miles from Burlington, on the Vermont Central Railroad, and south of the city. This is decidedly the most picturesque camping-ground yet selected in New England, except Temple Heights, in Maine, and has the best arranged and most appropriately constructed improvements; but not as extensive or capable of the extension or convenience and suitable grounds as Onset or Lake Pleasant, and yet sufficiently so for many years, and all that can be done in them within that time. We had excellent meetings, but not so large as at the other grounds, as the season was late, running into September, and many had spent all the time and money they could spare at the others, and earlier in the season, when heat had driven them from the cities; but those who came to Queen City Park were delighted with the scenery, the cordiality, the good feeling and hearty welcome given them by these genial sons and daughters of Vermont, who know as well as any people in the world how to make homes happy and comfortable for themselves and visitors. Dr. E. A. Smith and wife, Fanny Davis Smith of Brandon, Vt., are the leading spirits in this enterprise, and deserve great credit for the work they have done, seconded and aided by several other families who are always present and active in their large cottages, providing for visitors, and looking after their comforts. Our friends who visit camp-grounds should not miss this beautiful spot and genial company. Here, Sept. 12, I closed my camping season for this year, and left the grounds, with many friends, for Keene and Hancock, N.H. In the latter place I gave the first lectures, on the facts and philosophy of Spiritualism, ever given in the town in a public hall, and had good audiences and close attention. Two weeks later I spoke in Peterborough, N.H., with still better success, and more alarm to the churches. Oct. 28, 29, and 30, we had a good State convention in Plymouth, N.H., and had a real good visit with my cousin Hansen Chase and family, himself and wife Spiritualists for many years.

In closing my seventy-fifth year of life, and fortieth on the Spiritual rostrum, in November, I spent a week in Lowell, Mass., where I had frequently lectured many years ago, and had again four good audiences on the last two Sundays, and a very pleasant visit with my old and esteemed friends Mr. and Mrs. Jacob Nichols, who had just celebrated their golden wedding, but only had one of their four children, — and she a widow with five children, — the other three being in the spirit world. These friends and others who formerly attended my lectures are as firm in the belief as ever, but many have gone to the better life. Among those still lingering here whose companions were gone were Mrs. Holbrook, Mrs. Hapgood, Mrs. Wood, Mrs. Hume, the two Mrs. Gowards, Mrs. Perrin, Mrs. Pillsbury, Mrs. Evans, and several others, showing a greater tenacity of life in woman than in man in many cases. In December I lectured in Brockton, Mass., for the first time; in Manchester, N.H., one Sunday; closed the month at Troy, N.Y., Sunday, the 25th, and returned to Worcester to close the year, but did not see it die out there. At Troy we had a grand celebration of Christmas, in the elegant hall which the second society had hired for the year, nearly two hundred persons taking dinner with us in the hall, and all a free gift by the society and lyceum.

In closing my seventy-five years in the paths of labor in this field, I received a highly complimentary letter from A. J. Davis, with the important fact that MINE was the FIRST order received and recorded for several (one dozen) copies of our first Spiritual book, "NATURE'S DIVINE REVELATION," in 1847, which book I received as soon as issued. For an account of my reception on my seventy-fifth birthday, and the close of my forty years, see report from the *Banner of Light*, on page 202.

CHAPTER VII.

WHAT I HAVE LEARNED FROM FORTY YEARS' INTERCOURSE WITH THE DENIZENS OF THE NEXT SPHERE.

"I have travelled far and wide, and waited time and tide,
And have learned a thing or two in my time."

"Shall I know thee again in the happy land,
Thou who hast passed to that brighter sphere?"

"The love that unites two hearts in one
   Cannot be broken by death;
But united again in the heavenly zone
   Shall renew the affections of earth."

THE first, if not the most important truth I have learned, and which is now fully confirmed, is, that the condition of the mind is not changed immediately by death. That the deserted case, tenement, or covering of the earthly body, is immediately changed for another of different materials, made up more or less perfect in form and expression, according to the condition of the mind, and that the mind resides, acts, works, or plays in that largely as it did in the deserted body. Next, that it does not leave the locality to which it was attached, nor the persons, objects, or business in which it was most deeply interested, until either crowded off by indifference on this side or drawn away by other attractions. I have learned that those with strong and zealous religious beliefs do not suddenly lose their faith or change at once their beliefs, although they do not see or hear, or know any more of God or Christ or the saints than they did here; yet they continue to pray in the same faith, and congregate and hold meetings and expect the miracles they looked for when here; and when such spirits get *en rapport* with, or hold control of, media, they pray and preach very much as they did when in this life, as they only change when the mind outgrows its superstitions; and this pertains to the disciples of other religions, the same as to those of the Christian. Hence death does not correct the religious errors much more than a removal from one section of this world to another.

Those who are mentally free from all superstitions are there, as here, in the best condition to enjoy existence. Buddha of this life is Buddha in spirit life, and Buddhists here are Buddhists there. The Mohammed of this life is Mohammed there, and Mohammedans here are Mohammedans there. Jews here are Jews when they get there, and know as little of Jehovah or Christ there as here. Catholics here are Catholics there. Methodists here are Methodists there, and engaged in giving such assistance as they can toward building up the sectarian superstition here till they are sufficiently enlightened to leave that work. The souls of Catholics are, not many of them, in *repose*, waiting for the resurrection of the body, although thousands are expecting it and still believe in the coming of Christ and a general resurrection; as there is the same ground there as here on which to found the absurd belief, and no more. The Protestant souls are not asleep in Jesus, as announced on tombstones, but are awake, and still looking and waiting for his appearance with as much faith and as little knowledge as when here. Whatever superstitious belief is a controlling influence of the mind here is the same after death as before for a time; in many minds it is as difficult to get freed from it there as here, a change being effected only by growth and development. Those poor souls who are relying on Jesus to take them into paradise at death are to be pitied, as they are terribly disappointed, but still hope on in vain, as there is no more prospect of his appearance there than here, where he has been looked for nearly nineteen hundred years, and in vain. There seems to be a strange fatality about many spirits which to me is as yet unexplained and unaccounted for, by which many spirits who are driven out of their bodies by murder or violent death, in great fright, in which the mind is intensely fixed on the place where it takes place, seem to be tethered to the locality by some sort of condition till they can be relieved by some communication with persons in this life. There seems to be something of this kind of fatality about the poor Arctic explorers who exchange worlds among the icebergs and amid the terrors of an Arctic winter; and also something of it in the case of those who lose their bodies in mid-ocean, and where no connecting line of living persons reunites them with their earthly friends on the land.

Cranks and hobby-riders after death remain for a season, long or short according to circumstances, in their respective fields of thought and feeling, and attached to the object that occupied their minds when in the body. Scholars and artists continue attached to what occupied their minds when in the body, and if *en rapport* with a sensitive on earth, manifest their peculiar attachment; hence there is no reason why religionists should not be governed by the same law, since there is no more of the presence of any God in that life than in this. So my spirit friends assure me; and there as here they ridicule the absurdity of praying to any personal God. The most reliable information I have received, and which is constantly confirmed and perfectly reliable, is, that there is nothing true as taught by any sect in Christianity about God or devil, hell or heaven, thereby setting aside the whole paraphernalia of the churches and their systems of faith as utterly useless, except so far as they induce persons to live better lives and deal more honestly and kindly with their fellow-beings and animals. I have also learned that the conversions of criminals after sentence, or while waiting for execution, are only valuable as they are real changes of purpose in living a better life; and that when they are only dependent on the atonement of Christ, they are worthless, as they find on entrance into that life; if their minds are not changed in the course of action toward the victim and others, the repentance is of no utility to themselves or others.

As the physical body does not have to be fed in spirit life, we are there relieved from many burdens and duties pertaining to this life; but the cravings of the mind are not lessened by death. Hence that mental craving for stimulants and tobacco are felt there, and bring many spirits into close relation with the conditions on earth where these cravings were once supplied, and the sufferings of such as are subject to these cravings are as intense as in this life when not supplied. Persons who starve to death for a time suffer the gnawings of hunger; and if they can get control of a medium, display a ravenous appetite, but only once or twice, as after it is satisfied the mind is changed and released.

I have learned that a natural law of evolution lifts us out of this life into a higher and finer element of forms, as it does the seeds that germinate in the soil where they are planted and covered in, that like the human body in gestation they may start in the dark to develop a materialized form and push up to the higher stratum. As the plants cannot blossom and fruit in the soil, so man cannot develop his higher and superior life in his earthly body, but in the spiritual can develop his true character of man and womanhood. But I have also learned that that life is no more a fixture and no more eternal than this, although it may continue in many instances for many millions of our years, and pass through many changes, before another transition, corresponding to the one that brought us here, or that termed death, which takes us hence, — evolution pertaining to that life the same as to this, with its lifting and revolving processes, carrying us along there as here.

I have learned that when persons die they do not become angels, and are no more so than before death, not even priests or so-called saints; and that the winged creatures, so often pictured by Christians as angels, are no more known to exist in that life than in this, the silly idea of angels hovering over us being a matter of ridicule in that life: not even the winged devil is known there.

I have also learned that the location of the spiritual globe is immediately over the substance of our globe, and the people of that country over their kin in this; that that country corresponds to this mundane plain, with an extension over the water, which makes it vastly larger than the inhabitable part of the earth, and that it is involved with the motions of the earth in its orbit and diurnal motions; that our friends in that life who can communicate with us can no more visit the planets and other worlds than we can. I have also learned that the transition to that life does not enable them to know more about this life and the things of earth than we do who live here, and that most of what they tell us about the affairs of this life is taken from minds in the body with which they come *en rapport;* hence the numerous mistakes in locating minerals and other objects in the earth, and in giving directions about speculations, in which many have been financially ruined by following the advice of spirits who meant no harm, but, like us, are liable to be mistaken.

Having learned from perfectly reliable testimony that the spirit sphere to which we go when we die has no more evidence of the existence of gods, devils, heaven, or hell than this world has, and having found none here, I have never seen any utility in supporting the churches in their work of what they call "saving souls." I have also learned that the mind, through a spiritual control of this body, often performs remarkable feats through it, when the external consciousness is utterly gone or at rest, sometimes in dreams, sometimes in somnambulism, sometimes in clairvoyance, and sometimes when controlled psychologically by another mind. All of which goes to show that the mind has an active existence independent of its consciousness in the bodily organs, and that consciousness is incidental, so far as it pertains to the body and its organs.

I have also learned that in what is technically termed spirit life the thoughts are depicted on the countenance, so that no person can "one thing think and another tell," and hence there is no deception practised there between spirits, however much may be practised on us mortals by one another, or by their playing upon us and taking advantage of our confidence, no doubt often amusing themselves at our expense. Long and close observation has proved to me that it is useless to ask spirits about business affairs that are wholly mundane, as they give only opinions as mortals living here do; but if they see anything of importance to us, and they can transmit the imformation to us unsolicited by us, and they give it to us in that way, it is best for us to heed it, as in this way we often get valuable advice when it comes uncontaminated by any action of our minds. There is something about the law relating to minds in the body acting upon and dealing with disembodied minds, that is not yet well understood, but observation has proved to me that our anxiety on any subject makes what we get unreliable, from some cause to me as yet unknown; but I have had many reliable messages unexpectedly and unsolicited.

So far as I can learn from my friends in the other life, their bodies seem to be made up of discreted materials that have passed through organic forms on earth, and thereby become etherealized, and they seem to be gathered around the soul to serve as a case, in which the mind has its depository as in the brain of the earthly body. It is plain that the brain is only a reservoir for the particles or globules of mind-element in both bodies, and that only the accumulations collected in earth life are carried forward to be used in commencing the life on the other side. Hence the peculiarities, and even idiosyncrasies, of individuals are carried forward, by which we identify them in their communications. That they have forms as real to the mind there as here, is certain; and that these bodies are material is equally certain. A very large majority of the people in this life are wholly absorbed mentally in matters that pertain wholly to this life and the body with its surroundings. When such minds are freed from the earthly body, the mind has no other food to feed on, and such persons are not happy in spirit life until they can engage the mind in something that pertains more directly to that life. Such persons are the ones that lay up their treasures in this life instead of putting them in the life beyond. "Before the world was I am," is true of many human beings, but applies to the soul and not to any body, earthly or spiritual; nor to the mind which is collected in the body; nor from particles as the body is, but by the soul, which is the ego of every person, of which we so often speak when we say, "*I* make up my mind," or, "*I* think." Both reason and spirit testimony teach that a false or heretical religious belief is no better than, if as good as, no belief, and hence if Catholicism was true, which it is not, all Protestants are no better situated at death than agnostics or atheists, if the moral character and conduct of life here is no better; and if any one of the Protestants sects was right, which no one is, all the others, and the swarms of Catholics, are no better than atheists at death, as both have to become rid of the errors and accept the truth, to realize its nature and enjoy its blessings. According to all testimony, superstition of any kind is a very great incumbrance and obstruction to progress. Thomas Paine is in a vastly superior condition in that life, and was upon entering it, to Cotton Mather and Jonathan Edwards; and Abner Kneeland far better situated than those who persecuted and imprisoned him in Boston for telling the truth, which, they said, he had a right to believe, but not to express, and for which no God would punish him, but bigots would, and did.

The erroneous idea many persons entertain of the spirit world lead to many a blunder in the intercourse, they seeming to think that when a spirit is freed from its body, it can at once see and find any spirit that has preceded it to that life, as if it was only a small village; but those that go find it a region many millions of times larger than the habitable portion of the earth; and as each person is limited to his or her personality and locality, with eyes and ears confined to the spirit body, as in this life to the physical, they find it far more difficult to find persons in that vast region than in this more limited sphere of life; the only advantage there, being a much easier and cheaper mode of travel. A spirit inquiring for some person who was distinguished in this life may not be able to find any one who knew him or her, and no one who can tell where such person can be found. Those who hunt for Jesus are surely disappointed, as no one who went from this part of the earth has been able to find him.

Another popular error about that life is that a spirit, as soon as free from its earthly body, can see into our condition of body and our surroundings, and advise us what to do to cure physical maladies, and give us valuable advice about our business affairs, when, in fact, with the exception of a clearer perception and relation with our minds and other minds, it can come *en rapport* with, he or she can give us no better advice than before. Surgeons and skilful physicians, who carry with them knowledge of the bodies of earth, can see more clearly the ailments, and can prescribe from knowledge gained when on earth, provided we can engage them; but there is no currency except love and sympathy with which they can be paid, and it is not all persons that can interest such as can assist us in this life; hence maladies and diseases do not all disappear under spirit guidance that could be relieved by them. We are often asked what is the occupation in spirit life, and so far as I can learn, the mind aspires there as here, or grovels in useless absurdities. Persons in this life who have every comfort that wealth can procure, and whose minds do not soar above fancy dresses, balls, theatres, and eating and drinking, will not be likely to soar much higher on entering a mental state where the mind has no higher inducement than it has here where higher objects are abundant. It is estimated on very good authority that about one-third of the cases of insanity are obsessions, by spirits who in this world had no higher ideas of life or ambition than what they get by this partial control of human bodies, which double action, the two individualities often conflicting, induces us to call them insane and shut them up in asylums. It is quite evident that a large part of the religious insanity is of this kind, — obsession by religious bigots and fanatics, who have been released from their bodies, and, terribly disappointed, are seeking the old channel of mental relief.

With the mental condition and personal relations unchanged so far as the affections are concerned, death produces but little more than a release from physical pain and release from involuntary bondage. When the mental bondage is involuntary, as in most cases of religious slavery, especially in the Catholic Church, where ignorance binds the victims, it is no release. To the freeminded spirit it is a grand release from the earthly load when that load is a burden. We are not sure yet whether persons who are the subjects of strong delusions are psychologized by spirits, or work up the delusion in their own minds from their conditions and surroundings. Many of the popes really believe they are superior in their infallibility to other mortals, and continue in this belief after death for a period sometimes short and sometimes long. Swedenborg honestly believed he was an especial messenger of the Lord to reveal a revelation that was no revelation until he revealed its meaning, and is none yet to ninety-nine out of every hundred that read the Word of God's revelation. He was not at once undeceived by changing spheres. Luther, Calvin, Fox, Wesley, John Murray, Alexander Campbell, and a score of others, each became infatuated with an idea that they had discovered a meaning to this revelation that had been hidden before from mankind, to whom it was given by God, who could not put the meaning within their reach until these inspired messengers were employed to reveal it; and still it is as much a mystery as ever to the great body of readers, many of whom became in some way infatuated by it.

Several persons have believed themselves to be a reembodiment of Jesus; but I have never heard of one who claimed to have come through an immaculate conception; and one man I knew who stoutly maintained that he was Jehovah, living among men to learn their ways and actions. How long these and other delusions remain after death I have not learned, but so far as I can learn they are not freed from them nor from any others by death, but only by evolution and growth in that life as in this. Where a defect is purely physical, and results from injury to the nerves or brain, we are told that the change very soon restores the mind to its normal and healthy action. Idiots and infants grow into mental man and womanhood there, the latter slowly and often far more harmoniously than here, and the former start as infants, and have no advantage from this life, but lose only the time spent here. It is an important item to learn that the spirit life has no more connection with the gods of any system of religion than this life has, nor they with it, but that theories and beliefs are held, and ceremonies are performed there in faith, hope, and belief, as here, while the gods and their thrones and kingdoms are as remote from that life as from this. Nature and her law of evolution works in the human mind there as here, which all ought to know before they go there. We are fully assured that persons who leave their affairs of this world in an entangled or unsatisfactory condition have more trouble with and about them after death than before, and often regret that they had not adjusted them satisfactorily before they passed to the new life; and we further learn that many persons of large fortunes deeply regret the disposal they made of them, and for a long time do so, because they cannot correct the mistakes made in the disposal of earthly wealth.

Speaking at Onset (Mass.) camp meeting, in July, 1887, on what I had learned that I did not know in early life, I stated that this life is éternal life as much as any, and that we are as much in eternity now as we ever shall be, and as much in eternal life as we can ever be, enjoying and suffering proportionately a heaven or hell as we shall after death, varying only under the law of evolution and circular and angelic changes. Accepting for each human soul the old passage of Scripture, "Before the world was, I am"; treating the sour as a unit both indivisible and indestructible, and hence eternal, of course having no beginning as well as no ending, which must be true if it has eternal life, as neither the earthly or spiritual body can, as they are subject to growth and change in both worlds, being an aggregation of parts and particles, both mental and physical. The mind like the body being gathered, packed, or stored for the use of the soul, the divine essence or the ego of each one of us, and of all organic forms that have mind or life in bodies that grow and decay.

Among the facts I have observed and noted, that few seem to observe, is that those who report as ancient persons whose names are familiar to us as distinguished leaders in any department of life, are in about the same condition mentally as when on earth, and largely teach the same theories and ideas as when on earth, and which they left in their writings, sometimes slightly modified by the advanced knowledge and theories of this life. Confucius and Jesus have not improved on the morals reported as coming from them when on earth. Solon and Pythagoras report nearly the same philosophy as taught by them when here, and Socrates has the same rational philosophy. Paul, Cicero, and Demosthenes have not improved in oratory, and the musicians and painters hold just about the same as when here to the work that attracted them. We are told that as they come down into living human organisms they cannot show their superiority and spiritual growth. If so, what advantage do we get from their visits, and what do they get or give us that we did not have before, and how can we know or even have reason to believe they are the persons they represent themselves to be? The medium cannot know; and as we are familiar with the teachings they left here, we cannot prove but that they may be other spirits who were familiar as we are with these teachings. In some instances we have had variations and more ridiculous stories about the works and ways of God, of creation, and the early history of the earth and man like that of "Oahspe," as strangely absurd as Bible stories, and of course no more reliable. Many people are strangely infatuated with marvels and marvellous stories, especially if accompanied with some ancient and distinguished name; and spirits know this as well as we do; and, like De Witt Talmage, who knows better, take advantage of this confidence and faith and play upon the credulity of honest people. Such I am led to believe to be a large part of what purports to come from ancient spirits. I do not say all, for some is rational and consistent with the progress of this world which peoples the other, and peoples it with such intelligences as we have here; and so far as I can learn, they keep very nearly in the line of our progress and knowledge here.

It seems that some who report as ancient spirits advocate reincarnation, as some ancient sages did when here, and yet they report as the same persons not yet reincarnated, although they say they lived here many hundreds or thousands of years ago. I have never been able to learn from any spirit advocating reincarnation what disposition is made of the spirit body, which they all claim to be as real and tangible and of about the same stature as here. I have asked if it is cremated or buried, and how they get out of it and into the cell where earthly bodies begin; but none answer, as it is a theory that cannot bear criticism. We often meet persons in this life who claim to know from memory that they have lived here before, but that is easily explained by spiritual psychology, in which a spirit may leave the impress on the mind of a sensitive of events that transpired in his or her life, or even of incidents known of another, and so impress it as to enable the person to feel that he or she had really lived it and done it in a former life. Under such circumstances the memory they purport to have of a prior existence on earth is no evidence. I have not been able to get any to convince me of its truth.

I have found that persons who used profane language while in this life for a time use it in that, or as they return through mediums, and see no reason why they should not, as there is no restraint there that does not exist here; and the same is true of vulgar and ungrammatical language; and those who had a very imperfect manner of expressing ideas here retain it for a long time after death, as the schools there are not educational to them in the use of our language. I learn that they have schools there, but not like ours, but differing in many respects, and much better. I also learn that they enjoy swimming, bathing, sports, and many games there as we do here, in their societies and groups, ranged and associated according to their moral, social, and intellectual development, and in which the enjoyment is also proportional to these qualities.

From all the hundreds of denizens of the spirit life, and many of them who possessed a good degree of intelligence here and have not lost it, I learn that there is no more evidence there than with us here that any such person as Jesus, the Christ of the Christians, ever lived as a man on earth and was crucified by the Jews, who never used that mode of execution. As a God or godman no one can find him, although there as here many believe he lived, and are waiting for him to appear, and these are sometimes imposed on by imposters, who take advantage of their credulity and faith. It is now a well-established fact that some spirits have been trying for many centuries to open a general intercourse between the two states of existence, and have been invariably beaten back by the clergy and religious teachers, when they could not utilize the messages or phenomena in aid of their own purposes and for their control of the religious element in human nature. It is a great mistake to suppose spirit intercourse began with the "Rochester knockings," or Hydesville raps, or that it began with A. J. Davis and the remarkable and beautiful as well as truthful messages that came through him in the early years of his mission. It is equally an error to suppose that Swedenborg opened the arcana of the heavenly spheres, and still as great an error to give Jesus and his disciples, including the agnostic Paul, the credit; and still an error to suppose these revelations started with the Jewish Scriptures, however much or little of spirit messages are in all of these. But it is certain that all except that which came through Davis since he began has been perverted and used by priests to build up sectarian institutions on earth and carry them into the other life to react on this, which they have effectually done. We have broken their power at last, and they cannot stop the progress the work is making, although they as usual are striving to either suppress or control it for the same selfish and ambitious purposes; but it has already gone too far, and is in the hands and hearts of too many people, whom they cannot control; and the constantly increasing variety of modes of reaching us with evidence of their presence and with the transmission of intelligence which is daily and hourly refuting the sectarian teachings about the condition of the other life and the people who go there from this, is making it impossible for them to either suppress or control it. It is certain that the Greeks had messages as early as the Jews that were equally sacred and far better in morals and justice; the Persians and Hindoos still earlier, and Egypt perhaps as early as any; but then as in Jewish and Christian times they were monopolized by the priests. The ancient messages that came through mediums in the temple at Delphos and other temples, were undoubtedly from spirits who, although attached to the nations and peoples to which they belonged when on earth, and usually communicated to them and through them, yet in an age of intelligence like ours, and when priests could not control them, would have soon opened a general intercourse such as we have now, that might long ago have removed the superstitions of all religious sects and doctrines, and given to the world a rational theory of another life based on this and evolution. Herein we see the evil influence of a priesthood, which in all ages has been an obstruction and stumbling-block to human progress and knowledge, and has ever, as it does now, stood in the way of all scientific discoveries that would remove its errors and enlighten the people. Since we have ascertained that the spirit world in correspondence with this is supplied exclusively by emigrants from this life, with no more and no less number of gods, devils, and angels with wings, and other beings than those around us here, and that they are governed by the same divine and universal law as we are, we have no use for preachers to interpret messages as words of God, and affix their mysterious meanings to them to frighten the ignorant into subjection. It is now time to rationalize religion and leave out the personal gods and words attributed to them, which they never spoke, and never could, as they have no existence within the reach of earthly intelligence.

For the first time in our world's history we have a rational system, theory, and revelation of a future life, as a continued or renewed existence after death, and it is based on correspondence with the denizens of that country, and in harmony with nature, reason, and evolution. It is not disturbed by any of the hundreds of personal gods mankind have feared and worshipped as ruling over a spirit world with terrific power, and greater severity than any tyrant on earth has ever shown, to which our orthodox God is no exception. It is now certain that no words have come to earth's inhabitants from any personal God, and none could come from any but a personal source. It is equally certain that no revelation has been made to our race from any source above or superior to itself; but that human beings have carried their mental attainments, theories, and beliefs, and their personal and local attachments through death, and often when they could find conditions favorable have given advice according to their feelings and the interest they had in this life in their nation or kindred; and it is probable they may have in some instances carried their object so far as to create insanity, and even lead persons to commit crimes. From all this and much more we should learn to treat them as we would if they were still denizens of this life; and when they talk nonsense, give it the same weight and be influenced by it as lightly as we would if from earthly source.

It is now believed by many intelligent thinkers that each organic form on our earth has an immortal soul, which makes up the form from particles within its reach. This theory supersedes the old Christian theory that the Jewish and Christian Gods make every human child directly, and indirectly every animal form. This new theory is that all souls with sufficient power, whether original or attained, secrete and develop new bodies in the finer and eliminated matter that has passed through organic life and been discreted sufficiently to form bodies that exist in the fourth dimension of space, which to us is the spirit world. How far this extends to the animal species is not yet demonstrated, but many believe the domestic animals put in an appearance there among their earthly friends. This is only one more step out of the old superstitious absurdities of Christian theories of creation and the origin of life and forms of organic existence. These theories teach that God made the plants and animals for man's use, and man for his own use, to praise and glorify him; and yet the old theories gave man no existence where the gods lived eternally; not even Christianity until lately, for it taught a resurrection of bodies and life eternal on the earth, renewed with a new heaven, so changed as to be adapted to an eternal life, in which there should be no more of that sexual sin which Adam and Eve committed, and by which they let sin into this world, and caused God to drown most of the race once to put a stop to it, which experiment failing to accomplish his purpose, he sent his son to make arrangements for a resurrection and restoration of all things to purity which is to be done at some indefinite time, in an infinite future, by fire, as our Adventists teach. This view is very near the doctrine of the primitive Christians, which, so far as it refers to a future life, is only a bundle of absurdities; but so far as it teaches morals for this life, is good, and in many respects suitable to live by, though wholly unfit to die by, as any such belief is a burden in the next life, as odious as the fabled one of Bunyan's Pilgrim in the Slough of Despond. The new light and life which Spiritualism has revealed to us, based as it is on nature, science, and the law of evolution, gives us a rational, consistent, and glorious opening for the future, where we can achieve our own glory, and work out our own destiny, and have plenty of time to do it, instead of praising a God that could not deserve if he needed our praise. Farewell to old theories.

It seems extremely difficult, even with science, to eradicate from the minds of the people the errors, fables, follies, and absurd ideas of a future state of existence, in which nearly the entire population of what are called Christian countries, have been educated by an interested clergy, aided by the psychological influence of pious mothers, acting on the children before and after birth.

All liberalized individuals are aware of this, and hence deal cautiously with these strong forces of resistance to the newly discovered truth of an intercourse that opens the other life to us, and sets aside all of their crude notions of a physical resurrection, and of a heaven where God reigns as a king, with Christ and his mother as assistants; and of a hell where a devil reigns as king, with millions of assistants who visit this world to deceive and capture the children of God, and get them into endless misery with himself, which could be no satisfaction except in gratifying his hatred of a God he does not seem to fear or avoid. The middle ground, or purgatorial condition of spirits after death, as taught by Catholics, may, with essential modifications, be accepted in the new discovery, but without the requirement of masses said for those in trouble there. We now know that the life after death is simply a result of the natural law of evolution, lifting up the mind and soul one step higher in the scale of existence, each one carrying forward whatever of jewels or rubbish he or she has collected mentally in this stage of existence, being in a condition to learn there as here, with no more or less of a tyrannical God or devil than there is here, and no more or less of divine assistance or presence. It is a terrible act to take all of these patent weapons from our clergy and leave them with the husks and straw of a theological education, to be burned out by the fire of truth in the hands of those who know the truth about the world and life beyond the gate of death.

The difference in human life in the two worlds or spheres of existence is very slight, except that that is mental, while this is both mental and physical, and the physical affects the mental here largely, while there the mental controls the spiritual form in locality and transfer, at least so far as I can learn from the testimony of those who live there. In opinions, theories, speculations, and feelings, likes and dislikes, attractions and affections, the two spheres are nearly the same and equally changeable from similar causes. This accounts for religious and orthodox opinions and theories returned to us from that state of existence by those who live there. Why it should not be so I can see no reason, and why it should I can see plenty of evidence in the law of mental evolution, which law is as applicable to minds as to organic forms on our planet. The mind evidently is a collection of elemental particles collected and arranged into the individual here, and passes intact to the next stage of being, where it assists the soul in forming the spiritual body and gives an expression to it according to its condition, which is partially true in this life and in the earthly body, where we can see sorrow or joy, grief or anger, orthodoxy or free thought depicted on the countenance of many persons. Good judges often assert that they can tell by the looks of a congregation whether they are Universalists or Orthodox.

Of the length, breadth, and thickness of the spirit sphere in which our race live on leaving this life, I cannot learn from them, but they seem rather to be like the earlier races and generations of this world who had not surveyed it. How far into the infinite extension they can go I know not, and I do not see how they can measure as we do by miles and furlongs, and they do not seem to. How far toward the other planets they can go and not get out of the motion of the earth, and thus lose their locality on it, no one has told me; but many vague and ridiculous theories have been given, and some published, which evidently came from the minds of spirits, but do not appear based on facts or knowledge more than the fictions in the new bible called "Oahspe," a spiritual work.

GUARDIAN SPIRITS.— Much has been much written, and more said, about guardian spirits, yet very little seems to be known about them. So far as I can learn, most persons have personal friends or interested relatives in spirit life, some one of whom is usually so far in sympathy with him or her as to be called a guardian spirit, and so much *en rapport* as to be able to often control the acts or even the thoughts of the friend in the body; many times there is good evidence that thoughts are injected into the mind that lead to actions for which we cannot account on any other principle. What we call imagination is no doubt often produced by some spirit *en rapport* with the thinker that imagines. Dreams are also often the work of spirits influencing some organs of the brain, and causing broken fragments of mental consciousness while the organs are mostly at rest. There is little doubt that we shall in a few more years the better understand the true nature of spiritual impressions, and then more generally heed the admonitions of our guardian friends, if they can properly be called guardians. It seems abundantly established that no one spirit watches over any one of us all of the time ; but that different ones are at times the watchers, — coming and going as our needs and their other duties require. It would seem that in that life, with its great variety of attractions and the varied interests for all its denizens, they would find more congenial and profitable employment than following us round in our daily avocations, when they find it difficult to influence us for our good ; if that is the object of the guardianship, I am fully satisfied that some of my friends in that life often visit me and often try to impress me with what they think is best for me to do ; but it is extremely difficult for me to know what, and when they inject thoughts or wish to control my actions, and hence I may not heed them.

It is a well-settled fact that many spirits who are not

guardians to any one are mentally turned downward to the earth and its inhabitants, seeking control of mortals, to get hold of earth life again, and many of us think that a large part of the insanity is from this partial control, which we call obsession, and in this mixed control of the brain unfits both for a rational life in either sphere. In the control of mediums we see their unfitness for this life when under the control of spirits; and if it remained, our wise M.D.'s and D.D.'s would have them in asylums very soon. We have much to learn about the other life yet to fit us to live there, and not torment the denizens of this sphere. There is, no doubt, a great variety of obsessions, some partial and some complete, and most, if not all, injurious to the parties obsessed, at least so far as this life is concerned. I have watched the insane (incurables) at the asylum in Worcester, my windows being nearly opposite its grounds, and was satisfied that at least one-half of them were obsessed by undeveloped spirits who though not evil spirits, were ignorant of what they were doing, and had got back to the condition of eating and drinking through the organism of the obsessed person, and deranged the normal actions of that person. They all seemed harmless, so far as I could see, but, of course, if an evil-disposed spirit gets control of the body of a mortal, he might do mischief, and some day we may learn that many crimes are committed under such influence, and we shall thus through hard experience be taught to be more charitable, and to do all we can to prepare all for a higher plane of existence before they are called hence. We have positive proof now that human nature is not depraved, for the influence of all children that return is harmless, and not even mischievous, the evil not being inherited even, but educated by society, its surroundings, our wicked institutions, and corrupting systems of religion, which hold up no punishment for crimes after death if repentance and faith in forgiveness is obtained before the culprit, however wicked, leaves this world.

When we become as familiar with the presence of spirits, and learn the condition of their life as we have the nature of this, then we shall deal with them and treat them as we do the citizens of this life, taking only those for guides and teachers who are qualified to guide or teach us, select our associates, and not consider all spirits as angels or devils, but, like ourselves, good, bad, and indifferent, and no longer wonder why spirits do not always guard us or guide us aright more than our teachers and guides do here. Then we shall no longer submit to the foolish and absurd teachings of our priests about that world and the life there, but know it is simply an extension of this life with the earthly part sloughed off.

It is quite evident to me, after long and careful study of the subject, that ancient personal gods, as well as the present, so far as they had or have any existence, were spirits so related to the nations that worshipped them, that they often did order and direct the cruel wars and persecutions attributed to them. In no other way can I account for the barbarities of the Jews, under the direction of their god and our Jehovah, or those of the Greeks and Romans, as well as other older nations. As we now know there are bad men who go into the spirit world, and have no more restraint there than here, except the impossibility of deceiving their fellow-beings there, we may at once conclude that in the old barbarous times there were persons equally so, and of limited knowledge and no wisdom, who, finding they could not rule them, sought mediums here, and used them to rule, so far as they could, on earth and over nations. Such, I think, were the gods of Israel, Babylon, and Egypt. In due time spirit intercourse will unravel many of the mysteries of ancient times, and we shall find out that nations had guardian spirits whom they worshipped as gods, as some weak minds now are inclined to regard such spirits as saints or angels, if not gods, and place implicit confidence in them, when in reality they are no more gods or angels than their earthly neighbors. Time will let in the light.

If it was, as I believe, the word of a spirit that came to Isaiah, Jeremiah, Rebecca, and many other Bible characters, and led Samuel to hew down Agag, and Samuel that really spoke to Saul and told the truth; and if it was materialized spirits that came and talked with Abraham and Lot, and a spirit that gave old Job up to a more wicked spirit to torment him out of spite to the guardian that gave him up, and a spirit that obsessed Samson and saved Daniel from the lions, and three spirits that stood in the fiery furnace, then we can look back to still more marvellous and far more cruel acts of spirits in those barbarous days than any we have now, and yet we have some marvels and some cruelties even now, but do not attribute them to a god. It is plain that spirits infested the temple of Apollo at Delphos, and controlled the Sybils in Rome, and the soothsayers, and why not the prophets and seers or clairvoyants of Jerusalem? To me it is evident that nations have guardian spirits as well as individuals, and that these were the gods that took part in the wars of Greece and Troy, as well as those of the Jews, and for which each nation had names as their gods — Jupiter and Mars and the Jewish Yahwe (Jehovah), Lord or Lord God, and the Christians have taken the Jewish names for their gods — but how far these have become the guardian spirits of Christian sects is not clear. Neither those of the Greeks or Jews were able to save their nations from being conquered and scattered; nor is it probable that the gods of any Christian sect can do better with their wards, but, like the guardian spirits of individuals, are often defeated in their efforts by others more powerful and working against them.

Jefferson Davis and his associates, he being a Christian, called on the old Jewish God for help, but he was as powerless there as with the Jews, if he was there; but it is more likely that Calhoun and Jackson or some other slave advocates were the guardian and inspiring spirits of that government and of their battles. It is quite extensively believed that Stonewall Jackson was a medium and assisted by some guardian spirit, and no doubt others on both sides were partially controlled. Lincoln was advised at least by some of the guardian spirits of our nation, and when he by such advice issued his emancipation proclamation, victory was from that day assured, as it was evidently the intention of our guardian spirits that slavery should go down with the Rebellion. There is much more of this kind of foreign interference with our affairs than we are aware of. That Napoleon was controlled by some ancient warrior is quite well established; and some day he may control some other, or perhaps has; and no doubt some one did Sheridan and others of our generals in their great feats. War spirits are still interested in wars, and peace spirits in peace; the old popes in the Church of Rome, and Luther and Calvin in their work of overthrowing it. Wesley and Fox and Murray are still engaged in the progress of religion, as they were when on earth, and Thomas Paine is as zealous as ever in rooting out tyranny and superstition. Why should they not be? Their work is not done more than ours, and we are all working in our respective spheres. That the leaders of each sect of Christians become, for a time after passing to spirit life, the guardian spirits of that sect, is plain enough; and as they advance and outgrow their creeds and dogmas, they go on, and others take their places. This is also true of individuals, as in my own case a mother, who for many years was a guardian spirit and almost alone in the care, has long since given up to others, and gone on in her studies of the life beyond and into other work. If this is irrational, I cannot see it. Such at least is what is taught me. We see in all of these cases of national or sectarian gods, which are only guardian spirits, fallibility and repeated failures. We are daily assured in speeches and messages from our zealous workers in the temperance cause and in evangelican and sectarian work that their "gods" are on their side and working with them, and I do not doubt it; but they are only guardian spirits, and often fail, as is to be seen in both of these cases. Their error is in claiming almighty power for their gods, when they are as finite, and work as the mortal workers here, and have others there to contend with, the same as here, for both and all sides have spirit aid and counsel indirectly if not directly. The prayers only reach these guides and often bring response in the minds and feelings of the praying parties that encourage them to act, and yet the expected effect does not follow in many cases, even though the spirits join in the effort to bring it about. In time we shall all learn that the two worlds may co-operate, but both joined cannot overcome a natural law or change the fate that is in that law. God is outside all these feeble and finite efforts of mortals and spirits, and has no partiality for either, and gives no special assistance to any government of either world, nor to any creed or system of religion more than to a form of government.

This subject of guardian spirits, which involves the whole catalogue of personal gods of all ages as well as national sectarian leaders, is one of much significance, and has been as yet but little studied or treated upon, but in time will solve many mysteries and open the eyes of many intelligent thinkers to a law of causes that has puzzled theologians in all past times. Why their gods did not do as they requested and expected, and as he promised, has ever been a mystery, and this solves it. Two nations or two persons, each aided by guardian spirits in war or personal conflict, cannot both conquer; and, when both pray to the same god, the vanquished must find some excuse for the god they relied on; this view of their finite power and weakness explains it. Injustice and wickedness have often triumphed in this life, as all know; and yet we are told a God of love rules. If this be so, and he suffers an evil like drunkenness to exist, then it is right, and there is no propriety in fighting against such a god; but if we are contending against the spirits of dissipated mortals transferred to the other life, there is use in the work as much as if they were here. In the conflict with intemperance we are constantly assured by the Woman's Christian Temperance Union that their cause is the cause of God and Christ, and all of the prayers are offered on their side, — I never heard one or heard of one on the other side, — yet intemperance and license and saloons prevail, and we ask, Where is the power of Christ manifest?

Sexuality in Spirit Life.

That sexuality is retained in spirit life is as certain as is the fact of that existence; its complete recognition in the minds here carrying it out in the spirit form. The peculiar characteristic of each individuality, so far as it pertains to the mind, must also be retained and renewed for a time after death. As the spiritual world is mainly a mental world, and but slightly physical, those whose sexual mentality ran in the physical and sensual channel of thought and feeling are as miserable as those whose minds were absolute in the use of tobacco and liquors; and they have to hang round the earthly dens of vice as the others do round saloons and dens of tobacco smoke; while those whose mental sexuality reached out to the higher and holier relations of affectionate and conjugal life, and now find a higher and holier treasure-house in the spiritual life than it is possible to reach in this. Perverted passions, like perverted appetites, lead downward in that life as in this, and sensuality, like profanity, clings to its victims after death. If it is rooted out of the mind before death, the work is done here; if not, it must be done there before true sexual life can begin. As each person is known there just as he or she is mentally in thought, there is no chance for the sensual to deceive the pure; and when the earthly body is destroyed in which the passions reigned and found a satisfaction, as the drunkard does in liquors, the mind is no longer satisfied, and in both cases seeks the earth for the lost gratification, but is not satisfied there, and cannot be.

A true knowledge of sexual life in the spirit world is among the most important items to be taught in this life, as it would do more to remove immorality and licentiousness than any other moral force ever applied to them. Such, to a less extent, is true of the use of tobacco and alcoholic liquors; but we must get our lessons from those who are above these debasing vices, and were when they went there, and can see clearly the contrast.

According to all testimony, propagation is confined to this stage of life and on this planet; but it seems to be fully established that some pass into that life that were not naturally born into this, but none before the human form was outlined in gestation, and the animal changed to the human. That the human form in gestation is preceded by that of several species of animals seems to be admitted by scientists, and this is used by some as a proof that the race derives its forms and existence from the animal; but I am not satisfied that this is an evidence sufficient to establish it as a fact, and I have seen no other evidence as good as this. That propagation is confined to, and ceases with this life, does not prove that any other or further conjugal relations of the sexes cease at death, nor that there are no conjugal affinities in the other life, although the words attributed to Jesus may be true, that there is no marrying in heaven nor giving in marriage. Of course there are no such marriages as we have here, which are frequently consummated in deception and soon lead to legal divorces, however much there may be of mutual and voluntary separations after long or short periods of happiness. That those husbands and wives who are mutually attached and each satisfactory to the other in this life, and both remain so till the death of each, meet and enjoy a higher and holier union in that life is to me a well authenticated statement; while those who have not been happy in that relation here will be released by death is equally sure; but how far each will find a congenial mate will depend much on the condition of mind. If sensuality rules the mind on sexual affairs, there is no peace or spiritual mating there in it.

In this life a very large part of sexual life is sensual, which, owing to the physical masks and deception, is not apparent on the surface of individuals or society. In the next life, where no such masks can be worn, and no one can deceive another, this social vice sinks to its proper level, and its votaries are cast out of good society. In this life people often misjudge the motives of others, and often judge them by their own feelings and desires. No such mistakes occur in spirit life, where the interiors become the exteriors and the inmost thoughts are radiated on the features.

Death will be a sad disappointment to many persons, especially those who here put their faith and trust in Christ, and those who have lived sensual lives here and relied on Christ to cleanse them from their sins, and who have not cleansed themselves, which a mere repentance will not do. The soul, which is the divine essence in us, collects and organizes the body without any action of the mind, for there is no mind with us as individuals at the time; and certainly the minds of the earthly parents do nothing about it for some time after the act of conception, and not until birth, except in the psychological effect of the mother, and that is usually involuntary. When the soul has completed the body, with the effects of the mother's psychological action on it, or in it, and brought it out into the sunlight and air, the soul starts its new forces in the act of breathing, and propelling the blood, and taking in food through the mouth, which had not been used before. None of these actions can be attributed to the mind, for the new-born babe has no mind; but as a depository has been made for it in brain, it soon begins to collect it in particles from the elemental atmosphere that surrounds it. The soul doing this as it collected particles for the body from the substance within its reach, the mind collected is stored in the depositories which are the organs of the brain, and through them we have the variety of characters. Man is like a steam engine, of which the fire is the soul, the mind the steam, the brain the cylinder, and the body the machinery. When the fire goes out, the rest is dead. The soul develops a new body in the earthly body, which is the gestation of the spiritual body, and carries the mind forward with it to the next stage of existence, which we call spiritual life.

In this life the soul pushes out its feelers through the mind and reaches after earthly enjoyments in the body. When there is an excess of brain in the religious organs, it pushes out in that direction; when an excess of benevolent organs, it pushes more strongly out in that direction; when combative, it runs to fighting and to witnessing conflicts; when sensual, it runs in that direction; and when alimentive, it runs in that channel: hence we see what we call the evil or the good propensity of each child, and following it, the man or woman. The more perfectly harmonious and uniform the brain, the more perfect is the character and conduct of the individual. When this law of nature is properly understood and applied to life, we shall not have so many criminals to punish, for we shall know how to keep persons in those places for which they are fitted, and put trust only in trustworthy persons. We shall then know how to restrain lust and licentious persons, and people who are honest and virtuous will shun them as they would poisonous serpents or dangerous beasts. In the spirit world this is so, and they are not troubled as we are in this life of masks and masquerades. The mind, like the body, is an organization made up of particles as the body is; in this life it conforms to the phrenological structure of the brain, and no religious conversion changes it, although it may exert a restraining influence, and in various ways exert through other minds an influence on the ultimated actions, as in the case of an old swearer I knew, who, after conversion used "durned" for damned," which was only an outward change, but not an inward or mental improvement. Scientists describe the process by which the soul makes the earthly body, but never describe the soul, because their instruments cannot reach it, they being made of materials belonging to the same stratum of matter as the body, and not reaching that of the soul. They also watch the growth and development of the mind, but cannot reach with their instruments the materials of which it is composed.

As they cannot reach the materials of which the spirit body is formed, and hence cannot even watch its growth, many of them are inclined to deny its existence, and hence have no tenement for soul or mind after death, but the result of death on the mind leaving it intact, enables us to learn from our friends much about the spiritual body, although they know as little about its growth, formation, or development as we do about our bodies here; and they and we know there are bodies, and in human form, both male and female, in both spheres; as of course they can tell us of the relations there, as we can of them here. They assure us that there are no rapes or even adultery in that life that cause much misery in this life, and that will be a release to many victims, both in and out of marriage as it is here. No spirit can know that there are any eternal conjugal or conjugial affinities, as they cannot know any more about eternal life than we do, and we can only believe it of the soul, as all forms of which we know anything are transient, and the essences only being eternal, so far as we know; and if the soul is an indivisible particle of the divine essence, of course it is eternal as a unit and individual. Professor Zöllner's fourth dimension of space gives us the only rational scientific idea of what the forms and objects are in spirit life, where the mind maintains its individuality, even as here, and though not having length, breadth, and thickness, as the body has, are tangible realities to our senses, and through them to the mind. How the spirits reach and realize our three-dimension forms when we cannot theirs, I do not know; they certainly do in many cases, but I do not believe that all do at any time they may desire. It seems plain to me that sometimes they cannot find us, and often cannot be found by guardian spirits of our mediums. The spirit world, or globe, being vastly larger than this, it is not strange that some persons get strayed away, and do not find, even if they seek, their old earthly homes, as all nations have their localities and peculiar institutions and attractions there.

Of animals in spirit life, our friends persistently assert

that they have the petted and favorite animals they had here, or others so much like them as to appear the same to them, and in the absence of any knowledge or facts to the contrary, I am compelled to believe and to attribute their organic forms there to the same divine soul-life in them as in us in a perfected condition of immortality, and as there is room enough for all existence, and time enough for all changes, I do not propose to limit existence in any form to this stage of being. It has always seemed strangely inconsistent in most spirits when they control mediums for lectures, prayers, or dissertations, that such always confine their discourses to this world, its affairs, beliefs, and conditions, but seldom give us on such occasions anything about the world where they belong. Why they do not tell us in such discourses about the life beyond is to us yet a mystery involved and left to conjecture. I do not speculate or theorize upon the affairs of spirit life; what I write is what I have gained from those who live there, and of course I take it as I would take accounts of China or Africa from those who have been there and seen for themselves. I have read the opinions of Mark Twain and D. M. Bennet, and several Christian travellers about parts of Asia. In what they agree, I believe, and where they differ I take that which seems to me most reasonable and consistent. I do the same about the spirit life, and when all agree that they have not seen God and his throne, nor his Son, I take it for granted they are not there more than here, and live only in imagination and are seen only with the blind eye of faith. I have no reliable evidence that any spirit that visits us can visit any other planet or star and return to earth, and it does not seem to me reasonable that they can, as it evidently would require a change of body nearly as much as for us to go there. But many spirits do pretend to have a knowledge of the planets, and by the same evidence that Christians have of spirit life.

The human soul is never polluted, depraved, or wicked. All these defects come from outside influences, and expend themselves in an outer form which in time will be brought into harmony with the rest, and then happiness will be complete through the entire being; but as no condition is permanent, in time it will require and seek a change, find and make it as we do here. I have no knowledge of where the old cider topers of New England are, or what they are doing, as I have not heard from or of them, but suppose they are somewhere, and not in the burning hell of Christian theology. The churches have not heard of them either, and hence they cannot tell what has become of them in the next life. They are probably not worse situated than the English beer-guzzlers or German lager-sleepers: all are somewhere, and probably sobered off and improving.

It is astonishing to see the narrowness of a majority of minds in this life, almost entirely absorbed in the daily routine of the affairs of this life, with scarcely a thought of the to-morrow of death, and leaving that to the priests, who actually do nothing to really fit them for that life; hence they are unfitted and unprepared for it at death, Catholics depending entirely on the priests, and the Protestants largely so, leaving such as so depend actually less fitted for the change than those who never heard the prayers and sermons, but live upright lives. Where and what the countless millions of human beings are who lived and died thousands of years before the Christian era, and even before the Jewish and Christian gods were created, invented, or discovered, and who never heard of any of them in this world or any other, is more than I can find out from the spirits that in our day and country pass to the next life; but none of those I have heard from believe these heathen and half or wholly civilized millions are tortured in misery by those later invented gods who are now claimed as being in that life by our modern theology. They are undoubtedly somewhere in the infinite space, where there is room enough and time enough for all beings to continue existence that are in it or ever have been.

For some, to us as yet unaccountable reason, there exists a very strong desire on the part of many, if not all spirits, who went out of this life in great trouble or suffering in mental conflict, as by suicide or murder, or in some sudden destruction, to obtain control of some medium with whom they can get *en rapport*, and in which they often seem to return to a somewhat similar condition of feeling, and manifest it through the medium. This no doubt causes many suicides, some murders, and perhaps carries some persons into places of danger that result fatally. What the spirit gains by this fatality, I do not know, as it can hardly be accounted for on the principle of malice or a desire to harm others, in many if any cases. There is certainly some fitting condition in such mediums, as are thus fatally controlled, or it could not occur; and it must be a condition in the medium that takes him or her out of the control of friendly guardian spirits at the time, and gives admission to the controlling influence which produces the fatal result on the body; but what the effect is on the thus disembodied spirit, I have not been able to learn. Much yet remains for us to learn to enable us to escape the evil effects of obsession, and much to learn of the value of mediumship of different kinds. From every great gift vouchsafed to mankind in this world there comes to us good or evil, as we use it. Take fire, for instance, and read the daily reports of the terrible losses of life and property where it gets beyond the control of intelligent minds; and yet it is the best of servants to humanity, and one which, were we suddenly deprived of, we should sink to the conditions of animals. Electricity, which we have now pressed into use, is a dangerous element to handle, and yet we could hardly dispense with it. Such is mediumship, which, like other great blessings, needs to be used carefully and properly.

In the spirit world are plenty of persons amusing themselves by controlling mediums, and giving through them ideal sketches of what does not pertain to that life or sphere of existence more than to this. Such are the stories often published in our spiritual papers about spirits visiting the moon and planets, and on them finding the homes of spirits who once had an existence on this planet, often representing this as the birthplace of the inhabitants of the planets and the sun, as if God had only created intelligent beings on this earth, made them immortal, and peopled the solar system from it. Such nonsense is the legitimate outgrowth of our absurd theology, as are a large part of our novels; and this is a class of spiritual fiction gotten up for the ideal amusement of the spirits, but imposing a seriousness on the mediums and some other dupes that gives the stories a sacredness, as if the matter was really true. Nothing coming from spirits that is not rational, consistent, and in harmony with the grand law of evolution, is to be taken for truth because it comes from spirits, any more than if it originated in the minds of theorizers on earth. We are fast learning that mentally and intellectually the two spheres of existence are very much alike, with no more of God or devil in one than the other to restrain or interfere with mental ramblings, and no more sacredness or seriousness there than here. It will take many years yet to disabuse the public mind from the theological absurdities imposed upon it by the constant preaching of evangelical and other ranting fanatics, and the influence of these and ignorant, simple-minded, pious mothers over their children, aided by Sunday-schools and Bible classes, and to get the mind down to a rational, natural understanding of the two spheres of life and the relation they bear to each other; but in time it will all be accomplished, and the whole system of Christian salvation be relegated to the shadows of superstition, ignorance, and bigotry. Birth into this life has already become recognized as a natural result of law, in which God has no more part directly than he has in the birth of birds, and soon the transition by death will be looked upon as of the same nature, and what follows that event be the same as what follows birth here, and have no more and no less to do with God in one case than the other.

I have found a great variety of opinions in both spheres of life about the relations of the sexes in spirit life, and yet all agree that sexuality is retained in that life; but many here have the opinion that sexual intimacy, such as exists here, ceases at death, if not before, and is never renewed. Such is the opinion of many people on earth and the teaching of the Roman Church, from which it is chiefly derived, and these people go over with such ideas prevailing, and the mind firmly fixed in them, and it is often a long time in changing to an appreciation of the fact that the natural relation of the sexes is not changed by death. The old Church also teaches that all sexual relations not authorized and allowed by the officers of the Roman Church are sinful and sins against God, and such disobedience as Adam and Eve were guilty of. The best authority I can gain from that life teaches that social and sexual relations in that life are much higher and far superior to any in this life, and rise entirely out of the sensual plane of thought and feeling, but are on a spiritual plane, in the blending of congenial minds in mutual life and enjoyment superior to any on earth. Of course, the sensual are left in the mire of their own making, and deprived of the higher society and company of the pure and spiritual life of those who go there fitted for its enjoyment. When the ignorant, or those in the lower grade of thought and feeling, communicate, of course they give their own views, beliefs, or experiences, and often give us to understand they are universal there, because they are not admitted to the higher societies. I have not learned that any priestly marriages are solemnized there, or that any bonds are entered into that cannot be severed by either party, but we are assured that those whose lives were united and congenial here up to the separation by death are often found as closely united there as they were here, and often more so, as they see and feel the devotion of each to the other better there than they did here. This is Swedenborg's conjugial life, but no one knows, it is eternal.

We have learned that all messages from the spirit world are to be estimated by their intrinsic value, without reference to the names that are attached to them, or the persons from whom they purport to come. Those that bring intelligence, establishing the identity of friends, are the most valuable, and are, so far as they contain advice and counsel, worth as much to us as they would be if those persons were still in this life, with very little additional sacredness or value. It is true that sometimes, and in some cases, our friends, after passing through the gate of death into that life, may be able to look into, or look up, some few passing events that we cannot see, or that he or she could not see when here, and give us some advice on such subjects; but these cases are very limited, and do not extend to matters of mental belief or speculations on religious beliefs, nor on principles of moral, social, or political life. Death gives us no advance on these subjects, and hence our pious and prayerful friends are pious and prayerful after death for a considerable time, and when they begin to open their eyes to the light they are often ashamed of their previous ignorance and superstition, and as slow to confess to us their change of belief as they would be if still living here. When we all understand that a spirit is a mortal, simply having changed his residence, and limited mentally there as here, confined to surroundings and controlled by environments there as here, we shall not be, as many are now, misled and fooled by their advice simply because they are in spirit life; while many here think they can know anything they choose to, and answer correctly any question, and they are often so anxious to communicate that they mislead their friends, not from bad motives or design to injure, but as people do here who heedlessly give advice that misleads friends, being themselves ignorant of results. It seems to be one of our greatest tasks to disabuse the public mind on the subject of the fallibility of spirits, so many seem to think all who go through the gate of death have gone into the presence and kingdom of God, and ought to be honest, sober, righteous, and truthful, and to know everything they wish to know about that life and the affairs of this life. The many errors taught, and the conflict between the teachings of spirits, and the many who have been misled by their advice, ought by this time to have taught all who communicate that that life is as fallible as this.

The visionary spirits in the next stage of existence seem to exceed those of this sphere, as they mentally roam among the planets and stars and speculate on the inhabitants of the "summer land" in the milky way, peopled from this little speck of gross matter, the earth, to which they are confined by its motions and its attractive belts. Many of them have the planets peopled from this earth, and so that one Saviour, the Christ, can suffice as a Saviour to all, and only have to be crucified once as a sacrifice for sinners to repent by. Others have generating conditions on the planets and new races there; none, however, with forms superior to the perfected and beautified human form, but with great varieties of defective forms inferior. When we can understand that these are only mental observations, the same as those here of which novels and theatrical plays are made, then we shall know how to estimate their value; but so long as we look upon spirit messages as Christians do on stories in the Bible, so long they will delude us as Bible stories do Christians. This has been one of the most important items I have gained by my long intercourse with spirits. Both spheres of life have their personality confined to locality much alike, confined by forces over which they have no control, but each leaving the mind at liberty to roam as it can, and form pictures and describe them the same in each sphere. We speculate on the inhabitants of the moon and planets and of the interior of our hollow globe, and why should not the mind continue to do this after death, when it is no more restrained than here? Christians see with the eye of faith here and there, and wait for Christ and the resurrection, and some of the Catholic spirits are in *repose*, waiting for these events and listening to the masses said here and there by deluded and deceiving priests, the same in both spheres, and neither there nor here will they listen to the voice of reason, and learn that nature and natural law is supreme in both worlds; that God is as much in one as in the other; and if they wait ten millions of years, they will see no more of him than now. Countless millions of human beings that lived and died before the Christian or Jewish era are still in the darkness of their religious superstitions.

At the Free Circle rooms, so long sustained by the *Banner of Light* in Boston, a wise and intelligent circle of spirits have kept control of the intercourse through the several different mediums selected and paid by the *Banner* office. Through these mediums they have given many answers to questions, showing in them clear, consistent, and rational views on most occasions, such as the most advanced minds on earth would give in similar cases, as the questions are usually more or less connected with the affairs of this life; and when they relate to the next life, the answers are consistent with what we should expect under a universal law of evolution. In the messages, the Circle has shown much wisdom in admitting to the list of communicants a great variety of persons in all stages of intellectual development, to show us how persons go through death and come out into that life in the same mental stature as they leave this, and that only by slow and steadily progressive steps do they in that life increase in knowledge and wisdom, as we do here. I have watched with deep interest the efforts of both parties in this work, the spirits and our faithful friends at the office, in their united efforts to give to the readers of the *Banner* evidence not only of the existence of those who go out of this life through the door of death, but of the condition of all classes of persons in that life. Little children are often given a chance to show their childish condition of mind and attachments to parents and playmates, and even the toys they left here. The colored slave, too, has a chance as well as the strong-minded men and women whose lives here were devoted to reforms. Quite a number of my personal friends have sent through this channel greetings to me, perfectly characteristic of them as they were in this life, and thereby fully identifying their personality to me.

My social, political, and religious creed, as partly derived from and wholly approved by my friends living in spirit life : —

Perfect equality between the sexes in all conditions of

life. Marriage, a civil contract, to be made, controlled, or dissolved wholly by the parties to it, under general laws. Legal restrictions and public records protecting offspring, wholly released and freed from sectarian and clerical control. All children legally the legitimate offspring of both parents, and both held responsible for their support and complete education until of age. Both sexes equally eligible to any office, all of which should be nearly equally divided between them. No military armaments maintained by nations or states, but all disputes between nations to be settled by arbitration in a congress of nations, conformable to international laws and courts of final adjudication, and the whole people bound and pledged to carry out the decisions arrived at, as they are in our courts, and every vestige of wars and weapons of human destruction destroyed; then justice would take the place of force and destruction. A legal prohibition of the manufacture and sale of intoxicating drinks, and of the production and importation of the filthy, poisonous, and expensive nuisance, tobacco, and the direction and encouragement of all industries in providing the necessaries, comforts, and luxuries of life. The land restored to the people to whom it belongs for homes and production, and no speculation allowed in it, occupancy alone securing title. This to be reached gradually by laws that will not rob any person of acquired rights of property in land, but by gradual transfer and purchase, limiting sales to occupants, and prohibiting them to speculators. Abolition of what we call capital punishment and reformatory institutions of industry for criminals, of which there would be few with the above reforms in our social system. Repeal of all laws for the forced collection of debts, thus throwing all persons who want credit on personal honor and punctuality to obtain it. All homes of families with children in them sacred, and never subject to forced sale or mortgage foreclosure. Public education provided for all children and enforced.

A purely and exclusively national currency, allowing nothing to circulate as currency that has not the fiat of the government, whether made of paper or metals, as a legal tender, and a supply of such currency sufficient to reduce interest to a rate below the actual increase of production in capital exclusive of the rise in property, in order to keep the industries in active operation, and enable the operatives to pay for, as they require the necessaries and comforts of life. All changes to be made so as not to produce convulsions in business, or robberies of accumulation of property, as now under our present false and wicked system, in which honest and upright persons are involved as well as speculators, and where accumulations have been made under bad laws. Government depositories for surplus money in savings, with government responsibilities to depositors, instead of our constantly failing deposit banks. Corporations held strictly accountable to public interests ; all watered stock confiscated, and no issues allowed of stock except for actual payments at the time of issue. No interest allowed on mortgages when there is no product from property mortgaged, and no interest on debts for the Sundays when labor is suspended, it being considered a legal day of rest, in which the note should rest as well as the laborer. All laws to protect labor and capital both, and with equal justice to both, as they do not now, being partial to capital and oppressive to labor, the producer of capital. All church property taxed the same as other property. No religious interference or participation in Congress or in the legislatures by chaplains or otherwise, and no sectarian teachings allowed in any schools for the secular education of children until they attain to years of discretion and reason, but no interference with parental teaching by example or precept. No oaths administered in any court to a witness, but all persons held responsible under suitable penalties for false testimony in trials, the oath being now only a farce, and punishment for perjury the only restraining force. No religious test for office or for a witness.

To me religion does not consist in any kind of ceremonies, beliefs, faiths, or ceremonial exercises for, or to, any foreign person or power; not in fear of God or love of God, nor in praising God, nor in glorifying God; not in praying to God, or asking favors of God, but in honestly and faithfully doing our duty to ourselves and our fellow-creatures, both to human beings and animals; and I consider it a sin to abuse a horse or other domestic animal which we have brought under our jurisdiction, or to do an injustice to man or beast, a sin that no Christ or ancient sacrifice of innocence can atone for or forgive. I do not believe there is or can be any forgiveness of sins except by the person injured by the sin; and as we cannot injure God, there is no sin for God to forgive; and as an animal cannot forgive us, we have that settlement to make sometime with our own conscience, which is the monitor within taking notes, and is sure to report sometime and somewhere, and to prescribe the penance. As there is no sin against God, there is no forgiveness from God, and we are left to be reconciled to our fellow-beings who move along the path of life with us, through death, into a condition of life where we see and are seen just as we are, with our earthly lives attached to us and plainly visible. As I have no confidence or faith in the fables or parables of the Bible, I have no fears arising from them. The moral precepts and principles there or elsewhere that my judgment approves are sacred, but no more so for being in the Bible than if in the Koran or in Shakespeare. Death has lost all terrors, and I no more fear it than natural sleep, from which I expect to awake in a short time; and as I never expect to see any of the gods or devils in the next life, of course I have no fear of them. I live my own life, and expect to meet it after death. I cordially forgive everybody that has injured me, and hope to be forgiven by those I have injured in this life or the next, for, of course, I have done some wrongs.

From all I can learn, religious beliefs and other beliefs, as well as peculiarities of character, extend into the spirit life, and persons there, as here, speculate on a future, and depend on events that exist only in their minds. It is so common for spirits controlling mediums to write out fictitious and conflicting theories of future events, that it is plain they have no more knowledge of the future there and to them than they had when here, or than we have; hence they may as firmly believe in the coming of Christ there as they did when here, and wait as patiently for the expected event. I cannot learn that there is much difference in the mental condition of persons there and their condition of mind when here, nor that they advance much faster there out of errors of belief than while here. As that life, although not eternal, is much longer than this, there is ample opportunity for progress and for getting free from the superstitions that encumber the minds here. This is one of the most important truths for us to learn from our intercourse. We find quite a number of our best mediums controlled by Indian girls and other girls and boys that lived here and passed on many years ago, sometimes hundreds of years, and yet seem to be like our children here, with the addition of sharpened wit and intellect, but as fond of toys and playthings as our children here are, and as much pleased with bright colors and fancy trinkets as when in this life. From this we learn how slowly the mind advances in that life. They also tell us their forms are usually small even when they have been there a century. They must also keep in the range of our seasons to be able to register the years as we do from the revolutions of our planet around the sun, as there is no other way to keep the measure of time in years. They may have calendars as we do to mark the periods of time ; but if they are the same as ours, they must be based on revolutions of the earth.

We are often told, what is probably true, that when spirits come into *rapport* with us and our earthly forms and affairs, they seem to largely return to a sympathetic connection of their life on earth, and when they return to the normal condition of that life, they are released from this sympathetic condition of life on earth. Many spirits seem so attached to earthly friends or places and events that they loose much of that life, and remain so entangled in the affairs of this life, and of those that live here, that they make slow progress in spiritual development. We often meet with spirits who, when on earth, were addicted to the use of profane language, who on returning and controlling mediums, use the same expressions freely, but they assure us that they do not use such in spirit life. If our ridiculous theology was true, they would not even come back and make such use of the name of God and of Christ, and call for such damning and endless hell fires. That spirit life is merely a discreted degree of outer and body life, with no change by death in the condition of the mind, except so far as it is in immediate relation to its surroundings. Those who change worlds in a state of great fear remain in a state of fear for some time after the change, especially if it be a fear of God, or a coming judgment and sentence from it to an eternal and unchangeable destiny. Those who fear a cessation of conscious existence usually are made happy by the fact that life continues after death, as such minds are usually without fear of God, or devil, or hell, and are ready for the new life, and such incidents as may follow the change of worlds. Of all classes of persons who pass through death's door, none are so well prepared for the change as those who, having heard from friends living there, expect, and are ready, to meet them ; and they are very little disappointed by the change, for they meet their friends and accompany them to their homes.

The knowledge we gain of the other life before we go there to live is as valuable as is the knowledge we gain of another country to which we are to emigrate in this life. Foreigners would rarely come to this country to make a home if they knew as little about it as our Christian people know about the spirit world and the life there, which is nothing at all, as they ignore all information from there, and there can be no other source of information about that world, any more than there would be about any country on earth whose inhabitants were never heard from, and from which no visitor returned. For myself, I am very thankful for all I have learned about the country to which I am soon to emigrate, and I think I can prepare a much better outfit than I could if I had never heard from it. To me it is not a leap in the dark, as it must be to all Christians who have had no messages from that life, and only rely on the priests and the creeds of Christendom. I rejoice that this time of intercourse has come to us in my lifetime here. Had it not come till my transition, it would have been most surely a leap in the dark to me, and I should probably have waked up to the fact of renewed life from death as the first evidence of such existence, as I never could accept any of the Christian theories about a future, as they are all, so far as they are based on the Bible, relying on a physical resurrection, and an eternal residence in a kingdom with absolute monarchy for its government, and either a God or a devil for a king ;

in either case an absolute monarchy. Our facts are a glorious relief from both Christianity and atheism, as well as from the leap in the dark theory of the agnostics. I am only one of many millions who are now relieved from fears of an angry God, or tormenting devil, or annihilation, and many who have passed through the gate report to us that it is even better than they expected.

CHAPTER VIII.

EXTRACTS FROM CORRESPONDENCE IN THE BANNER OF LIGHT
AND OTHER PAPERS — BRIEF SKETCHES
FROM MANY YEARS.

"Thy task may well seem over-hard
  Who scatterest in a thankless soil,
Thy life or seed with no reward,
  Save that which duty yields to toil.
Yet do thy work: it shall succeed
  In thine or in another day,
And if denied the victor's mead,
  Thou shalt not lack the toiler's pay." — *Whittier.*

"You can sow to-day; to-morrow will bring
The blossom that proves what sort of thing
Is the seed, the seed that you sow."

"The main point of conversation is to state one's own opinion without exaggeration or platitude."

"CHICAGO, September, 1860.

"Large and intelligent audiences on each Sunday of this month assembled in a large hall in Chicago to listen to Warren Chase. The first lecture of the course was on revelation. Taking Webster's leading definition, he contended it could only extend as far as *knowledge* goes, and could not include any subjects of faith or belief, however sacred they are claimed to be. That no words, however sacred they might be claimed to be, could ever convey knowledge, and hence no words in the Bible could be a revelation; nor could the book be a revelation from God. That it had never made us *know* anything. That under our rules of evidence in our jurisprudence, no testimony of Bible or priest could be accepted to prove the condition of any soul or spirit after death, as there was no knowledge conveyed by either on which a rational belief could be founded. He also took the position that teachings were utterly unreliable, and conscientiousness as ready to accept error as truth, and hence the variety of religious beliefs.

" The evening discourse was on inspiration and not less radical or unsectarian than that of the morning, and yet both were listened to with evident satisfaction, showing the weakened power of the clergy over the public mind in that city. He claimed that while the laws of God were just, there was no sign of mercy in any of them toward man or beast, nor to man more than to beast, plants, or rocks. That so far as we can discover in this life, God treated the man who prays and the man who curses alike in all of the gifts of nature, and as yet we have no evidence of any change in God's dealings with man in the next life, but there and here leaving him subject to laws that ultimately punish or reward."

" These lectures were given in Kingsbury Hall, one of the best in the city, and well attended through the month, and quite well reported for the *Banner* and good notices given of them in Chicago papers. The second Sunday's lectures were not as radical as the first, but explained the mental and internal identity of each person which was maintained in spirit life, and he explained mediumship and the relation of the two worlds, as he has many times since. He maintained that the principal obstacle to a general belief in spirit intercourse was a belief in a devil who was capable of doing all that is done in the name of spirits. According to the lengthy reports of these lectures, they were very similar to those given now, with variations and increased evidence and knowledge, but equally radical, and his audiences maintained to the last."

"TOLEDO, O., Dec. 31, 1860.

"Amid the political, social, and commercial convulsions of the country, and while South Carolina is settling up her affairs with Uncle Sam, I may as well send in to the *Banner of Light* the footings of my running account with the world for the year which leaves us to-day for that unknown region 'from whose bourn' no year ever returns (see footing for 1860 for report). This little city of 14,000 inhabitants, closely united and roped to the Union by rivers, lakes, and canals, and riveted by railroads, is not likely to secede either from Ohio or Spiritualism (it did secede from Spiritualism and let it freeze out). Mrs. Laura McAlpine (later Laura Cuppy) lectured there with good success, and Mrs. S. M. Thompson and Mrs. Ada L. Hoyt (now Mrs. Foye), giving tests, are all good and faithful workers and doing good work there, as reported in this article. During the year I have seen our cause spreading, deepening, and strengthening, and taking hold more firmly of the public mind. (So I wrote then and have often since, and it is true to this day.) The union of the two worlds is growing closer, as I anticipate the union of our States will after the convulsions and the political storms are over, and the second sober thought of the people comes to the rescue of rights, duties, and obligations of justice. (So I wrote in 1860, and so it has proved, as I more clearly expressed it in my little book 'The American Crisis,' published about that time.) The calling on God in a storm and neglecting him in fair weather is ridiculous in this enlightened age." (So I think yet, and see no advantage in calling on God in any weather or in any emergency, as he never interferes to save us from fatal calamities in this life or any other that I have heard from.)

In February, 1861, I wrote an article for the *Banner* on "Mind and Matter," in which I stated, "I leave to physiologists to decide where human beings begin existence, both as a race and as individuals, and when they have decided, I will then endeavor to show that then and there the human soul began to 'live, move, and have a being.' As they never did, and never could, even find the origin of life or the origin of souls, because there is none, both being eternal in duration, I for myself, settled this question some years later in life, and gave my conclusions in my late work, 'Essence and Substance.'"

July 8, an interesting letter was written to the *Banner*, from Geneva, O., too long for insertion here. It speaks of general complaints, of windy days, frosty nights, short corn, thin grass, and scarcity of money, and yet many pleasant homes in the four States recently travelled over on my missionary work, and increasing interest in spirit intercourse, which has ever had many friends in the Western Reserve, where Joshua R. Giddings and Senator B. F. Wade defended it. This letter gives a graphic description of the free love society at Berlin Heights, O., and of a convention held there by the Spiritualists, to which very few of the society belonged, and speaks of them as well behaved, free from tobacco and liquors, profanity, and quarrelling, and the prevailing social evils of our large cities, and yet as abused and lied about by their pious neighbors, as if they were drunkards and thieves. It speaks of the convention as a most harmonious assembly, free from all disturbance and largely attended, and of the able speeches given by Seldon J. Finney, Mrs. H. F. M. Brown, Mr. Barnum, Mr. Loudon, myself, and others, and the good impression made, but not indorsing nor condemning the society of free lovers quietly residing there, as the Oneida society did in New York; but as they were strongly opposed to the popular use of tobacco and intoxicating drinks and pork, and to profane language, quarrelling, and law-suits, as well as to fashionable Christianity, they had too many reforms for the age and country in which they lived, and by the society with which they were surrounded. The result was they dried up and scattered after a few years of trial, while the Oneida society, which was Christian, but had all of the other obstacles of outside society to contend with, lived on for years, though it at last had to yield its social practices to the church regulations.

BATTLE CREEK, MICH., Aug. 22, 1860.

A letter says, "Once more under our own roof is the family circle complete, and glad hearts are joined in feasting on the ripened and abundant fruits of our Michigan soil. In our little garden (which consisted of one acre only) may be seen growing apples, pears, peaches, plums, figs, and grapes, and the various garden vegetables. Since I last left the cottage, I have travelled in all of the free States east of the Rocky Mountains, and lectured in all but Maine, and in Missouri and Maryland, which were then slave States. Have visited hundreds of happy homes and some unhappy ones, have found the *Banner of Light* in many, and many more needing it. . . . A brighter day is dawning on this benighted world, even in the midst of the political, social, and religious strife, commotion and turmoil. We can see the day-star that gives promise of a brighter morrow (this was just before the election of Lincoln). . . . I have occupied the pulpits of several prominent clergymen, and have there often taught our philosophy unconsciously to their audiences if not to themselves. . . . To be a true, consistent, and rational Spiritualist will soon be an honor in any intelligent community (so it is). . . . Have been absent over a year and lectured every Sunday but one, and given on an

average over four lectures per week. . . . In a few days
I return to my wandering work, and my eldest son to his
college studies."

"SYRACUSE, N.Y., Oct. 3, 1853.

"*Editor of Oshkosh Democrat:* As I journeyed along
my winding way to the Gotham of the East, I left the cars
at the depot in this city to call on some friends and spend
a few days at the great 'Salt-lick' of our nation. I
soon found myself in the midst of many noble hearts
which beat for human progress and liberty, gathered here
to celebrate the 'Jerry Rescue.' I soon met my old
friend Gerrit Smith; then an old veteran in the cause of
freedom, Samuel J. May; then the soul-inspiring face
of John O. Wattles; then a bright and noble soul in Lucy
Stone; and another in Antoinette L. Brown, who was
duly installed and had a right to 'preach.' Friday
morning a crowded house of earnest souls gathered to
listen to Lucy Stone on human slavery. Soon her small,
delicate, but well-proportioned form, with a living soul in
it, was in the desk, and the silvery tones of her persuasive
voice, in well-chosen words fitly spoken, was sending its
thrill through the audience. I wish we had a hundred
like her in the field. She spoke with much ease of the
hard and *soft* shells of this State; the soft were dough-
faces, and the hard had scarred consciences, and the fire
of truth, she said, was already heating with a prospect of
cracking both shells. Being registered as one of the vice-
presidents, I became quite well acquainted with the platform of the 'Jerry Rescue,' and with deep interest
listened to the eloquent speeches of Gerrit Smith, Antoinette L. Brown, S. J. May, Lucy Stone, and others, during
our three days' convention, held for and donated to the
cause of freedom. Saturday we had to go out into the
open air, as the hall would not hold the three thousand

people assembled to listen to these noble and devoted advocates of human liberty and the emancipation of the millions of slaves held in the South in apparently hopeless bondage. A rain-storm and a circle prevented my hearing C. C. Burleigh Sunday."

In the *Oshkosh Democrat* is also a lengthy letter from me dated Oct. 7, 1853, with a description of the Crystal Palace and its contents, in New York, in which I held a commission from the Agricultural Society of Wisconsin. But as that great exhibition has been eclipsed by the Centennial, and nearly gone out of the memory of our people, it is not worth while to repeat or read it now. The vast amount of my correspondence would fill several large volumes if collected, as it never can be. Only a few fragmentary scraps are in my possession, as much of it was never even seen by me after it was printed. My next letter to the *Democrat*, dated Oct. 22, 1855, describes a visit to the last lingering remnant of the many Phalanxes, or Fourier Societies, then still holding out at Red Bank, N.J., which soon after succumbed and followed the others to oblivion, to wait a renewal in the other world, as society here was not ready for that state of social life. As none of them tolerated tobacco or liquor, gambling or laziness, they were sadly out of sorts with popular society and soon dried up. This letter speaks of spending some pleasant hours in New York with Horace Greeley, O. S. Fowler, Judge Edmonds, T. L. Nichols, Henry James, and others interested in some if not all of the reforms I then as now publicly advocated. It also describes my visit to the Nutmeg State, as Connecticut had not then outgrown its early reputation for working up wood into clocks, hams, nutmegs, and cucumber-seeds. A visit to Winsted and Hartford is alluded to, lectures briefly noted, and a description given of A. J. Davis, whose home was then in Hartford; and also of that remarkable medium, Mrs. Semantha Mettler. It mentions the strong hold Spiritualism had at that time on the people of Hartford, but which does not seem to have held out as well as it has in many places. A visit to the old Charter Oak is also recorded, but I did not, like many others, rob it of a fragment as a relic. It has long since gone, root and branch, and only the sacred ground is left where it stood and was a sacred monument.

In my next letter, dated Oct. 28, 1853, is a description of the seven Cheney brothers of Manchester, Conn., their silk factory, and the improvements they had made by co-operative industry and united efforts, which was wonderful. The elder brother was among the early Spiritualists, and a friend of A. J. Davis and Mrs. Mettler. Their business outgrew the place, and was partly moved into Hartford. This letter says, " No sectarian bigotry is in the ascendant here, but the principles of the harmonial philosophy shed their genial influence over the place. No liquor is sold or used in the place. My soul has been refreshed by my visits here, for I see that degradation is not a fundamental part of a manufacturing business, but only incidental to an undeveloped condition of mind. I never saw such bright and cheerful countenances in any manufacturing establishment as I saw here, and I have visited many. Every sign of human progress and redemption from poverty, ignorance, and crime gives me encouragement to work on, and ever for the redemption of the race." My next, dated Nov. 1, 1853, was written at the Hutchinsons' home on High Rock, Lynn, Mass., giving a description of the tower and the circle around the wonderful image, built there by spirit direction given through John M. Spear. It was quite a curiosity, and went far toward showing me that there are spirits as fanatical as some denizens of this life, and as eagerly seeking for wonders and marvellous developments. This image was first supposed to be for perpetual motion, and later it was claimed that it would be endowed with life; but, of course, all failed, and only served to educate us on the conditions of those who inhabit the next sphere of existence. The image was mostly metallic, and built at considerable expenditure of time and money, and if for any other purpose than to educate us in the direction above stated, I never saw any evidence of it. All parties were at last ashamed of being duped in the enterprise by spirits.

My next letter seems to be largely devoted to Adin Ballou and his Hopedale Community, which was then quite successful, and a pleasant home for reformers in social life, but, like other premature efforts at a higher social life on a communitive basis, has gone out, or at least out of notoriety, like the Shakers. The society had then been eleven years in existence, and showed no signs of dissolution that I, a visitor, could discover, but I have heard little of it since. I think Brother Ballou, if not his community, parted from the Spiritualists on account of the free love craze, as he feared it might lead out of the orthodox teachings on the marriage subject. My next takes in Western New York, and the former home of Mr. and Mrs. Love, then the celebrated Mary F. Davis, and later the Mary Fenn, recently passed on to celestial life, for which her labors and disposition in this life fitted her, and where she can be happier than she could be here. A later letter describes graphically the "war of the gauges," which has gone into the history of Erie, Penn., the post and battle-field of the broad gauge and narrow gauge in the greatest railroad war our country has experienced. Then comes a description of the home of Grace Greenwood, at New Brighton, Pa., the home of her childhood; her home name was Sarah Jane Clarke, and there, too, lived one of our early able and faithful workers, Milo Townsend, and an old anti-slavery pioneer also. My next gives a graphic account of a railroad smash, with one death and many hurt on the train I had decided to go on, but was, contrary to my usual custom, persuaded to wait till next day. Only an incident, people said, giving my spirit friends no credit; but they do not need it. My next describes the Ohio legislature trying to elect a United States senator, and finally electing Salmon P. Chase, who had only two abolition votes for a long time, but by Democratic strategy was chosen.

Next comes L. A. Hine, a bold writer and liberalist of Cincinnati, and his pamphlet on the tallest steeple, and also a graphic description of the city and its suburbs, and slaughter-houses for swine. Joseph Barker was there, lecturing against the Bible, a powerful speaker who afterward became a convert, and blew hot out of the mouth that once blew cold; and at last nobody had confidence in him, as he deserved none. In 1854 I returned to New England and kept up this correspondence till the paper expired, as I have with many others before and since. An old scrap-book contains many more of those letters to different papers during the years before the publication of "The Life Line" in 1857, from which much of the interesting incidents is taken for that book; it does not need a place here, and I move on to later correspondence.

A letter from the greatest physical sufferer I ever knew, and my answer, from a *Banner of Light* of 1870 : —

"TO WARREN CHASE.

"DEAR BROTHER: From your article, 'Whence are we?' I see you 'believe' man had no beginning, and so can have no end. I had desired to know your belief on the subject. I can think of nothing which to me is more absurd, even in the old theology, than the doctrine of *pre-existence*. If the doctrine were true, you and I may have been through the same in an earthly body an indefinite number of times. We are, at least, *liable* to be forced through an earthly body any number of times in the endless future. I might stand a good chance to get better bodies than the one I am in. I might get worse bodies. On the whole, brother, I prefer the assurance of an endless and dreamless sleep. Yes, sooner give me non-existence than such a liability. I say this coolly and deliberately. I think few men have experienced more real mental and social felicity. Still, I ask nature and the gods to save me from another such a life. I do not fear it; I have so far borne this with courage and patience. I shall get through with what I believe to be the material hell of my existence; then I expect a better life for a season. For many years your life was one of great hardship, but I hope it may never be such as to enable you to fully realize the justification of my words. Brother, what do you do with the doctrine of progression? Have we been *improving* during the endless past, and only reached our present mental and moral stature? If so, about how much — or *how little* — will the endless future do for us? In love, I am your brother,

"AUSTIN KENT.

"STOCKHOLM, NEW YORK, April, 1870."

"Yes, brother, you and I exist. This is an admitted fact. We were not consulted about our existence, or at least, we have now no knowledge of being a voluntary party to it, nor of fixing the conditions and surroundings, so we have not much more chance of our choice in the future, whether it be annihilation or life. Fixed and immutable laws govern us in all stages and conditions of existence. We cannot if we would put an end to our existence, nor can any other power. Intelligence is eternal in its most minute particle, and there is one in each of us that will maintain its individuality through all eternity; it is divine, and as pure and perfect in degree as the aggregate, which is God. Your painful body can be and *must* be borne only for a brief season. I, too, have beat the bush and been pelted by the storms all my earthly life, and feel, as I near the goal, that a reward is sure. Progression! What a use is made of that word! God — mind —spirit-essence, *never* progress, being always perfect; bodies grow and decay and renew, and that is relative progression; and all progress is relative change, universal and eternal. Where we were and where we are to be in countless eons of past and future, are not now within the scope of our knowledge. That we are, is nearly all we know. We do not even know fully our relative position to each other, hence can scarcely say what progression is in ourselves — children — men — children again — dead — spirits, and then what and where? Our rules are too short to measure further. Many spirits come to earth to learn, and to grow better. Eternal progress from a starting-point is an absurdity, unworthy comment, as would be the starting of a ball in a direct line and continued with eternal speed in a straight line from that point; no such motion can be. All motion is in circles, and all periods rounded by the meeting of two ends. The ancients had a symbol of eternity fitting well. It was a snake with his tail in his mouth, and forever swallowing himself. It is not probable you or I shall ever have just such bodies or lives as we have here, nor is it likely we ever had such before; but the time may come when we shall be thankful for this experience, and glad we lived and fought it out. Let us take it all and bear it, and be ready for the next turn of Fortune's wheel. I have already been a thousand times thankful that I was not born of rich, popular, or of *Christian* parents. Not because my life here has been easier or more pleasant, but because I already realize my advantages in the next stage of being; and I feel sure, brother, that you too, will rejoice over your earthly lot, however hard it seems now."

From an article in the *Banner* of April 28, 1860, I extract the following: —

"I believe love is an element as free as electricity or magnetism, and no more intelligent or responsible, but, like them, subject to laws. It cannot be God, and does not rule the world or mankind. The human mind or will, however free and voluntary in its action, does not always control this element in the organism of the body and mind. The human heart is often as mercilessly destroyed by it as the fruit-tree is by lightning, and its shocks are often as violent as those of electricity and even as destructive. It seems to me the only safety is in discerning its laws and guarding against injurious effects, as we do against those of electricity. Then we shall soon discern how far we are like Leyden jars, voltaic piles, or galvanic batteries, and protect ourselves and society from the evil effects now attributed to God or the devil. Speculations, experiences, prayers or divorces will never remove the evils experienced by the ungoverned use of this potent element in the human organism. I wish we had some Galva or Franklin to experiment with the social and religious manifestations of this element, and searching find the laws that control it and the instruments necessary to govern it."

In the *Banner* of May 12, 1860, is a long article by me, on the social discords among Spiritualists, from which I have only room for the following extract: —

"One part of the mission of spirits is sympathy with the suffering and afflicted, and I do not know where they could find more deserving or greater demand than in some of those oppressed victims of domestic tyranny. 'Steps to heaven are fire-paven,' says a poet, and I think many can bear record to its truth, and none more than some victims of social discords. That there are some unworthy subjects, and some who 'flee when no man pursueth,' I have no doubt; but we have been long taught that there is no effect without a cause. Those who think spirits or Spiritualism the cause of the social discords of spirits, are as much mistaken as the ancients who thought the sun went round the earth and caused day and night. The cause and effect both exist; it is the suffering that brings the sympathy of the spirits, and I am glad to say of Spiritualists also, and often, too often, when it could not be found in our Christian churches and their adherents."

In the *Banner* of May 26, is a letter written at Geneva, O., with a scathing review of an editor of a local paper at Conneaut, O., who had attacked Spiritualism and its speakers. He long since passed to the shades, while Spiritualism goes marching on, conquering and to conquer. It says of his allusion to me that if I had not more friends in the county than he had, I should not stop there to lecture. He said Spiritualism was "endemic and epidemic," and the letter says he had better take it, as "hair of the same dog cures the bite."

In looking over the files of the *Banner* of twenty-five and thirty years ago, and its extensive correspondence, I see names of but few who are still among its correspondents, and this notifies me that my time is nearly out. In the issue of July 21, 1860, is an article of mine on the wicked practice of taking little children to Sunday-schools, and teaching them falsehoods they have to unlearn in riper years, or remain in ignorant submission to the church,—teaching them about God, and heaven, and hell, of which the teachers know as little as they do, which they will at some time in riper years find out. In the issue of Aug. 4 is a long letter written at the home of Hon. S. J. W. Taber, an old correspondent of the Boston *Investigator* from Independence, Iowa, and some years an auditor in the United States Treasury, where I also visited him and his valuable library. This letter gives an account of our convention held there when our sister, Mrs. H. F. M. Brown, took part — she and Brother Taber, both now in spirit life, of which she knew much, and he nothing, as he often told me; but he found it all the same, and enjoys it as he deserved, for he was an honest and upright man, a great reader, and a good scholar and citizen.

Nearly every issue of the *Banner* of 1860 has a letter of mine, and quite a number from our young brother, F. L. Wadsworth, who came into our ranks in Maine, and flourished brilliantly for a short time, and then left us for paths and pastures more congenial to his tastes. Dec. 31, 1860, a long letter from Toledo, O., closes my year with its footings of lectures and scanty pay, but keeping up expenses, leaving me no excuse to leave the cause, which I never wished to do. January, 1861, I report from Baltimore, Md., when the war spirit was up, and the fever running high, with Brother Danskin in it to some extent. This year I was on the war-path, as elsewhere related, but kept my Sundays sacred to our cause. In the issue of March 2 is a long and labored article by me on " Mind and Matter," conveying some of the ideas I have since extended and varied by study and observation. In the *Banner* of March 9 is the following, which gives some idea of my work: —

" Warren Chase lectures in Oswego the five Sundays of March; in Utica first Sunday in April; in Troy the second Sunday in April; in Providence the third and fourth Sundays of April; in Putnam, Conn., the four Sundays of May; in Stafford first Sunday in June, and will be at the convention in Worcester, Mass., in April."

A letter from Penn Yan, N.Y., dated March 26, 1861, says : " Here I met Brother Toohey, whose name does not appear as often as it should for one doing as much in the cause as he reports. He says he has given over twenty lectures in the last month. To-day he still lives, but seems rather played out for so young a man." March 29 a writer from Oswego, N.Y., says: "We have been blessed this week with a visit from Professor Grimes, and a course of lectures against Spiritualism, and, as Brother Chase says, 'amusing the children with his funny stories, and getting their money, which is what he is after.'" A description of this discussion between Messrs. Grimes and Chase follows, for which the committee had to pay Mr. Grimes $45, and Mr. Chase got nothing but the victory, and both were satisfied." The writer also says, "Henry Ward Beecher gave some lectures nearly as radical as those of Mr. Chase." We had evidently been approaching each other for some years, and since his change to spirit life are much nearer than before. In the *Banner* of May 20, 1861, is a long letter from me, largely upon the war spirit in the old Quaker city of Providence, in which I approve the loyalty, but deplore the war spirit that called it out, and made it necessary. No place I had visited showed more zeal and devotion to the Union than this old home of Roger Williams. I speak of the military parade as a pitiful sight, and say I had hoped our country was above the war plane, at least a fratricidal war and believe much of it is, but not all, and do not know whether a war can bring the lower and fractious part up; and it now seems to me, by the way the military spirit is kept up, that it has not done it, as our congressmen and the leading papers are talking war, and for war preparation on land and sea for naval and harbor protection; but, as I believe, largely for the vast appropriations and expenditures of money which they hope to have a share of in some way, direct or indirect. As I turn over the pages of the *Banner* of the long ago, and read the names among its correspondents, with my own, of Judge Edmonds, Henry C. Wright, S. S. Jones,

Mrs. H. F. M. Brown, Achsa W. Sprague, Dr. H. F. Gardner, S. B. Brittan, Rufus Elmer, John M. Spear, L. K. Coonley, Abel Underhill — all in spirit life now, — with many others whose names are also there, I almost conclude I too ought to be there, having been here long enough, and done my little share of the work in introducing the new dispensation. In a letter dated Providence, June 7, 1861, speaking of Thomas Gales Forster, than whom we never had a more eloquent man on the rostrum, I say, after hoping he might recover his health, one word that will encourage him is "victory," and of that we are sure, however many of us may fall in the conflict, killed by disease or the masked batteries of the churches, by persecution and slander, or whoever may run off the track, or stand on side issues. We will conquer, and each laborer will have his reward in the grand hereafter.

A letter dated South Hardwick, Vt., July 5, says, evidently in a sorrowful tone, "There is rest for the weary, a balm for the wounded heart, sympathy for the sorrowing soul, even in this world of strife and conflict."

"What we sow, that we shall gather;
Or grapes or thorns it boots not whether."

The letter closes with a motto, "The Banner and the Union." May they together float and prosper. In the *Banner* of August 24 is a long and graphic description of a visit to the top of Mount Mansfield, the highest of the Green Mountains, and of one of the grandest scenes I ever saw, in looking down on a shower whilst the sun was shining on it and us, and the lightning playing on the cloud that shed the rain. So there was, as ever with me, sorrow and joy intermixed in life. From Glover, Vt., Aug. 8, an article of mine on "Government" is deserving a place here, but I can find room for only one extract. It begins: —

"Backward, ye presumptuous nations:
Man to misery was born."

The Christian argument applied to the North from the Southern church, — "But whosoever shall smite thee on the right cheek, turn to him the other also. And if any man will sue thee at the law, and take away thy coat, let him have thy cloak also." If the planters of the South take the government of the South, give them the government of the North also. If they take the national capital, give them the state capital also; if they take your house, give them your farm also; if they take your brother, give them your children also; if they make slaves of your sons, give them your daughters also, for you are all commanded to "resist not evil." That this is Christian precept and authority, I do not deny, but it is not Christian practice, and I hope will not be till this terrible conflict is over. Suppose our sires had acted on this Christian principle, what should we have had for a government to-day? The noble spirit that prompted them to resist evil, and make Boston harbor a teapot, was not Christian, but it was true patriotism, and I trust will enable us to save this country from becoming a home where the few aristocrats have all the wealth, and the producers are chattels, or worse, oppressed as wage slaves. A letter from Marblehead, in November, speaks of old Salem being shaken by the lectures of Emma Hardinge, and says, probably the theological cannon that silenced the witches will be pointed at her, and she will be shown "witch hill" or "gallows hill," and pointed to the old elm, and the story of Mary Dyer, and bid to "depart out of these parts." A letter dated Boston, January, 1862, and headed "49 and 25," has a graphic sketch of my life, and forty-nine years, and twenty-five in Spiritualism, and truly says the first forty years of life had very little in them to comfort and satisfy me, or pay me for my efforts to live and let live, and only with Spiritualism came any satisfaction with life, and such as no church could give me.

April 5, 1862, my article on "Affection" says: "There is a free, spontaneous, and almost universal expression of affection and love for children, general or partial in our race. Men and women may caress both boys and girls under a certain age, and it is all right, proper, and a sign of goodness, and not of depravity; but as soon as these children begin to develop man and womanhood, and when they need it as much for guidance and protection, it suddenly turns to evil and is all wrong,— a sure sign that nature (for it is nature) is totally depraved. Love, then, becomes lust, and must be restrained by both Church and State. Hence people taught by both restraining powers that they are totally depraved by nature, and this love is the sure sign, it is no wonder they largely become so, and are so very wicked. If a child of ten years needs affection, one of sixteen or twenty needs it more, as the temptations are greater; and the shield of love and affection should protect both sexes till intellect is ripe."

My April letters show that I had completed and published my third book, "The American Crisis," long since out of print, but which sold well during the war. In the issue of May 10 is a very critical letter on D. J. Mandel, who, with his best muzzled gun loaded with fine shot, was permanently located at Athol Depot, Mass., as the Army of the Potomac had been all winter anchored in the mud. It says my brother seems to take exceptions to my views of prayer. I am glad of it. I should have nothing to do if everybody agreed with me, and I would as soon have him differ from me as any one. He objects to my calling it a crutch or staff; he calls it a wing; and I accept it as useful to collect dust in the kitchen or carry a bird in the air, but useless on the body of man or spirits, for either body or soul of mortal. The issue of May 7,

1862, contains an article of mine on "Marriage," which says: "True and real marriage consists in the harmonious blending of two lives in unitary duality in four departments of one nature, — the intellectual, affectional, passional, and pecuniary; and the discords in social and domestic life arise from a want of harmony in one or more of these departments." In the issue of August 23 is an article on "Slavery, Polygamy, and Land Monopoly," classing them as kindred systems in our social life. In 1862, writing up my half-century of life, I said, and ever say, with the negro recently executed in New York, "This has been to me an unfriendly world"; only the light and life of, and in, Spiritualism had given me comfort and hope. In the issue of January 3, 1863, is a letter of mine on "Abandoned Women," which severely criticises society for having such a class of women and no corresponding class of men. No abandoned men, but plenty of abandoned women, of which we should be ashamed.

March, 1863, the following was written, and published in the *Banner of Light* of April 18. It is more appropriate now than at that time, in some respects, but not in all, as some deep sorrows and bleeding wounds of that time are healed.

"FAREWELL TO NEW ENGLAND.

"I leave thee, if not out in the cold, to go out in the cold myself. Sorrows and joys are intermixed and closely woven among thy hills and vales, and around thy rockbound coast. Grief cankers in many a heart, and sorrow drapes the family altar in many a home. Many are the causes and varied are the hues. 'Every heart knoweth its own sorrow,' and many can exclaim, 'the powers I have were given me to my cost,'— the power to enjoy, which carries with it the shadow with suffering.

Many have I met who have wished themselves back nearer to a rock, or quite to a rock in feelings, and, although often reproving them, I have been in the same condition, and often wished it myself, when my grief, too, seemed more than I could bear. Then the angels came, and one bright spot, though small and distant, appeared in the heavens, and Hope hung her anchor there.

"The proof-sheet from every ledger, the account current of almost every family and person, whether made quarterly or annually, will show a debt and credit side that will not balance without borrowing from the future joys to offset the sorrows, especially in these trying times, when homes have been desolated and hearts have been broken; when discords have riven the closest ties, and misery has walked into the most quiet parlors and stirred the smouldering embers of the most quiet firesides. It sometimes seems as if God was scourging the earth; certainly our country has borne a scourging, and how can individuals escape? If Jesus bore the sins and sorrows of the wicked in his day, shall the good of our day escape? Shall the burden fall only on the wicked? No, no, New England; you have given birth to the principle that is now being tried on the battle-field and in the school-house, on the rostrum and in the parlors, in the dens of thieves and by the quiet firesides, in the cabinet and in the kitchen. Born and hardened among your rocks, I carried your principles, which were ingrained in my education, to the westward. I have travelled and traded; have exchanged thoughts and feelings; have returned to your homes and been welcomed and spurned; felt blessings and curses, and thanked God for blessings and affections, and that I can join in and share with you pleasure and pain, misery and delight, sunshine and storm, poverty and wealth, purity and crime (*if crime must be*); and I only ask strength to bear with thee my share; be equal to the duties of each hour; carry my crosses; fulfil my mission; grow better and wiser as life wears away. And I hope, if I never visit your shores and mountains again in the body that has so often walked your streets of city and town, and securely slept in your homes, that my spirit may often come to your homes where suffering is, and administer words, if no more, to the sorrowing hearts that linger and long for deliverance; and that I may be permitted to meet many of you at the threshold of the other life, as you have met me at your thresholds here, and share with you there, as you have shared with me here, whatever of good we can reach. I often feel as if my earthly work was nearly done, and the golden gate was already being opened by a mother's hand, that shall let me into the realms where this weary heart can rest from its life of sorrow and toil; for to me life has been a 'wheel of pain at best,' although I have found sunny spots along the shore and among the mountains, in the groves, in the cities, and in the cottages; and have found loving hearts, and vile, unhallowed ones; and all the children of God are, for aught I know, equally sacred and dear. I have long since ceased to envy the good or despise the bad—if indeed there are any wholly bad. I bless you all, and wish you all happiness, and feel sure there is a law of compensation awaiting every soul for every sorrow and every joy. Many of you who have smiled or frowned on me will see my face no more, even if I should visit New England again, and to you all I say, Good spirits bless you, as I do and will, in this life and the next. Even envy, malice, spite, and lies have done me good, if not so designed, and schooled my soul in lessons I could not otherwise have learned. Yes, yes, New England, I love thee still, and still my heart is with thee, turning there; and I could not if I would, would not if I could, tear it away. With thee I have seen my saddest and happiest hours; drank deeply of the cup of sorrow, and from the Ganymede cup of nectar. . . . Once more farewell, home of my childhood, land of the brave and true. Let me pass in form away, but in spirit let me dwell among you still and share your joys and sorrows."

The above is not all, but most of that letter; all I can afford space for here. In my letter of December 2, 1863, is a description of the fruit-hills in the Egypt of Illinois, where I located a rude home for myself, son-in-law, and daughter, and where we have ever since kept a home, or they have, and one for me in old age at South Pass, now Cobden, Ill. April 3, 1864, my letter from Princeton, Ill., speaks of attending the funeral service of the Hon. Owen Lovejoy; sermon by Rev. Edward Beecher. Later I made some speeches to aid in electing as his successor the brother of Col. R. G. Ingersoll.

In *Banner* of May 28, 1864, my report says I have just closed a third engagement in Chicago, making in all ten Sundays, and sixteen lectures to the best audiences I have ever addressed in the West. I was then preparing to move to our new home in Southern Illinois, now Cobden. During all these years nearly every week a letter of mine in the *Banner* reported progress and the work I was doing. In its issue of July 9 I report a grand success in a convention in Geneseo, Ill. From New Boston, Ill., I report the Boston *Investigator* having done much to enlighten the minds and prepare them for Spiritualism, which is true wherever that paper has been read, as was the case in my family. In the issue of September 10 is a very interesting letter on "A Change of Base"; political, social, and religious, somewhat prophetic, but too long to copy here, as are many others; although some critic calls my articles "finger-length articles," not knowing they are generally read, while his with superfluous verbiage are left out in the cold. A series of articles from me appear in 1864 in numbers of the *Banner*, embodying much I have since published in "Essence and Substance," and other works. In a letter of December 24 is an account of the ways and workings of the Oneida Community, of which the late John H. Noyes was the founder, and then the chief. In a letter of May, 1865, after describing two poor women who supported themselves by work for a pious Boston man, and which they had to continue seven days each week to make expenses, and which he took from them because they worked on it Sundays, I mention another case which I knew, where a very pious lady refused to sell milk to a poor woman for her babe because the woman was not married, when she knew she could not get it elsewhere, remarking she did not sell milk for such children; and I wondered if she would have sold it to Mary for Jesus, whose mother was not the wife of his father. October 23 records a very pleasant visit at the home of Thomas Garrett, in Wilmington, Delaware, often the resting-place of the abolitionists. My letter of January 1, 1866, reports an average of about $3.50 per lecture for the preceding year, scarcely paying personal expenses. In the *Banner* of April 28, 1866, is graphically described a vision, if it was a vision, of the future of Philadelphia, in which city I got it in some way, in a partially abnormal state. It spoke of it as a great city with clean marble streets; not a horse, not a cow, not a dog, not a cat, not a pig in its clean streets; no steam, but electric motive power; free cars for passengers and separate freight cars. No intoxicating liquors, no tobacco. A neatness and splendor no pen could justly describe; both sexes beautifully and comfortably dressed; buildings of glass, iron, marble, and many materials not now known; parks with shade and fruit trees in abundance, and most delicate flowers. City completely under-drained, and no sign of filth anywhere. Much more is described in the letter. January 1, 1867, announces my taking charge of the *Banner* branch-office in New York, which I retained till they closed it up. From this office, 544 Broadway, my articles were regular in the *Banner* during my agency, and often spicy. March 23 No. 1 of Vol. 21 of the *Banner* entered my name at head of New York department as local editor and agent. In that number my article showed up the great folly and absurdity of the effort — still continued — to unite Church and State in this country, when the tendency all over Europe, and in all enlightened countries, is in an opposite direction. Sunday, March 18, my letter says: "The first Sunday of rest for two years, and that because I could not get to my engagement on account of a storm." April 17 I send a report received of a praying-machine made to go by water-power instead of by wind, as most of them do. It is said to be used in some part of the world, and so far as I can yet learn, as effectual in securing foreign aid as any human machine-praying. The modern discoveries might easily be made to utter or print in large, visible letters the Catholic and Episcopal service from the books, and thus save the priests much labor. May 11 speaks of a man "down in the mouth" because he was out of tobacco and no money to get it with.

My articles made reading-matter items for from one to two columns each week of my stay in New York, while every Sunday my voice was heard in some public hall. To this day I think it a mistake in breaking up the New York office, but it was too long in getting upon a paying basis of business. For some reason, to me then unknown, my spirit guides evidently wished me to travel more as an itinerant, and hence moved me out of New York City, and later out of St. Louis; but I think now, at the age of seventy-five, they will let me settle down and become local, as I wish to do, and in the West, probably St. Louis.

Sept. 3, 1867, we attended the Eighth National Convention of Spiritualists in Cleveland, O., but, like our location in New York, this experiment to establish a national and central organization was premature, and it had to be abandoned later. The final bursting of the bubble is generally attributed to that blazing comet that went through our social sky, Victoria C. Woodhull, and finally fell in England, landing in London. An effort in which I engaged at that time to get up State organizations failed. Oct. 20, 1867, in my articles about Christianity, I do not include Jesus or his disciples, who were not Christians, nor even called so; they were heretics and infidels, and he was crucified as such. They were utterly unlike modern Christians, who do not do the works they did, nor live as they did, nor teach as they did, but instead, follow aristocracy and Roman rituals and dogmas. I hold the same ideas now. My graphic articles on New York and its "upper ten" Christians, and the suffering poor in the streets, gave a picture of Jesus with the poor, and the old and new priests with the aristocrats. In my department for June 27, 1868, is an account of a motion made by Gen. B. F. Butler in the House of Representatives in Washington, to have mediums taxed as jugglers, but which, by a close vote, was defeated. Probably the general is wiser by this time; if not, he soon will be. On the first day of May, 1869, the office in New York was closed, and all business transferred to the home office in Boston, and I started again on my itineracy, but retained a place in the *Banner* as correspondent for several years regular, and later irregular to this date. After two years and four months of busy life in New York, a change was no doubt an advantage to me. My articles were next entered as "Editorial Correspondence." In the autumn of 1869 I opened our bookstore in St. Louis, and lectured there most of the time for three years, and continued my editorial letters to the *Banner* all of the time. In my letter of March 20 is this quotation from Theodore Tilton, " We have never yet seen any evidence that evangelical Christians are better men and women than liberal Christians"; and I add that in my fifty years of life and observation I have never seen any evidence that either were better men and women than many who do not believe in Christianity at all, and have generally found that most of the wicked, including nearly all murderers, were believers in Christianity. In my letter of March 23, 1870, is a reference to a saphead by the name of Arnel, who chanced to get into Congress, and offered a resolution stating that as the Christian religion was recognized as a part of the common law of the land, therefore the reading of the Bible in our public schools is eminently wise and proper, and tending to encourage and foster virtue and morality; and I add, especially the history of David and Solomon, of Lot and Noah and Job and Elisha and Samson. Had he confined his resolution to Congress, and declared it to be a Christian body, needing a chaplain and prayers and the daily reading of a portion of Scripture and selections as above, the country might make no objection to its passage; but to declare the absurd falsehood that Christianity is part of our common law, when it is not and never can be, is the height of folly and ignorance, and was thrown as a sop to the most ignorant Christians, to show his piety. Dec. 10, 1870, my letter speaks of the softening of brain of the Catholic Church, as its heart did when it lost the power to persecute and execute its opponents. Recently its brain seems to be recovering.

There are many valuable items in these years of regular correspondence, but there is room for very few in these extracts. Jan. 25, 1871, I mention attending a lecture to the Sunday-school scholars by a pious brother of Charles Partridge, who had just returned from a visit to the Holy Land, in which he told them he had stood on the very roof where Peter stood when the sheet was let down from heaven, with all manner of four-footed beasts in it, and had stood on the bank of the Jordan, right where the children of Israel stood when Jehovah rolled up the waters, and let them cross without wetting their feet, and several more such stories, and informed them where they could find the accounts of these miracles in the Holy Word of God; and I thought of the "Fool's Errand, by one of the fools." A description of the fountain from which the water was drawn which Jesus turned into wine at Cana, is also another item of another writer who had visited that Holy Land. July 1, 1871, one letter speaks of a judge who, in sentencing a criminal to be hung, said God saw the motive and the act; and I thought he ought to hold God as accessory and equally guilty, as he saw and knew it all, and could, but would not, prevent it and save the victim. Another item of ours speaks of the grasshoppers eating up the wheat-crop in Paradise, which is now a section of the new holy land of the Mormons in Utah, and advises people not to go to Paradise. Another item of ours, copied from authentic statistics, shows the death-rate in the eight largest cities in the United States. St. Louis the lowest, and San Francisco, where they cannot stop to die, the second. Another item of mine describes Thomas L. Harris as being like Absalom, suspended by the hair of his head between the two worlds, and of no benefit to either. A letter of March 16, 1872, speaks of the deserters from our army of brave defenders of the unpopular truths, but thinks they will be fully punished by their own consciences; but this has not stopped it, as several speakers have since gone, the last being our able writer, J. M.

Peebles. "Second Advent of Satan" is the heading of an article on Spiritualism, which the churches call such. My article in the issue of May 18, 1872, announces the fact, with reference, that the Supreme Court of Ohio has decided unanimously that "neither Christianity nor any other system of religion is a part of the law of this State"; a godless state in a nation claimed to be Christian, but is not legally recognized as such. When the city of St. Louis licensed houses of ill-fame, my pen put them on the same respectable — or not respectable — basis as licensed saloons. The former is ended, and the latter ought to be in all cities and States, as a curse with no good in it. On the 9th and 10th of November, 1872, the terrible fire in Boston swept the *Banner of Light* office and all its valuable stock of books and papers into oblivion; but the indomitable spirit of its proprietors, and the aid of friends, soon put that paper on its feet again, and long may it run with its good news. In December of that year Horace Greeley left his body for the higher life, and when I had one of fifteen electoral votes for Missouri for him for President. April 5, 1873, my letter contains a description of a Christian family, regular attendants at a Catholic church, the man a miserable drunkard, and the wife a broken-hearted and careworn mother of several ragged and half-starved children, who are kept out begging evenings, and yet the church can send missionaries to the heathen, and have the poor with them, that the Scripture may be fulfilled. In June I sold out and closed my business in St. Louis, and devoted all of my time to lecturing, taking with me most of the books and selling them at my lectures; but I had lost money all the years of our business in St. Louis, and only sustained myself by lectures outside of the business, and assistance from the *Banner of Light*, which, with Brother Colby, has always been the best friend I have ever had in New England. In the fall of 1873 my editorial correspondence with the *Banner*, which had lasted over six years without a word or note of discord, closed. Since then I have been an occasional correspondent only, as I have to many other papers. A letter in the *Banner* of November 22, 1873, says, in the last three months I had travelled over fourteen States, and lectured in seven of them. No one but myself can know the estimation in which I hold the *Banner* and its editors, publishers, and its whole corps, and no one else can know the assistance it has been to me during its entire existence. I continued my correspondence in its columns mostly from the West, quite regularly through 1874–75, and its publication was a great help to me in my itinerant work. In August, 1875, I made my second and last trip to the top of Mount Washington.

In the *Banner* of December 11, 1875, is my notice of the transition of my wife, Mary P., to her new home in the summer land, with my tribute to her faithful and useful life here, and glad release from a suffering body. After spending some weeks in '76 at the Centennial, and visiting my home in Illinois, I proceeded slowly westward, closing the year with a course of lectures in Salt Lake City. December 31 found me in San Francisco, and, after my eventful six years' residence in California, as elsewhere related, I returned to close my eventful life in the East. I close this *Banner* correspondence with the following report of my seventy-fifth birthday reception, as published in that paper, Jan. 21, 1888 : —

"SEVENTY-FIFTH BIRTHDAY OF HON. WARREN CHASE ; FORTY YEARS IN THE FIELD ; CONGRATULATORY TESTIMONIAL AT PAINE MEMORIAL HALL.

"As set forth in these columns last week, a delegation of the Boston friends of Hon. Warren Chase celebrated with appropriate exercises, on Thursday evening, Jan. 5, his attainment of the age of seventy-five years of mortal experience, and the rounding out of a forty years' term of service on his part as a public advocate of the New Dispensation.

"The exercises occurred at Paine Memorial Hall, on Appleton Street. Dr. H. B. Storer officiated as chairman, with his usual tact and skill, and all present seemed filled with an appreciation of the occasion and its lessons.

"Shortly before eight o'clock the people were called to order by Chairman Storer, who proceeded to explain the meeting, and what it proposed to emphasize in eloquent and concise fashion : —

"Brother Chase, he said, was indeed to be congratulated at having attained the age of seventy-five years of earth-life — forty of which had been devoted to the wearing cares incident to the path of the pioneer in the cause of truth — with his faculties still undimmed, and his full ability for active service in the field still capable of demonstrable proof. Some thirty-four years ago he had made the acquaintance of Mr. Chase in the city of New York, whither he (the speaker) had gone as a delegate to a Spiritualist convention ; and the friendship then formed had endured to the present hour.

"Brother Chase commenced life as a free-thinker, or materialist; he did not hesitate to give expression to the agnosticism which then ruled his mind; when he did *not* believe the existing order of thought regarding human life and its probable outcome, he did not hesitate to proclaim it; and when the time came that he *did* believe in a future life and in the bearing of the present upon the next, he showed equal courage and persistency in making that fact known also.

"The speaker believed that Brother Chase was the first advocate of the Harmonial Philosophy as set forth by Andrew Jackson Davis; and did valiant service for the betterment of human conditions at the time when the glamour of a false theology blinded some of the keenest intellects of the world, and any reform, if it hoped for a hearing, must approach the people, hat in hand, through church channels, and 'for Jesus' sake.'

"He referred to the bigotry of the churchmen who, in the early days of the great temperance movement, refused to allow women, the wives of reformed drunkards, to tell from the pulpits of the land the story of their great temporal salvation! It was because of the earnest efforts of Brother Chase and those of his class in this country, that the pulpit at last became open to the voice of Temperance, whether it used the lips of a man or of a woman in the expression of its measurably Apocalyptic message. Brother Chase went into the fight for temperance on moral, not on religious grounds; then he went further, and demanded equality of the sexes and freedom for the slave! Of him it might be said, as of one of old time, 'the common people heard him gladly'; his long life had been devoted to the righting of their wrongs, with a sturdy fidelity which told that underlying principles, not the shifting influences of 'every breath of doctrine,' were at work in his mind.

"Dr. Storer recommended that all who had not should read the book of Brother Chase, entitled 'Life Line of the Lone One,' and also keep in mind the sequel thereto which he is about to bring out; since by such action they would become much better acquainted with the true and sterling merits of his (C.'s) character than any words of the speaker could accomplish toward making them so.

"The little stream which took its rise among the rugged hills of New Hampshire three-quarters of a century ago had since spread from the Atlantic to the Pacific, had extended into every department of reform connected with human progress and well-being; and the present assembly was convened to bear witness to the practical worth of its enduring influence.

"Dr. Storer noted the disappointing absence of Horace Seaver, Esq., and then said he had a letter to read (which would explain itself) from another, who, purposing to attend, had been rendered unable so to do through illness : —

"BANNER OF LIGHT OFFICE, BOSTON, MASS.,
Jan. 5, 1888.

"DEAR MR. CHASE: We congratulate you that Dame Nature has kept you physically intact up to the present time; we are thankful to the spirit-world forces for thus protecting and encouraging you in your able advocacy of the grand movement through whose revealments we and others have for many years, and in the midst of much tribulation, sought to enlighten a benighted world.

"Your forty years of incessant labors, by both voice and pen, all over this country, in conjunction with other able co-workers, have resulted in placing before mankind *a mighty truth* — no more nor less than the *grand fact* of immortality; the *fact* of direct spirit communion between the world of causes and the world of effects; the fact that we still live after the dissolution of our physical bodies.

"Should you pass to spirit-life ere we are called up higher, it is our earnest wish that you report to us promptly. Should we go first, we shall make it a point to report to you whenever the first opportunity offers.

"Enclosed you will find *material* evidence of the appreciation in which you are held by
"Your humble servant,
"LUTHER COLBY.

"N.B. — I should have been present in the form at your ovation had not illness prevented.

"Mr. J. T. Lillie then favored the audience with a fine vocal selection, after which Miss Lucy Barnicoat was introduced to the people.

"Miss Barnicoat prefaced her remarks by reading ' My Birthday,' by the poet Whittier, and then proceeded to note, in advance, the fact that as it was due to the efforts of Mr. Chase, and such as he, in the past, that women had found admission to the public rostrums of the several reforms, the presence of Mrs. Lillie and herself on an occasion like this was eminently appropriate. She spoke of the service which she personally knew Mr. Chase had performed, at camp meetings in Maine and elsewhere, where she had met him, and where the young admired him, the middle-aged appreciated him, and the old honored him.

"She regretted the enforced absence of Mr. Colby, whom she considered a valued personal friend and a stalwart bulwark of the cause of Spiritualism which was so dear to the hearts of those present.

"She closed by thanking all who had given the encouragement of their presence to this testimonial, and by the expression of hearty wishes for the success of Brother Chase in the future.

"Dr. Paxson, of Philadelphia, gave several interesting personal reminiscences of the temperance and anti-slavery reforms and reformers, and bore witness to the fearlessness which Brother Chase had ever manifested in the expression of his views all along the line. He (the Doctor) had found that a man, firm in his convictions, and calm but determined in their presentation, would as a rule escape from permanent injury when brought into collision with heated opponents. Dr. P. had been, himself, tried in that furnace, when a Philadelphia mob threatened to burn his house over his head because he had at the time William Lloyd Garrison as a guest; he refused to turn that great apostle out of doors at the cry of the rioters, *but* his house was *not* destroyed, after all! The mighty inspiration of that hour had gone onward, and Spiritualism was now its point of objective expression; he adjured all to be true to its uplifting power; prophesying that by the aid of female intuition, which the New Dispensation had so strongly emphasized in its public work, the character of men and nations would be thoroughly changed ere another century had passed away.

"Mrs. J. T. Lillie spoke of Brother Chase as one who by the peculiar conditions attending his early life, had been commissioned to right the wrongs of women, and thus do valiant work for the good of general humanity. She compared him to John the Baptist, crying in the desert of human scepticism forty years ago: 'Prepare ye the way for Spiritualism—the revelation of immortal life, and sure progression for all mankind.' Her controls then delivered an inspirational poem appropriate to the occasion, and instinct with recognition of what the guest of the evening had accomplished for the cause when once it had *made* its cheering advent.

"Mr. Lillie then sang, 'One Hundred Years to Come,' and on being *encored*, gave in response, 'My Sweetheart when a Boy.'

"Mr. Chase followed; he was warmly received, and commenced with congratulating himself: There was a vast improvement in his conditions over those which existed early one morning amid the bleak hills of New Hampshire seventy-five years ago. He had then been ushered, at the very threshold of life, into a moral and social atmosphere which equalled in keenness and cruelty the wintry blasts that swept the gloomy heights around, and found none to welcome him to the mortal plane save his mother.

"The life of hardship to which he was exposed in his earlier years had produced a lasting impression on all his subsequent career, making him, through a fellow-feeling of sympathy, always a friend of the poor and the oppressed on every hand. He had thus been led to champion anti-slavery, temperance, woman suffrage, and had in turn, according to his light, been a materialist, and latterly — for the forty years just closed — a Spiritualist, and a platform advocate of the claims of the New Dispensation. It had been mentioned during the evening by a lady speaker, that he had been privileged to do a great work toward opening the platform to women and breaking up the prejudice which had so long existed against woman's speaking in public; and, judging by the remarks which had been made by the lady speakers on the present occasion, and the eloquent sentences for justice and reform which were finding expression from the women of the present day, he was proud to have so grand a compliment paid to his life labors. 'Perfect equality between the sexes' had been his motto for half a century, and he should hold to it till his life on earth was done. The principle involved in this motto, he believed, would become world-wide in its power as years proceeded.

"He announced that by reason of unexpected detention, Horace Seaver, Esq., the venerable editor of the Boston *Investigator* (whose presence had been expected), had not been able to attend. He was much interested in the *Investigator*, as it was the first paper with which he (C.) had had any journalistic experience; his *first* article on Spiritualism was published in the columns of the *Investigator*, before there were *any* Spiritualist papers; both himself and Mr. Seaver had been progressing since their acquaintance; he had known that gentlemen when he (S.) was calling on men to 'come to Jesus' to be saved, and when he (the speaker) was teaching exactly the materialistic views which Brother S. *now* entertained; but since then he (C.) had stepped forward and taken up the knowledge of immortal life from and through the demonstrations of Modern Spiritualism, while Mr. S. had become an agnostic; thus both were moving progressively over the same track, though he (C.) thought he was as much in advance as ever of Brother Seaver.

"He regarded the service of the *Investigator* in the past as having been of great value — by its stalwart denials of then generally accepted views — in clearing away the rubbish, and preparing the ground for Spiritualism in its modern advent. Its work had, therefore, not been one of negation alone, but was full of a grand activity.

"He spoke of the old leaders of spiritual thought who had gone to higher life since he took upon himself the responsibilities attending the promulgation of the new truth; and said, when the ground had been prepared, and the time had become ripe, the angels raised up his friend and brother, Luther Colby, who had fought the fight for Spiritualism with his *Banner* ever turned toward the sun; amidst abuse the most virulent, and suspicious and misrepresentations the most cruel, that brother had maintained his way victoriously, and still held up the *Banner* to the breezes that blow in upon us from over the borders of the heavenly land. The speaker had an abiding friendship for Brother Colby, which the fleeting years of this transitory life were totally inadequate to measure.

"He spoke appreciatively of his mother, and what she had tried to do for him; of the aid and comfort which the spirit world had extended to him in the past through hundreds of mediums; and of the inspirations which came to him personally, and ofttimes from the denizens of the higher life. He referred to the political triumphs which had been accorded him in several States of the Union, and said whatever position he had held in the past as to public office, he never for a moment had hidden his views, but had openly lectured on Sundays upon Spiritualism and its revelations, and he was sure his outspoken course in this regard had done him no harm.

"He believed that Modern Spiritualism, if fully understood, — as its primal facts were sure to be in coming time, — would elevate and purify the race till angels and men, unfettered by present untoward conditions, would clasp hands in practical efforts to rid the world of poverty and crime.

"He closed his remarks with a feeling expression of thanks to all present who had assembled to bid him farewell previous to his removal to his Western home.

"The meeting closed with a few appropriate words from Chairman Storer, and the audience then resolved itself into a 'committee of the whole' on hand-shaking with and general congratulation of the venerable guest of the evening."

SCRAPS FROM MY SCRAP-BOOK.

"The biggest coward in the world is that man who takes grumbles instead of kind words home to his wife and family."

"Every grown person who is afraid to die is unfit to live."

"A majority of our greatest blessings come from disappointments."

"When some Christians reach the judgment-seat, they will wish they had run their religion through a fanning-mill before they left home."

"Not one man in ten dares to express his honest opinion of the man he talks to. Not one in five tells the truth of him he is talking of."

"At the dedication of an Episcopal church in Denver, Col., the dean stated that the sons of God who were the founders of the church there, and who were called home to heaven, and of the first twelve who went, and who were buried by good Father Kehler, two were executed for murder, five were shot, one shot himself, one died of delirium tremens, and only three died natural deaths."

"A little Boston boy was brought into court for a witness in Cincinnati, O., and the question arose as.to his knowing the nature of an oath, and the judge questioned him. 'Well, Wendell, do you know where bad little boys go when they die?' 'No, sir,' he replied. 'Goodness gracious! don't you know they will go to hell?' 'No, sir; do you?' 'Of course I do.' 'How do you know it?' 'The Bible says so.' 'Is it true?' 'Certainly it is.' 'Can you prove it?' 'No, not positively; we take it on faith.' 'Do you accept that kind of testimony in this court?' asked the boy. The judge did not answer, but turned the boy over to the lawyers for his testimony."

"So sometimes comes to soul and sense
The feeling which is evidence
That very near about us lies
The realm of spiritual mysteries:
The sphere of the supernal powers
Impinges on this world of ours."

"A wonderful thing is a seed,
 The one thing deathless forever;
 The one thing changeless, utterly true,
 Forever old, forever new,
 And fickle and faithless never."

"The cherished ones for whom we mourn
  As lost in death's embrace,
Are living still in realms of bliss,
  In God's eternal space.
Then let your voices sweetly blend,
  This grand old anthem sing,
'O grave, where is thy victory?
  O death, where is thy sting?'"

"The love that binds two hearts in one
  Cannot be broken by death,
But united again in the heavenly zone
  Shall renew the affections of earth."

"The groom lies parted from the bride,
But life and love that here divide
Are joined upon the other side."

"Twenty years ago no photograph was more often seen than that of President Lincoln sitting with a big book on his knee, and his little son Ted standing beside him and looking at it with him. The book has been thought to be a Bible, but it was not. It was photographer Brady's picture album which the President was examining with his son while some ladies stood by. The artist begged the President to remain quiet, and the picture was taken. This has been largely used to prove that President Lincoln explained the Bible to his boy, and, of course, believed it sacred, which he never did."

"Do not keep the alabaster boxes of your love and tenderness sealed up until your friends are dead. Fill their lives with sweetness. Speak approving, cheering words while their ears can hear them and while their hearts can be cheered by them. The words you mean to say when they are gone, say before they go. The flowers you mean to send for their coffins, send to brighten and sweeten their homes before they leave them. I would rather have a bare coffin, without a flower, and funeral without a eulogy, than a life without the sweetness of love and sympathy. Flowers on a coffin cast no fragrance backward over the weary days."

"The matrons of ancient Greece and Rome adorned their rooms with the finest paintings and statuary, representing physical strength and perfection, they could obtain, and they became the mothers of a race of heroes. Many women of to-day have as the leading feature of their rooms their pug dogs, and the result is a race of dudes."

"Some books are lies from end to end,
And some great lies were never penned."

"'Tis pleasant sure to see one's name in print;
A book's a book although there's nothing in't."

"Cards were invented in 1392 to divert the melancholy of Charles VI. of France. The four suits are supposed to represent the four orders of the state: hearts, the church; spades, the military order of nobility; diamonds, the mercantile part; and clubs, the peasantry."

"When men speak ill of thee, live so no one will believe them." — *Plato*.

"The most dangerous of wild beasts is the slanderer; of tame ones, the flatterer."

"He is a worthless being who lives only for himself."

"They declaim most against the world who have sinned most against it, as people generally abuse those they have injured."

"That which to-day is not begun
Is on the morrow still undone."

A sensible prayer by the chaplain of the House of Representatives, in Congress, March 27, 1887 : —

"Give ear, O God of Jacob, and awaken us to see the danger which threatens the civilized world with a revolution more tremendous than any of which history tells, in which the scenes of the reign of terror may be enacted in every capital of Europe and America. For long the few have mastered the many, because they understood how to use them; but now the many have learned the secret of organization, drill, and dynamite. Rouse the rich of the world to understand that the time has come for grinding, selfish monopoly to cease; that corporations may get souls in them with justice, honor, conscience, and human kindness. Teach the rich men of this country that great fortunes are lent them by Thee for other purposes than to build and decorate palaces, to found private collections of art, to stock wine-cellars, to keep racing steeds and yachts, and find better company than hostlers, grooms and jockeys, pool-sellers and bookmarkers. Teach them, O God, that it is Thee who has given them the power to get these fortunes; that it is to prove them, to know what is in their hearts, whether they will keep thy commandments or no, and that those commandments are, 'Thou shalt love the Lord thy God with all thy heart, and thy neighbor as thyself'; that if the rich men of this land keep these commandments, the poor will follow the example, and we at last will be saved from the days of tribulation that are fast coming on the world. Help us, O God, and save us."

I do not think the God of Jacob heard the prayer, or could change the policy of the monopolists, if he did; and the rich have not heeded it.

A new version of the Lord's Prayer, recently published in Rome about the time of the Œcumenical Council:—

"Our Father who art in the Vatican; Infallible be thy name; Thy temporal sovereignty come; Thy will be done in Europe and America as it is in Ireland; Give us this day our tithes and titles, and forgive us our trespasses as we give plenary indulgence to those who pay penitently unto us; and lead us not into Œcumenical Councils, but deliver us from thinking; for thine is the crozier, the key, and the tiara, Rome without end. Amen." This seems to be for the priests only.

"There's a germ of good in every ill,
Like the bur of the nut with the meat in it still."

Hindoo prayer: "O God, have mercy on the wicked and unjust, as thou hast already had mercy on the just and innocent."

"Man's demands are God's commands."
Henry C. Wright.

"I do not hate the man who has rheumatism, but I hate the rheumatism that has the man."— *R. G. Ingersoll.*

"I do not hate an orthodox preacher, but I hate the doctrines he teaches, and is bound by, in his articles of faith."

"He can't be wrong whose life is in the right."

"Praises on tombs are titles vainly spent;
A man's good name is his best monument."

"To do good is to be good."

"Is it love that commits the murders in jealousy?"

"Is God love, or love the god of this world?"

"AN ADDRESS TO THE VOTERS OF SANTA BARBARA COUNTY.

"Since the passage of the Act calling a Constitutional Convention for the State, I have been repeatedly and constantly urged by many citizens of the county to submit my name to you as an independent candidate for that Convention. Believing my experience in two Constitutional Conventions and two sessions of a State Senate, together with thirty-five years of public discussion through the press and on the rostrum, of the questions involved in Constitutional and Statute Law, in which I have ever taken the side of the people and the producers against tyranny, monopoly, bigotry, and oppression, I have, and hereby do, submit my name for your suffrages.

"Should you elect me to that office, I can assure you that whatever ability I possess will be faithfully used to secure equal justice to all citizens, to restrict and control monopolies and corporations of all kinds in the interests of the people, and to prevent by constitutional provision those unjust laws which have so largely driven the wealth of this new State into the hands of the few, for the support of which condition, they have imported Mongolian labor to reduce our own citizens to their standard of labor and domestic life, and have kept out of the State a large population that desire to make homes among us and would be most valuable, industrious citizens, for which the whole State has most ample room.

"As the time is so short that I cannot meet many of you, I shall be glad, so far as I can, both in public and private, to give you my views on any question that may rise in said Convention, and should be glad to have every voter know my opinions and vote understandingly for or against me, as I do not desire to be elected to misrepresent any constituency.   WARREN CHASE.

"SANTA BARBARA, Cal., May 21, 1878."

Defeated by the Circuit Judge and efforts of both political parties.

The following is from my reply to W. F. Jamieson, published in *Light for Thinkers*, Atlanta, Ga. : —

"We agree on so many points there seems little necessity of a controversy over one or two IFS which we both admit to exist. We both agree that all forms are ephemeral, and all matter in its essential state is eternal. We both agree that whatever has one end has two, whether measured in time of duration or extension of space. We both agree that the existence of spirits in forms is no more evidence of eternal life than the existence of forms in this life. We both agree that while the forms dissolve and disappear, no particle of the matter is lost or annihilated. We both agree that the essential elements into which forms are changed by dissolution, are as really material as when combined in the form. We both agree that material bodies cannot be moved or controlled by nothing, and that matter only can act on matter. We both agree that the material in the universe never has been, and never can be, increased or decreased in quantity. We both agree that belief in the human mind is involuntary, and hence we cannot be accountable for it. Now after this agreement is it strange that we should, from a wide range of different experiences, arrive at different conclusions on some subjects in points of both belief and knowledge. We both admit the senses to be the channel through which we derive all knowledge in this life ; and as we do not have the same experiences and evidences through these senses, one may know what the other does not, and what the other may not have sufficient evidence to believe. Here we may part on the evidence which to me is sufficient to enable me to *know* that spirits live and communicate."

The articles from this point to page 266 were written and contributed by me to the *Spiritual Offering*, formerly published at Ottumwa, Iowa.

"THE WORD OF GOD — WHAT IS IT?

"I think the New Testament says, Jesus, who was the Christ (or Kreshna), was the only begotten Son of God, and that he was the *Word*, and that the word was with God, and the word was God, and came on earth and dwelt among men, and that he said, 'Before the world was I am.' I do not pretend to quote word for word, but think I do not misrepresent. Now if Jesus was *begotten* he did not exist before he was begotten, and certainly could not be a word or *the* word and come to earth before he was begotten, and hence the Old Testament could not be the word of God if Jesus was the word or ' Holy Bible — book divine, precious treasure, thou art mine' [fetich], — which so many hug to their hearts and pray over in times of fear and trouble, and which with their prayers has as much and no more effect in case of cyclones, earthquakes, and pestilence than would the hugging of a wooden image and praying to Jupiter Ammon. Talmage and Moody, Harrison, Sam Jones and Sam Small, and a score of other revival cranks read the stories of Noah and the ark, of Jonah and the fish, of Balaam and his beast, of Samson and his Delilah, of Job and his Satan, of Daniel and his lions, of Elisha and his bears, and lots of other nonsense in the Old Testament, and try to make their ignorant hearers believe what they do not believe themselves, — that all this is the word of God, and must be true, and must be believed and accepted as truth, however ridiculous it may seem. As all in the book is the word of God, the words said to be spoken through Satan are words of God, and it was God who spoke through Balaam's beast, and the words which Samuel spoke after he was dead were the words of God, and those the medium spoke at the time were God's words, and all words in both Old and New Testaments are words of God, through whatever channel uttered, even those from the devils that Jesus cast out, and those spoken to Jesus on the mountain and pinnacle of the temple.

"If Jesus was himself the word of God and was God, I do not see how any other words could be. I do not see how the Gospels of Matthew, Mark, Luke, and John, and the Acts, written by no one knows who or when, can be the word of God, since they certainly are not Jesus nor his words. They are ·evidently somebody's words full of contradictions and widely different stories of events not authenticated by any reliable history of the times to which they refer. They are said to be 'according to,' but no one knows how much they accord or how much they differ from the original stories, if there were any original stories or events. If they had been written or even superintended by God, they would have told straight stories, and agreed at least in the history and geneálogy (if he had any) of his only begotten Son and the mother. Were the words which John, the Patmos crank, which he said he heard spoken in heaven, when he looked in and saw the dragon and the vials of wrath, the words of God?

"If any part of the Bible contains words of God, it would be wise to have these words separated from the rest and put in a book by themselves; but to me none are."

"THE CYCLONES.

"When I read of religious revivals and especial providences of God, and the partiality of the Christian's God to different sectarian churches in aiding them to build up societies and temples, and hear or read of their prayers, praises, and thanks to their God of *mercy* and charity and universal love toward all of *his* children, and especially little children, who are invited to come to church and receive his blessings and love, and then read of the terrible cyclones, railroad accidents, pestilence, famine, and misery caused by drunken fathers and husbands, where innocent persons, largely children, who have committed no crime, suffer, I wonder where this merciful and loving God is, with his special providences that help to build churches and support preachers and keep up revivals.

"These questions arise in my mind, which I wish our clergy to answer, as I cannot: — Did this loving and merciful God know of these cyclones and other terrible calamities, in which the innocent suffer, or did he not? If he did, could he stop or prevent them by a special providence, such as he used to convert Sam Jones or Sam Small and other sinners, and by which he saved guilty persons from death and hell? Can he intercept natural law and control it, or is it above his reach or power? If he can, is it not a lack of goodness and mercy that he does not do it? Was he present and looking on at these cyclones, or absent? Would prayers or masses have any effect in inducing him to avert these calamities if he could? Do the masses said on the Pacific coast prevent the earthquakes that disturbed that region before Archbishop Zadoc ordered them in 1879? If so, why not apply the same remedy to cyclones on this side of the Rocky ridge? If this merciful God must have cyclones to show his power, why not let them fall on the saloons and dens of vice and wickedness? Can this Christian God do as he pleases with cyclones? If so, 'his ways are not as our ways.' Does this God do anything to alleviate the sufferings and misery caused by these terrible calamities? Are the Christian worshippers of this God any more charitable and kind in such cases than those who do not believe in him or the Bible? If he cannot prevent them, he lacks power; if he will not, he lacks goodness and mercy: let Christians answer which."

"SIN — WHAT IS IT?

"Everybody is supposed to know what sin is, and yet there is no well-defined meaning to the word. Lexicographers define it to be a transgression of divine law, a neglect of duty, etc. No two distinct religions in the world define divine law alike; and most of our Christian sects differ on the subject, as they do on duty, etc.; so it may be safely said no one *knows* just what sin is, or what duty is such as God requires of us; hence, no one can know when he or she is sinning unless we go by conscience, which, being a creature of education, is in great variety. Most Christians will admit that a premeditated and cold-blooded murder is a sin, and yet most of them will join in wars, which are premeditated and cold-blooded, — wholesale murders of innocent persons, — and they will pray for victories, which can only be obtained by murder. They will also uphold the gallows, which certainly is a premeditated and cold-blooded murder. Even in private murder, which the law punishes, and which they call a sin, our churches hold that the sinner may be forgiven without punishment (except that the law inflicts), by confession to God and repentance, which comes from the murder of the innocent Jesus, who consented to be murdered for our sins, as an atonement to appease the wrath of God. If Roman Catholicism is the true religion, all are sinners who do not attend mass and make confessions to their priests; and they also have a longer list of sins than any other sect of Christians. Most churches have what they call sins of omission and sins of commission. I suppose all or any are fatal if not forgiven through the blood of Christ. Most Christians teach that all people are sinners by nature, having inherited a totally depraved nature from the Adam parent of all nations, — black, white, red, and yellow; so by this doctrine all are sinners, even if they commit no sinful act. How much of this is atoned for by the death of Christ is a matter of dispute among Christians. The Romanists have the power of forgiveness handed down to the Pope, and through him to the under-officers down to the priests; they can get any sin forgiven, and they declare none can be forgiven except through their church.

"Outside the churches there is no definite meaning to the word 'sin,' as it is purely a church word; and they hold all outsiders to be sinners, and are constantly calling people to 'come out and be separate from sinners and sin,' which means, Come and join our church. There are no outward signs that church members are better or less wicked in the aggregate in our country than those who make no profession of religion. If we turn to conscience for a guide, how wonderful is the variety!

"To me it would be a sin to use tobacco in any form internally, or to get intoxicated, and yet a large majority of those around me would not include the use of tobacco, if they did the other. I should have no faith in Jesus forgiving me for either of these sins. I do not believe there is any sin against God, or that we can violate his law, but it will violate us if we put ourselves in conflict with it, as we do in using tobacco or getting intoxicated. There is said to be a sin against the Holy Ghost. To me my own soul is my holy ghost, and I try never to sin against that, as I could not expect forgiveness. If sin is doing wrong, we should have a uniform and reliable standard of wrong, and certainly there is none. I cannot allow any priest to fix a standard of right and wrong for me, nor could I submit to any but the one within me, which may be called conscience. I could not find any authority in the commandments said to be given by the

Jewish God, and which he almost invariably commanded them to break—by murders and in many other ways. Neither can I accept the New Testament authority which makes involuntary belief a virtue, and unbelief—equally involuntary—a sin. Such sins are not sins to me. If the word is made to cover all acts not in accord with natural laws, then any injury to ourselves or our fellow-creatures is a sin, and I can see no reason or justice in a third and innocent person dying to atone for such acts."

"WHAT HAS SPIRITUALISM DONE?

" When I began to lecture on the existence of spirits and their ability to communicate with us through some persons in certain peculiar conditions, which was in 1847, and soon after the publication of our first and best book of communications, ' Nature's Divine Revelations,' through A. J. Davis, and which confirmed some of my own experience, and that of others with whom I was in correspondence, there were probably from three hundred to five hundred in the United States who believed in modern spirit intercourse, and very few even of these *knew* it, as millions do now. Now there are not less than five millions that *know* it is true, and many more who believe it on testimony, but who have not the knowledge through their senses, the only source of knowledge.

" At the start, and before the raps, there was very little clerical opposition, though I had a discussion with H. H. Vanamringe, a clergyman, on the spiritual origin of the messages in that book, he denouncing it because it had no Christ in it, and nothing from Christ. This was before the Fox girls began to talk with ' Old Splitfoot.' Up to a short time before the issue of the book referred to, I had no evidence of a future life that was to me in any way reliable, the same being the condition of many thousands who have since had positive proof of a continued existence beyond death, and have prepared for it in accordance with advice and instruction from friends living there, instead of relying on the foolish and conflicting theories of the churches. Spiritualism has made many thousands happy by imparting this knowledge; a good work, the value of which cannot be estimated. The opposition of the clergy, backed as usual by the vulgar and profane rabble, began very soon after the rapping and other modes of intercourse brought to us direct information, differing from the teachings of all sects of Christians, which relating to that life were false and utterly unreliable. Of course this endangered the entire basis of all creeds, and put the preachers and their salaries in danger; and as our numbers increased and our evidences increased, as they yet do in a geometrical ratio, our enemies became more bitter. Seeing as they did the natural results and just deductions based on these messages, they were compelled to modify their sermons, and leave hell entirely out, with its devil, and to drop many other of the absurdities, so that a great part of the good Spiritualism has done has been in the churches, and the preachers, in modifying sermons and general belief among Christians."

"WHO WAS JESUS? WHO WAS THE CHRIST?

"The prolific but unreliable Christian historian, Goodrich, says, according to the best authorities Jesus Christ was born in the twenty-sixth year of the reign of Augustus Cæsar, four years before the date of our Christian era, which is founded on the fabulous record of his birth. So the old Catholic Church, founded in the third century, fixed the date of his birth and founded our timetables on it. How comes it that Protestants have to set it back four years? It is supposed to be because Herod, the last king of the Jews, had died four years before the date fixed by the Church for the birth of Jesus. This sets aside the fabulous story of the edict of this king against the boys, to escape which Mary and Joseph fled into Egypt for the safety of God's son, as the power which had so often and so miraculously saved King David, and others like David, seemed to have ceased to be used.

"This writer, Goodrich, says, after his return from Egypt Jesus dwelt with his parents. Not God, who is now reputed to be his father, but with Joseph, through whom, the record says, he was descended lineally from David, that the Scripture might be fulfilled, and his wife, the celebrated Mary who ceased to be a virgin when married, as all unmarried women then and there were called virgins, and no others. This author further says that from Nazareth, where he lived with his parents at the age of twelve years, he made his celebrated journey of about six miles to Jerusalem, and confounded the priests as any twelve-year old scholar in our time can our priests. After that he went back and worked with his earthly father till about thirty years of age, in obscurity. Rather a singular experience for a God who was the God of all the universe! A very slight and unreliable story of one or two miracles was all known or heard of him in these long years, while thousands of poor sinners were dying daily, with no hope of a resurrection or of salvation, and yet the Saviour was right among them, quietly working at a trade which he is supposed to have mastered, and abandoned when he took to preaching. This author further says there never was but one church in the world. If so, it must have been the Catholic, and all others are now heresies. If what this author says was the mission of Christ on earth is correct, it is, and ever must be, a failure, as it is an impossibility. As there is no Roman or Jewish contemporaneous history of any such person as the Christ, there is ample room for speculative theorists to fix dates and events with no positive authority to contradict them satisfactorily to those who are trained from childhood to accept any testimony of the existence and marvels attached to him, with scarcely a scrap or scrip written within one hundred years after the dates fixed for the occurrences. Everybody should read the Apocrypha of the New Testament to strengthen or reduce a belief in the person and miracles recorded in the canonical."

"THE LORD AND SATAN — WHICH?

"Our priests on Bible authority assure us that God forbade man to eat of the tree of knowledge, and Satan persuaded him to eat; and as the fruit was not poisonous, he did not die from that cause, as God had told him he would, but long after from a natural cause. By this disobedience of God and persuasion of Satan he arose, named the beasts and had shame, which he before had not, and learned to clothe himself, which he never had, and in fact gained all the advantages and superiority he has ever attained over the beasts which did not disobey God. By this knowledge he has been able to select articles suitable for food and medicine, and exclude poisons and evils like tobacco and alcohol when he has knowledge enough to avoid them. There can be no conjecture of what the race would have been if Adam had obeyed God instead of Satan. The same Bible authority says God ordered man not to kill, and soon after ordered his chosen people to commit the most cruel and unjustifiable wholesale murders that were ever ordered on earth, such as Satan never was guilty of by any record we have of such a being. We were for a long time assured by the authorities of the Church that Satan was the inventor of printing, which was to destroy the Holy Bible by giving it to the people to discuss and wrangle over. We pass over many valuable discoveries charged to Satan, and finding none credited to God, we give Satan the preference in conferring favors on mankind, especially since his last great and good work in opening to us the intercourse between the two worlds in Modern Spiritualism, as this is still by most priests laid to the Satan of our time, which, we suppose, is the same one that tempted Eve. Our Catholic Church has discovered that our godless public schools where children get knowledge are wicked and Satanic, and hence take out their children and put them where knowledge is limited and proscribed."

"Is the Leaven Working?

"Every year and every month, if not every day, there are new converts made by our mediums to the knowledge of spirit life and spirit intercourse, or to the latter if they were already aware of the former. So far this leaven is working among those in and those out of the various churches, and when on those in the churches, of course it brings them new light which is thrown on the next life, and it seems to me it cannot fasten them in or to any of their creeds or doctrines of the life after death. What puzzles me and what this article is after is, how those already free from all creeds can go into the bondage and join a church that has a creed, utterly and entirely in conflict with the united testimony of the spirits that communicate with us.

"A respectable if not a large number of those who know the truth of spirit intercourse have joined the Universalist churches, no doubt somewhat crowded that way for want of society and social life, which I acknowledge we sadly lack in many places; but how any one, after hearing many times from the spirit world, can join a church that has a trinity in its personal Godhead and three persons in one, each and all without body or parts, and yet personal in each and in the union, and also holds strictly to original sin, for which Jesus atoned by his death and on which our salvation depends, is the puzzle.

"A still more respectable number have joined the Unitarians, seeking for society in the 'cultured free thought' of that church, where there are not nearly as many absurd mysteries connected with the Godhead or even personality, and where they do not teach so much nonsense about Abraham's bosom and the arms of Jesus and gold-paved streets of the New Jerusalem; but still they are Christians and take in the Bible with its description of heaven where John saw the seven angels, each with a vial of wrath to pour out on this earth, and seven more with seven trumpets to blow destruction on the earth; also the dragon and the great beast and many other marvellous sights, none of which our spirit friends have seen, not even Jehovah sitting on his throne with twenty-four elders and the beast for personal guards. To me it looks strangely ridiculous with others who have not the knowledge he has, for a rational person, after hearing from the spirit world, joining in support of such nonsense and those who teach it.

"Brother R. P. Ambler backed into one of these churches in the early days of Spiritualism, and several of our speakers have followed, and yet I do not see that they have leavened the Universalist church or its creed, and the Unitarians are certainly far ahead of them, as they always have been, and yet we have not leavened that sect. Past experience and history will satisfy any one that some churches will take in anything, as the fish did Jonah in the fable, if it will not disrupt them or break up their societies and set their creed and preachers aside; so if they can get help from Spiritualists to support their system, they will gladly take them in, and I think they are generally taken in if not thrown out as Jonah was. I am satisfied that we shall never leaven the churches by going into them and subscribing to their creeds and by supporting them and their doctrines so entirely at variance with what the spirits teach about the life they live. I shall not walk into any of these parlors, as the fly does into those fitted for it, but will still watch for the leaven to work outside sectarian bonds."

"SURVIVAL OF THE FITTEST.

"Slowly the laws of nature are asserting and establishing their superiority over the perversions and antagonisms of man. The hell fire of alcohol is fast burning out the lives of those who take it in to pervert the reason, stupefy the faculties, and destroy the moral rectitude of the conscience. The longer life, better life, happier life of those who wholly abstain from it, is fast gaining the ascendency in our country through efforts now made to expose its evil effects, after a long time of its rapid progress in corrupting the morals and distracting the reason of millions of American citizens, and causing an immense amount of crime and expense for the innocent to pay for the punishment of, and that too often a failure. Close observers of society can see in this direction the working of this principle in society, and we may look for greater results from the education of the children in our schools on the subject of alcohol and its effects. Another step in this line of progress is a knowledge of the evil effects of tobacco, that slow poison that steadily saps the foundation of natural health and plays havoc with the nerves, setting them into a tremulous motion, and ultimately affecting the brain and through it the reasoning powers. Not as bad as alcohol in its effects upon the morals, and not causing the crimes that the more stimulating poison does, but still with no beneficial effects and at enormous expense in the aggregate, producing only evil and perverting nature and good health, which ought to be sufficient when understood to exclude it entirely from every family and person, and thus aid the progress of the 'survival of the fittest,' for surely the purer and better the bodies of parents, the purer and better will be the offspring, and it is about time we looked into the question of propagation of the species of our own race, as we long have in the propagation of domestic animals, and as nature does in the undomesticated.

"Excluding these two utterly useless and greatly injurious and very expensive articles from our bill of fare and from our orders for supplies, we may next look carefully into the nature and effects on the human body of the different kinds of food, and exclude as far as possible those which bring disease into the body, and when we exclude alcohol and tobacco, we shall nearly all be able to select the most healthy food, even if it does cost more than that which is less in conformity with health and happiness. In time, through intellectual growth and the application of science and knowledge to physical life, we shall have the survival of the fittest and a better and healthier and more moral condition of mortal life.

"This law and line of progress to a more rational, natural, consistent and intellectual condition of moral, social, and religious life is equally sure to prevail. Slowly but surely the effects of superstition, bigotry, and intolerance are being understood, and they will be eradicated with their evil effects like those of alcohol and tobacco. Sectarian Christianity has been as destructive of life and happiness as alcohol, and though greatly modified since the days of the Inquisition, yet its bitter effects linger in the minds of those who, like old topers and chewers who have come down to beer and cider and cigarettes, still have the lingering effects of the poison in their organizations. We have many Spiritualists who want to keep a little of the old superstition for a medicine, as the liquor-drinkers do a little of the firewater to taper off on, and they must have a little of the Christ or St. Paul spirit, mixed with the Spiritualism as a tonic — bitters ' for their stomach's sake.' Some want us to retain the morning mass or evening vespers, say our prayers, ask for blessings, or thank the Lord for every good thing we earn, or learn, and bless the church for favors received from other sources. They would have us look in the Scriptures, which have led everybody astray that has relied on them, for evidence of the truth of what we never learned from them and never could, but have learned from other sources and entirely without them. But this hold on the old fables and parables is steadily loosening and giving way to the law of the survival of the fittest in religion and morals as well as in physical life, and it gives us pleasure to see our race gradually coming out of the fogs of Christian superstition with a sure sign of leading all other nations out of their equally deep, but not greater darkness of religious ignorance. The grand work began with the telescope, which peered into the heavens and was soon followed by the microscope, the crucible, the retort, the scalpel, and the cabinet of fossils collected from the crust of the earth; and as the telescope revealed the heavens to astronomers, so geology with its fossils revealed the past ages and changes of the earth's crust and the ' races that perished to pave the granite slab with a floor of lime.' These sciences turned the attention to the theological history of creation, and a ' peep into sacred traditions' soon revealed its fabulous character and utter unreliability. Later came physiology, and later still

Spiritualism with its intercourse and correspondence with the denizens of the other life, which is to be the next revealment for us; and then we turn to the churches to see what they teach about that life, and find them as much in error as is the Old Testament in its teachings about creation and the origin of man.'

"We find the pessimism of the New Testament which teaches us to ignore nature and disregard all social and domestic duties; to hate our relatives and our own lives, and take no thought for the morrow what we shall eat, drink, or wear, and that it is not what we take into the mouth that defiles us; and that it is entirely wrong for us to suppose tobacco and liquors and other filthy and poisonous substances taken in the mouth defile us, and that we should take thought for the morrow and provide for, care for, and love our families and let our duties begin here, and that it is not the way to bring peace on earth for every man to have a sword even if he had to sell his coat to get one. From our friends on the other side we learn that 'he is not wrong whose life is in the right,' and that such a one has no need of Christ or Christianity any more than he has of Paganism or Mohammedanism, alcohol or tobacco, — that whatever perverts, distracts, and misleads the mind and intellect of man in this life, whether taken into the body or mind, draws him away from a true and natural growth and progress into harmony and health of body or mind. If the laws of nature — which are laws of God — are supreme, then ultimately they must triumph over all of these obstacles by the survival of the fittest, and when the physical evils are eradicated, the moral, social, and religious will soon follow, and in time not a vestige, except the fossils of our theology, will remain to obstruct the progress of the race, and then even our Christian Spiritualists will dispense with the little they keep as a medicine."

"Which, shall Leaven the Whole Lump.

"Many persons speak of Christianity as the leaven spoken of by Jesus, that the leaven is to leaven the whole human race. Even if that was so, no one can tell what true Christianity is that is to do this great work. Catholicism is undoubtedly *the* Christian Church, as it is the oldest, the richest, the largest, and the most popular, and even in our free country going up to the head, as shown by the unsurpassed splendor of the Catholic wedding of a congressman in Washington recently, and the great value of presents and distinguished guests, and a valuable and noted present to the bride, blessed by the Pope, which, it was thought, added greatly to its value. President Cleveland's wedding, which had no church back of it, bore no comparison to this one with the Pope and his emissaries to sustain it. This is the church, if any, that can leaven the whole lump of humanity, for it requires no conversion or change of heart, as most of its members are birthright members, being taken in soon after they are born by christening, and requiring no consent on their part, which they could not give if required, and then trained and educated just enough to hold them in its sacred precincts, which is very little education, and equally safe without any if duly christened. Not allowed to reason on religious subjects, they are safe if they will not think on the subject, except to accept the words and authority of its priests. To this church, our own and all public schools are dangerous, because they 'teach the young idea how to shoot,' like buds into blossom and to ripen intellectual fruit. The Catholic Church is the most complete system of mental slavery on the earth, equalling the tyranny of Russia, of whose people it is the sole religion, and in harmony with its government, and all other tyrannies that will accept it.

"Protestant sects in this country protest largely against this tyranny, and yet it holds its head as high as any of them, and pecuniarily gains on each one of them, as it is second in wealth in the United States, and fourth in numbers if we double in the factions in each of the Calvinists, Methodists, and Baptists, thereby putting them ahead in numbers, and yet it is evidently gaining on each of these. If we put the sects all together, and give the large majority to the Catholic which belongs to it in the world, there is yet not the remotest possibility of the whole lump of the race being Christianized, for after nearly two thousand years of propagandism it has evidently reached its culminating point, and passed, or is passing, its perihelion, from which it will pass away into oblivion, as older systems have. Its temples, however holy, are going to destruction in earthquakes and cyclones like other buildings not holy, and its societies quarrel and divide, and go to pieces; and they furnish as many criminals in proportion to their numbers as those without its folds, and the people are fast learning that its prayers are useless to effect anything in any of the great causes of reform in which there is so much need. It only requires education through a reading of history, and the study of the sciences, to show that its pretences and claims are without foundation except in fables.

"Every reader of the *Offering* interested in Christianity, temperance, and other reforms should preserve for reference the very valuable articles of Brother Mendenhall, as they contain statistics in figures and authority of the Bible that cost much research, and they show the drift of popular life in our country. He will pardon me for extracting a few figures from his table taken from the census to show how fast Christianity in the aggregate of all sects is leavening the lump of humanity in our free country. His statistics on the temperance question show us the necessity of every person rising and taking an active part in the temperance cause to save our country from utter ruin, and they also show the utter failure of Christianity to save us. To show the leavening process I make the following extracts: From 1850 to 1860 the increase of churches was proportionately seven per cent less than the increase of population. From 1860 to 1870 the rate of increase in churches was five per cent less than the increase in population. From 1870 to 1880 the churches gained and were six per cent over that of population, largely a Catholic gain by immigration and increase in manufacturing cities. In thirty years population runs six per cent ahead of churches. Population in thirty years gains 140 per cent; churches, 131 per cent; grogshops gain 2122 per cent. In 1850 there was one church for every 551 persons, in 1880 one church for every 571 persons, and yet they are not half filled, and on an average not one-fourth of the seats are occupied on the Sundays of the year, and not nearly all that attend are professing Christians or members of the church they attend. The Catholics are the most punctual, the most devout, and the best paying, as their priests have a way of extracting part of the wages obtained by a large part of the operatives in the shops and mills of our country, especially from the foreign-born laborers.

"In England, France, and Germany the religious showing, from the best evidence I can get, is not better, if as good, as here. Protestantism, science, and last, but not least, Spiritualism, have taken the power of the Catholic Church, and there is no fear from any other sect, as they soon break apart, and a house divided against itself cannot stand now any more than it could in New Testament times. The salt has lost its savor, and the leaven its power to leaven the lump. Now let Spiritualism try its power as a saviour of life unto life and life *into* life."

"BACKING OUT.

"Some years ago, Elizabeth Stuart Phelps discovered that the gates of the spirit world were ajar, as many of us know who knew that by and through Modern Spiritualism they were being pushed and pulled open, and even at that time they were so far ajar that many of our friends were looking through and whispering to us and telling us of the beauties of their home on the other side of the death-gates. Our sister, seeing, or feeling, this fact, used her extraordinary talents to express her joy in putting out that valuable book, 'The Gates Ajar,' which was eagerly sought for, earnestly read, and highly appreciated, especially by Spiritualists, and it soon crept on to the tables of many families who attended churches and contributed to their support. As it was proving to be an introduction to the spiritual facts and philosophy, the clergy were alarmed, and many of them condemned the book as leading people to look at the opening through which the spirits could 'peep and mutter,' which was condemned in the Scripture. The author was severely censured, and the book likewise condemned by many zealous fanatics, but not till it had reached a large sale and circulation, which gave her a good reputation as an author, and registered her among the *literati* of our country. The outside pressure was now brought to bear on her to save her and her reputation from falling into the ranks of that unpopular class of writers and speakers known as Spiritualists, and she began to hesitate and back into the ranks of sceptics, till she might have found herself where Peter was in the story of Jesus and Peter, when Jesus told him, 'Get thee behind me, Satan;' but still she had not said or done enough in her later works to satisfy the sectarian bigots who held her reputation on their tongues and pens, until she came out through the leading secular and pandering prejudiced press and ridiculed the subject of spirit intercourse; like Peter of old, who, when the pressure was brought to bear on him, denied, and even cursed and swore to prove he did not belong to the unpopular class of cranks of which Jesus was the leader. It is an interesting story; true or false, it applies well to Sister Phelps, and the sequel may turn out as well, or she may be like that other character in the story, whose repentance led to a widely different result.

"It is interesting to see how sensitive some persons are to the pressure of orthodox influence when it touches their reputation. They seem to think that reputation makes character, and to save the latter they must secure the former, and go with the current of floodwood, or be beached on the dry sands of unpopularity. If this life were all there is for us, their policy might be worth considering; but it is so short and unsatisfactory that it is not worth while to sacrifice truth, or knowledge, or conscience to gain the good will of the multitude, and especially that of the bigoted and superstitious leaders whose life and luxury depend on keeping the masses ignorant enough to gain their support from them. I am sorry for Sister Phelps; but of course she will not care for my sorrow, as she has now the sympathy and support of the orthodox clergy, and they can give her a reputation."

"CENTERSTANCE, CIRCUMSTANCE, AND SUBSTANCE.

"Centerstance is the inner, or radiating centre; the germ of all organic life and crystallized forms. Circumstance is the outer belt to the centre; the moving and circulating particles or forces gathering around the centre or centres in organic or crystallized forms. Substance is the under or inferior condition, as the prefix *sub* denotes, and applies to the lowest condition or inferior part of the universe, or, as some would term it, the base, as the crystallized rock is to our earth with its soil and water and living forms above it. Our philosophy in its history corresponds to our earth and its strata, with its rock base and spirit realm at the top. For more than a thousand years after our Christian time-table began its dates with its Divine revelations, this earth was supposed to be the centre of the universe and the sun, moon, and stars, made by the God who made it, and all for his glory, especially to minister to the earth. This was hardly up in correspondence to the silurian era, with its flora and fauna; and if the Christian Church could have prevented progress and mental evolution, this would still be the true and God-revealed theory of the creation; but the world moves and drags Christianity after it in progressive thought and discoveries, but not by God-revealed revelations.

" From this fabulous centerstance of the universe Copernicus, Galileo, and the burned Bruno and Kepler, pushed the centerstance out to the sun in spite of the Church and its fagots that burned Bruno. Later, philosophers with the improved telescopes pushed the centre out to Alcyone, and now they are speculating on a still farther away centre of which, or where, no one knows, but only guesses there is one. Now let us turn to religion and theology, and see the correspondence. First, the stone and wooden gods as the religious centres; next, the horrible beasts and monstrosities; next, the sun, moon, and stars; next, the multitude of personal gods of which we have three in our mental image, and to which we are now building temples as the ancients did to their gods, with equal zeal and devotion. We are on the eve of another move forward, which is, as it ever has been, resisted by the idol-worshippers and gold-beaters as of old, who cry 'Great is the goddess Diana of the Ephesians,' of which we have Talmage, Moody, Joe Cook, Sam Jones, Sam Small, and a score more of the money-seeking and money-making servants of him who required his followers to sell all they had and give to the poor, and even to sell their coats and buy swords,—which our anti-war Christians say meant swords of truth to fight error with. This latest move, which many preachers have reached, is dispensing with all personal gods as centres or centerstances, and supplanting them with an Omniscient, Omnipresent, and Omnipotent Soul of the boundless universe which cannot be personal, or local, or partial to this or any world, or to us, or any grade of being in existence. As this is as far as my mind can reach for a centerstance of organic life, I cannot even conjecture what next, if there is to be a next, and I anchor here and call this 'soul of things' God, with the elements as circumstances, and substance as a base of forms in the lowest stratum of what we call matter, or material life. We have in our reach, first, mineral with forms, vegetable with life, animal with sensation, human with religious aspiration, and spiritual as an outgrowth or another step in the infinite rounds of circles and cycles of being.

"Our theological 'gold-beaters' will keep us and the race back as long as they can, as their trade pays well, and 'the fools are not all dead yet,' and Spiritualism, although a giant, is yet young, and yet bracing up to these Sullivan sluggers in the pulpits with the man-made divine revelations for gloves. The gods which were once in the rock images are now in imaginary heavens located in the minds of the preachers, and with some progressive minds they are centred in one great *Oversoul*, binding all in with a circumference to each and all, — if there is an *all;* but to me God is the inner soul of all existence, the centerstance of all forms in worlds or atoms, the force and motive power in all motion, life, sensation, and intelligence."

"NEW METHODS OF SALVATION.

"To increase the power of the several churches to save souls in our day, many novel measures are resorted to, such as would have been condemned in the old Puritan days by all Christians, as, for instance, the more liberal policy of Christ, claimed by some of the Andover professors, is by the old fogies of the present Orthodox church. Myself and wife attended an Episcopal festival last evening in the largest hall in the State, which is in Worcester, Mass., and where we crowded round in a jam of over three thousand persons admitted at twenty-five cents each, with extras inside at exorbitant prices, and in great variety, from which enormous sums were raised, mostly for little or no consideration, and largely by obtaining money under false pretences, one of which was a fortune-teller (handsome woman) telling the fortunes by looking in the hands, and squeezing those of the gentlemen, and smiling in their faces to keep them good-natured while she spun out some silly yarn to get money for the church to save souls with. Another part was Punch and Judy as a side-show, with extra admission, which, silliest of all silly performances, brought something like $200 in the two days and evenings, illustrating the old saying, 'the fool and his money are soon parted,' — but, in this case, for Christ's sake, which made it all right. The elegant music was timely and good, and the dancing, especially the Highland Fling. The ballet and surf dance would have done credit to a theatre, — which the performance must have resembled, — had there been seats and order, and the goods for sale at exorbitant prices left out. In one corner was a windmill, which reminded me of the church and its preachers, and it ground out grists for each customer for ten cents. There were no liquors sold, but other drinks and food of most kinds and ways of feeding, including fresh milk, and, by the milkstand, a cow calling for her calf; she had been got up the two flights of stairs, and gave her milk for the church as we did our money,—all to save souls by a church that has never been able to prove that man or woman has a soul, and ignores the only evidence to be had, which Spiritualism furnishes. Fancy and funny costumes were among the attractions, and handsome stage girls selected, as the theatres do, and which churches are imitating, because that is a way to get money, if not religion.

"This is only one of the lines of progress in Christianity, or churchianity, in old Puritan New England. In Boston they have had the two Sams,—Sam Jones and Sam Small,—getting up a Methodist steam by blowing off the most ridiculous strings of nonsense ever let off in old Hub of the Universe, and they did it to the tune of over $3000, besides private presents, and of course saved a large number of souls to the churches that paid it, and the leading papers published the ridiculous sermons of these great revivalists as they would reports of theatrical performances for the information of the public ; their whole parade being much like that of the Salvation Army, which I call the tail of the Christian kite, which is now so long it drags in the mud.

"The old Catholic Church, too, has gone into the show business and selling fancy things to raise money, as selling indulgences to sin does not bring in enough in these extravagant times. It is wonderful to see how popular this church has grown in New England within the last century, it having, in several of our manufacturing cities, got control of the municipal governments and taken the Catholic children out of the public schools, and put Catholic teachers over most of the public schools also. All is for Christ's sake."

"TRY THE SPIRITS.

"If this sentence has any meaning, it seems to me to apply to the intercourse of spirits with mortals, and in our time, when the intercourse is extensive and daily increasing, it is worth looking into.

"The subject is brought to my mind by the excellent article in the *Offering* of Feb. 5 by H. K. The thought at once occurred to me that a standard was necessary by which we could try them, and my mind at once started in search of one. It strikes me, as it is an established fact that death serves only to change the spheres of life very nearly as they are changed here by removing from New York to Paris, and does no more change the mind, the opinions or beliefs in the one case than in the other, either in religion, politics, or moral and social affairs, that a standard would be very difficult to obtain by which the fallibility or infallibility of an opinion obtained from a spirit could be tested. It is a well-established fact that Mohammedans are Mohammedans, and not Christians, after they pass to the other life, and the Chinese and Indians are the same there as here, as is daily proved of the latter who once inhabited this section of the earth and come daily to our mediums, and are no more Christians now than when here. It is also proved by the fact that Thomas Paine, Benjamin Franklin, Professor Hare, and others are no more Christians now than when they lived here. We also know that Roman Catholics who die full in the faith and belief of that church remain in both long after death, and often communicate to Catholics and urge them to stick to the church, while they, on being questioned, confess that they have not seen Jesus or the Virgin Mary, but expect to at some future time. Calvinists who are firm in the faith, passing on, carry it with them, and there as here it has to be outgrown by progress in thought, as in all doctrines and dogmas is true of finite minds, and that growth is slow there as here, but perhaps not as slow — we must take each one's opinions of what they do not know, as we do the opinions of our fellow-mortals on such subjects. So far as I can learn from spirits they actually know as little about the infinite intelligence and wisdom that govern the universe, or about the extent of the universe as we do on earth. Many persons live here nearly a century and know no more about these things than at twenty or even ten years of age, so far as actual knowledge is concerned. The Calvinist or Methodist would set up his standard as the test of value or correctness of the opinion or message from a spirit, and thus each would try the spirits by his own standard. It is probable that those of us who are not Christians or Mohammedans, would have a standard that would not accept the opinions of either of these sects of worshippers. In our estimates of the value of opinions here we should probably think those of Herbert Spencer superior to those of Spurgeon, and those of Ingersoll superior to those of Talmage, and those of Beecher superior to the rantings of Sam Jones and Sam Small, who are just now converting the rabble in Boston about as the Salvation Army is all over the country.

"By these rules I do not see that we can fix up any one standard by which we can any more, or any better, try the spirits in their messages than we can the different creeds of the Christian churches. I try the latter and reject them all, and yet find some kernels of wheat in nearly every one of the piles of sectarian chaff. I have heard as orthodox prayers from spirits as from any on this side of death, and seen messages as ridiculous as Sam Jones' sermons, and I have no more respect for them and no more confidence in them than if uttered by Sam Jones or a member of the Salvation Army. I have also had and read many of the most beautiful and to me rational, natural and truthful messages, that equal the sermons of Theodore Parker, or the letters of John Stuart Mill or Herbert Spencer. How can I try the spirits except by my own standard and the condition of my mind? If the Catholics are right, I am wrong. If the Calvinists are right, I am wrong. If the Methodists are right, I am wrong; and if I am right, they are all wrong. If I am wrong, I cannot see it now, and spirits have not yet given me any evidence that I am wrong. When I find I am wrong on any line of progress, I shall abandon it and take what seems right to me. As I have never been a Christian either by birth, baptism, or education, and was never taught the *ca*techism, I have never accepted the *dog*matism of any church, but have been an outsider, seeking and collecting what I could, and I readily caught the *facts* of spirit intercourse and by it gained the knowledge of a life succeeding this, into which all go from this and, so far as I can learn, unchanged in mental capacity and opinions by the change we call death. Hence I take the opinions from these as I do those here, and try them by the best standard I can find."

"PEACE ON EARTH AND GOOD-WILL AMONG MEN.

"We are so often and so repeatedly told by Christians that the mission of Jesus to this earth as a God was to bring peace on earth and good-will among men, that it is well to look up the record and follow the trail of Christianity which claims to be carrying out and fulfilling his mission. It is now nearly nineteen hundred years since this Jesus, who is said to have been a God with omnipotent power to do what he pleased, came on earth to bring peace and good-will, and to-day while I am writing, our Congress, and other Christian nations with Christian governments (which ours is not, although we have chaplains in both branches of Congress and most of the State legislatures, and thousands of costly churches and seventy-six thousand Christian preachers), are discussing great questions of armies and navies and the most destructive instruments for destroying one another, and all preparing for war. This has been the history of all Christian nations and Christian governments since the Christian Church was organized and united with the governments under Constantine, and the more powerful the church and the government with which it has been united, the more cruel and the more warlike and despotic its history. Russia is to-day the most devout Christian nation on earth, and has the worst and most cruel government, and Spain the next in both respects; ours, with a liberal Christianity and largely infidel, is, as our congressmen declare, in the most peaceful condition, and it has the least Christianity of any, and yet under the sanctions of our chaplains and churches our politicians are urging preparations for war, and many are trying to get us into a war with Canada, and consequently with England, over a kettle of fish upset on a Nova Scotia coast, which to the whole nation and people is of less importance than the overflowing of the Mississippi River each year.

"It has ever been the policy of the Christian nations to take up the slightest occasions for war when they felt that they had power to check the growth or crush out a weaker nation, as Russia did Poland, and Spain the South American and Mexican nations, and as we have the Indians. But wars have not been the only way our Christians have interfered with this pretended mission of Jesus to bring peace on earth and good-will among men. Persecutions and the most cruel executions for no crime but the honest expression of an unbelief, when belief was involuntary, have marked its entire history from Constantine to the present time, only ameliorated and modified as the churches have lost power to execute it by the growth and strength of unbelief and infidelity; but the spirit and disposition is the same, as is evinced every day in cases of church quarrels like that of Dr. McGlynn of New York, and one we are having to-day in Worcester in a Baptist church, which is divided against itself and cannot stand, if the Scripture is true.

"Divisions, discords, wranglings, anger, and disputation are the prevailing conditions of our churches in place of good-will, and are a modified form of the hatred that prevailed for more than a thousand years, in which millions lost their lives, even reaching down to this country and tapering out in the hanging of six Quakers in Massachusetts, and the execution of nineteen mediums in Salem, accused of making league with the devil and being witches and warlocks, because phenomena occurred around them such as do now around our mediums, and over which they had no control, and the sources of which were unknown to them. It has been growth and strength of infidelity that stopped these cruelties tapering out in Massachusetts from executions through the imprisonment of Abner Kneeland for blasphemy in saying 'the Universalists believe in a God which I do not,' which only showed that he was honest enough to express his unbelief over which he had no control, but for which, our Christians tell us, God will torment us forever. Such kind of good-will as God is said to have is such as orthodox Christians have manifested in the past, and Catholics still maintain in countries where they control the governments. Preach peace and practise war is Christian nations' history; preach good-will, and practise enmity is church history. Get the heart changed and be no better is individual history."

"CHRISTIAN SCIENCE.

"A Christain scientist is a misnomer. I never knew and never read of a genuine and thorough scientist that was a Christian, and it has rarely been the case that a scientist has accepted Christianity, even for friends or popularity; and when one has, it has been like one I once heard say when lecturing on authority, and remarking that he did not accept it except in religion; and on that, he said, 'I shut my eyes and go it blind.' *Faithist* is a proper name for a Christian, as faith is proper evidence in Christianity, but not in science or courts of law, where we have to prove a fact by evidence. Faith being 'the evidence of things not seen, and the substance of things hoped for,' is good enough for a Christian, but is neither evidence nor substance in science or law. What faith can do that science cannot, is evidenced in the many (over 300) creeds which it proves true by the Bible, no two of them being alike, and many directly contradictory. Neither science nor law could do this, nor prove by its rules of evidence even one of them true. The rules of evidence in science and law are similar, and entirely distinct from those of Christianity, hence the misnomer. No amount of metaphysical nonsense can ever unite science and Christianity, or prove anything by faith except its own existence and absurd claims as fictions. W. F. Evans, in his work on 'Esoteric Christianity and Mental Therapeutics,' has dabbled in more of this metaphysical nonsense than I have seen in so short a space for a long time; beginning with an absurdity, he runs the gauntlet of nonsense successfully for those who cannot reason. He says: 'The human mind is dual. There is an active intellectual department of our being, and a passive and receptive nature, and the union of the two constitute the mind. The one is masculine, the other feminine.'

"If more nonsense can be combined in as few words, I have never seen it. Read on: 'This bipartite division extends down through the three discrete degrees of the mind, and even into the body. The function of the one is to act, of the other is to receive and to react. When we turn the receptive and passive intellect toward the realm of light, the "intelligible world," the light of truth will flow in according to our degree of receptivity.' He ought to send this profound philosophy and grand discovery to Herbert Spencer, and to De Witt Talmage; the latter could weave it in with the old Bible stories in his inimitable sermons, where it would fit nicely. But a child might ask some questions that would spoil it, as a question did the darky's sermon on Adam and Eve and the garden fence. What and who is the 'We,' or *ego*, that turns the two facts, male and female, of the mind, toward the realms of light, the 'intelligible world'? and what is the realm of light, and what the intelligible world? Science defines, and is made up of facts, not fiction or assertion.

"Let us know what we are that turn the crank, and face the mind about and catch the light of truth which, we are to suppose, shines like an electric light or a distant star. How much of this dual mind does the child have when it is born? Is it masculine and feminine then? How much mind would we have if we had no senses? So far as I can discover, and so far as science has gone with its evidences, we are born without any mind, but with a small repository for it to be stored in, as it is collected from the elemental universe through the senses, and collected particle by particle, and some retained and some passed off as are the grains of coarser matter that compose the body at different stages of life. The body may determine sexuality at birth, but in the mind it is developed in some years of growth, and in most cases settles in one or the other sex, but not always in either, and but rarely in both. The mind is no more a unit than the body, and no more a quality, but like it, is a combination of particles collected through the senses, and stored in the varied and various repositories of the brain. Large religious organs are filled with what we were stamped with along the path of life by seeing and hearing and reading, and this makes faith, sometimes equal to a grain of mustard seed, but not quite enough to remove a mountain into the sea, or to cure a cancer or typhoid fever or the cholera. Even those who rely on the faith cure often get baffled, as Jesus did with the figtree and the faithless people. Science never depends on faith or belief, but on the immortal laws of nature, and its facts are demonstrated the same to sceptics as to believers. It is religion that relies on faith to set it out for acceptance.

"Spirit intercourse is a demonstrated scientific fact. No creed in Christianity is, and faith is an *ignis-fatuus*, that too often leads into swamps of superstition and absurdities of doctrine. The human body has been analyzed and dissected, but the mind so far in experiments eludes our grasp for experiments, as we have no crucibles or retorts that will hold it, and the vague theories and speculations about it, and about what it can do and cannot do, are without scientific evidence. Its existence in different quantities and varied effects and expressions in individuals, is what we know of it, and we may say of it what the ancients said of nature's laws, '*causa latet res est notissima.*' If each mind is male and female, we are more than double in marriage, as there are two males and two females in each conjugal pair, and there would hardly seem to be any necessity for marriage even to perpetuate the race, as we should be like some plants, especially our maize.

"What are we to understand by the 'intelligible world,' toward which the mind is to be turned by something that can turn it, and may turn it out in the cold if it can turn it at all? I can recognize an intelligent system of laws by which all existence, so far as I know of it, is governed, and I do not see any exception in mind so far as I can trace its effects, as I cannot deal with it as I can with minerals, or even as I can with the gases, and have read of no scientist that can, but have seen plenty of ridiculous theories about it, and its origin and destiny, its power and effects; but science ignores them all, as they are not based on facts. I make up my mind; but what am I, the *ego,* that owns and controls the mind and makes it up? My answer is in my last published book, 'Essence and Substance.'"

"POST-MORTEM LIFE.

"There is a vast amount of speculation about that life, and many even deny its existence. There are over three hundred and fifty creeds and theories about it, all based on divine revelation, or what is claimed to be such, and no two alike, and yet all supposed to be based on the infallible words of God, who is supposed to live there and know all about it. The conflicts of these theories are such as to lead any careful writer to reject them all as coming from any God who knows what that life is, and was honest in the report of it. There is not one particle of reliable evidence that any word about it has come from any God of knowledge and wisdom and honesty, and hence the conflicting creeds of mere speculators on what they call divine revelation. That persons who were enjoying that post-mortem existence have through all historic time been dabbling in and often directing the affairs of this life, while giving very little information about their own, seems to me a plain fact, and that these messages should often be called the word of the Lord as it came to prophets and seers, who were no doubt what we now call mediums, is also plain to me, judging from the records. These messages from Jews in the post-mortem life to those in the ante-mortem life were received by the priests as authentic, and were generally accepted and too often followed out in the cruel and barbarous practices of that people. Those of the Greeks were better because the Greeks were a more enlightened people, and the Greeks in both worlds were more advanced in literature, science, and poetry; but Greeks and Jews and Persians each peopled a section of the spirit world near to and closely allied to their native homes on earth.

"To me it seems strange that no more was given relating to the life and world in which they found themselves living after death, as that is the first thing we write about now when we discover a new section of this world and land on it; but this neglect is still more marvellous if it came from gods who knew all about that world, and this also. To me it seems plain that we have learned nothing about that life that was reliable until what is now called Modern Spiritualism opened an extended and widely varied intercourse between the two states of existence. As yet there are many and varied reports about its locality and its scenery, showing the great variety of conditions in which its denizens live, and we also find the same varied and widely different opinions and theories on subjects of which they know no more than we do, such as the origin of our world, of life, of man, etc. It is plain that they have no more access to God and the source of knowledge of these things than we have, and hence the theories there as here. Like writers and speakers here, they like to have their theories and opinions accepted, and hence often assume names that we venerate and accept as authority. In earlier times it was the word of God, or the Lord; and now it is Jesus, or the saints, or some distinguished philosopher, statesman, or poet; and with such sanction of a sacred name many vague and ridiculous theories of our future and of the post-mortem life are palmed off on the people, some of them as ridiculous as the Christian creeds. In time we shall sift this subject and rationalize the whole matter, as we are doing with this life and its duties and results. When I was young, it was taught from the pulpits and in the catechism that the chief end of man was to glorify God and praise him forever; and yet we were told that a great majority would go into eternal misery and be made to praise him there. I remember well when it was said we must be willing to be damned before we could be saved, and I could see no chance for me in that course. To me some of the theories of that life, and the beliefs entertained there of God, are as ridiculous as those taught here by the churches; and when they conflict with nature, with reason, with justice, I am no more ready to receive them. When a spirit talks of things as ridiculous as those John said he saw when looking into heaven from the Isle of Patmos, I put that spirit down as a crank; and when one writes out a new Bible history of creation, etc., as in 'Oahspe,' I put him in the catalogue of those who wrote the Old Testament and other fables like the Samson, Noah, and Jonah stories, and by such I learn nothing of that life, except that it is a continuance of this with the cranks, and Christians, and Faithists, and believers there as here."

"CHRISTMAS DAY — WHAT IS IT?

"That it is a holiday, and especially the children's day, we all know, and are all glad their dear little hearts can be made glad and merry at least one day in the, to them, long year; and I have tried to do my part in such work, although in my childhood there was no

Christmas, especially for me, in that old Puritan section of New Hampshire where the new revelation of Spiritualism had not appeared in public. None of the merry-made children and few of the merry-makers ever inquire after the origin of the fabled Santa Claus, or the reason why this day is selected from the 365 of the year for his visits. That it was a day of rejoicing and a holiday of the sun-worshippers many centuries before the origin of Christianity, is a historical fact; and likewise that it had its origin in the fact that on the twenty-fifth day of December the sun-god started back north on his journey to resurrect the dead vegetation that had died of cold from his journey south when his slanting rays could not sustain them. During these short days the evil god, Ahrimen, had the partial control, and, bent on death, he stopped the production of food, as it was the sun-god that gave the daily bread.

"This old record and practice could not have given it the name of Christmas, as that comes only from Christianity with as much of a fabled origin as its distinguished visitor, Santa Claus, has, neither having any fact for a basis as the sun-worshippers had. The unquestioned Roman Catholic statement that it was the birthday of Christ is wholly fabulous, and unsupported by a single historic fact or item of reliable history, even if there is any of his birth at any time, which is now closely questioned, and by many, with good reasons, doubted. The mule shed and manger story, where the sheds were only ledges of rocks which constituted the wilderness of that bleak and barren country, and the mangers only hollows in the rocks where the jacks and mules were fed, and the fabled birth of a God in such a place at that time of year, is a little too steep for rational minds in this enlightened age. It only adds another link to the fabled story of the priests turning the Holy Virgin out of the temple, because she was miraculously with child by their God or his Holy Ghost, which, of course, would and should have secured her the best of care in the temple.

"Up to the year three hundred and fifty of our era, no day had been agreed upon as the birthday of Jesus, who had then become the Christ and a God in the Trinity of the old Mother Church. Many dates had been suggested up to that time; some in May, some in April, some in November, and various other dates, but no one authentically agreed upon. Somewhere about 352 or 353 the Church writers discovered that God made the world and sun, moon, and stars, and the garden, and man in the spring, as that was the time the grasses began to grow in the northern hemisphere, and they knew nothing of a southern hemisphere then; as the day and night were divided equally in the evening and morning, it was fixed at the spring equinox; and as that was the time of God's first work on earth, making it out of nothing, with the sun, moon, and stars to light it, for it was as flat as a pancake then, with a bottomless pit under it, and the home of the gods on the next flat above, and above the blue waters of the sky as well as above the sun, moon, and stars, and the gods then went up and down from the mountains and broke up the plan and effort to build a tower with steps up to it as related in the Holy Bible. Taking this as a basis, the holy Fathers, full of the Holy Ghost, and with great wisdom and foresight, saw that this must be the time of year that God made his last visit to this flat of the universe, and that that must be the time of the visit to the holy temple and the wonderful event that led to the redemption of man from original sin, at least to all that were reached by the atonement and blood of Christ through his church on earth and no others, as they were and still are hopelessly lost, and I find myself among them and prefer to stay there.

" Now we have the key to Christmas and the reason of its date in the deep winter by counting the time of gestation from the vernal equinox, and most fortunately, and no doubt accidentally, it fell on the very day that had been so long and so generally used as a holiday and day of rejoicing, as the sun-god's start back to save the frozen world, and hence it was at once and almost universally accepted, and the old church made glad that it had so miraculously discovered the very day on which Christ was born, and we sacredly keep it yet, and will keep it with old Santa Claus."

"DANGER SIGNALS.

"The constantly increasing and renewed attacks on our best public mediums of the most attractive and convincing class — the materializing — is a subject for every true Spiritualist to interest himself and herself in. A bigoted public prejudice built up and sustained by the churches, and a subsidized press ever seeking sensation articles to feed this prejudice, are at the bottom. A clergy and its revival preachers all the time obtaining money under the false pretence of saving souls, stands ready to use the law to persecute some poor, honest, hard-working medium who is not obtaining money under *false* pretences, but is trying and often succeeding in convincing sceptics that death does not separate those who love each other, nor put the person passing through it out of existence or to 'sleep in Jesus,' but leaves the person mentally in a condition to study nature's law, and when these laws allow it, to make themselves known. This fact, so fatal to the many theories of our churches about the destiny of the souls they claim to have saved, or failed to save, is what arouses their bitterest prejudices, and they at once join with the writers for the papers that only seek sensational items to feed the prejudice and sell their issues. These papers which so eagerly catch up any pretended expose, and often get them up and employ reckless and rascally persons to go prepared for their work, carrying with them the very articles they scatter in the dark and pretend to find, and taking with them the persons they pretend to grab as accomplices, get well paid by the extra sale of the papers containing the lengthy and well written stories of the exposure, but which, when it is shown that the fraud was all in, and by the exposers, they will never explain, as that would not aid the sale of the paper nor satisfy the popular prejudice. There is a day of reckoning and retribution for this rascality, and we can afford to wait; but it is well to have up the danger signals for the mediums, as this kind of treatment and abuse of many of our best and most sensitive mediums has driven them out of the useful field of labor, and often out of the body through the gate of death to a better world where pulpit and press can persecute no more."

" ANCIENT AND MODERN CHRISTIANITY.

"To a seeker after religious truth a history of Christianity is highly essential, and entirely unsatisfactory as a foundation for a philosophical religious belief. There is but one thing original in its history as a belief, and that fabulous and absurdly false, and that is a bodily resurrection as the basis of a future or renewal of life after death. All of its moral precepts are taught and embraced in more ancient religious teachings. The Egyptians, Hindoos, Chinese, Persians, and Jews had them, and they have nowhere any evidence of a divine origin. They are natural and instinctive in mankind. All intelligent people with no religious creed, or even belief in any God, know as well as Christians do that it is wrong to murder, rob, steal, lie, or covet a neighbor's property, as do the most devout Christians, and if they obey the dictates of their own consciences, live as righteously and wisely, or even more so, than do those who do it through fear of a God who commands it and whose punishment they fear. It is questionable whether there is merit in a good act or life, performed or lived through fear of punishment. The Mohammedan moral code is nearly the same as the Christian, and may have been largely borrowed from it, as the Christian was from the Jewish and Persian, and these from Egyptian and Hindoo, or Grecian and Roman in later models. It does not require a God to tell us it is wrong to kill or steal, nor does it even require a spirit from the other life to teach these truths that are instinctively implanted in our nature, and they are no more sacred because found in ancient scripts than they are when found in savage language or in the illiterate, or vulgar rabble and profane dialect of the prize-fighter.

" Separating our morals from religion, to which they do not belong, we can look up the history of Christianity as we do any other religion, but not with the same reliable certainty that we can Mohammedanism, which is five or six centuries younger and more accurately traced to its mediumistic founder, and the phenomena and messages that came through him from the spirit world. Those which came through Jesus, if they ever actually occurred in any manner, are more remote, more uncertain, and much more unreliable as facts, and often so extravagantly exaggerated in the records as to create discredit of their having occurred at all. That those of Mohammed are also exaggerated is unquestionably true, as all ancient mediumship is in the narrative except perhaps that of Socrates. It requires a strong taint of fanaticism to believe that a God or the '*very God*' of all creation and existence lived on earth thirty years among boys and men as one of them, working with them at mechanical work, and only in two or three instances after his childhood gave any signs of the infinite power he possessed, but lived and labored in the most obscure part of the world, and yet came to enlighten and save the whole race, or to offer them salvation from endless misery to which they had been by himself sentenced, and to which all must go without this pardon from their own acceptance of him as a sacrifice of himself to himself, as he and his Father are said to be one. The 'mysteries of Godliness'— whatever they are — are said to be wonderful and, so such as these certainly are, and beyond my comprehension or acceptance, whatever the consequences may be to me.

"So far as I have been able to trace the history of religions, they all seem to have started, even down to many of our modern sects, in spiritual phenomena and messages, running backward from Mormonism and Millerism, Universalism, Methodism, Shakerism, Quakerism, Protestantism, Catholicism, to Primitive Christianity, which is as distinct from all of these forces as Shakerism is from orthodoxy. To me there is no doubt of spirit manifestations and messages among the early Christians, the Jews, the Persians, the Hindoos, the Chinese, and the Egyptians, and that the priests of all ages have deceived the people with these as coming from their gods and being providential and of divine origin and supernatural, while they ever showed their finite and fallible origin as do those of our time.

"During the first two hundred years of the Christian era, mediumship, phenomena, and messages were quite common, and worldliness, pride, ambition, tyranny, and persecution were almost, if not entirely, unknown among the followers and teachers of the Jesus doctrine. They were mostly itinerant mendicants, poor and despised by the rich aristocrats with other religions and gods. Even the Jews despised them and utterly ignored their pretensions and stories of Jesus and his miraculous origin, which none but Jews and Jewish priests could know of, if it occurred as related in the second century by the writers of Matthew's or Luke's Gospels. That these primitive teachers of a new religion lived pure lives generally, and made great sacrifices of comfort for a cause in which they were conscientiously honest, there is no doubt; and although disputes arose among them in matters about Jesus, it was not until the third century that they became generally corrupt and tyrannical. When Constantine, that most cruel, wicked, and corrupt of all Roman rulers, exceeding even Nero, got control of the Roman power and took Christianity for an ally and wedded it to the Roman government, it at once became even more corrupt, more tyrannical, more wicked, and more cruel and relentless than any Pagan system of religion then in existence. It caused, created, and sustained the darkness and crimes of what is known as the dark ages, which spread over Europe, but not over Mohammedan countries, and until the Reformation and astronomy broke its power of persecution, it was the worst religion the world was ever cursed with. Since the Reformation it has been gradually, but very slowly, growing better, and as it loses power by its division into sects, it grows more tolerant, but yet retains its persecuting spirit, as is shown even now by its persecution of our mediums; but it is softening as the popular mind is fast getting out of its control, so it cannot use the persecuting power it did in the earlier Protestant ages. It runs now almost entirely into pride and temple show. It saves the rich now which it ignored in its early history, and neglects the poor it then saved."

"CHRISTIANITY AND CIVILIZATION.

"We so often hear and read how Christianity has civilized the world that it leads a critic to examine history to see how and when it did it. In tracing the history of Christianity back, it terminates with Constantine and his mother in the third century of our era, in which he established the Christian Church and its trinity, and she miraculously discovered the true cross on which Jesus was fabulously crucified, and many other holy objects and places, which are still held sacred by the Catholic Church. Christianity proper does not include Paul and his co-laborers, and still less the Jesus, whether real or fictitious, and his poor fishermen disciples, who are said to have opposed the private and popular religion of that time and country as much as Spiritualists do those of our day, and to have been persecuted by them in the same way, while he and his poor, ignorant, and mendicant followers were poor and powerless, and they rich, proud, and haughty. Leaving out the two hundred years in which the heresy in and among the Jews, for some cause, spread in Western Asia, we come to the foundation of the true Christian Church under that most wicked founder, Constantine, who, unfortunately for England, was born and educated there, and with his sainted mother founded the Church, after he, through a bloody path, had reached the head of the Roman Empire and had his seat of government at Constantinople. If any honest student of history will take up the history of Christianity as it was organized, established, and founded there and then, on murders, persecution, plunder, and rapine, and tell me where civilization began in its history, I will be greatly obliged to him, or her, as I cannot find the point of time nor the *civilized* steps in its progress. History informs us that Mohammedanism, which started four hundred years later, spread more rapidly and has held even pace with it ever since in the promulgation of its religious devotion and in numbers, and it also informs us that both were propagated, extended, and enforced by wars, murders, persecution, and confiscation, and that civilization was checked and retarded by the cloud of superstition and ignorance which the Church spread over its dominions, in the dark ages, when the Saracens gained rapidly upon them by letting in more light through the interstices of their religion. If any one can find the footprints of civilization in Christian history, from Constantine to the present Pope and Victoria, he, or she, can do what I cannot. I have read up the history quite carefully, of the murderous and plundering wars of Christian Rome, in its subjection of Europe and its crusade attempt to take the Holy Land from the Saracens, with the help of the Christian trinitarian God and the blessings of the Pope, and prayers of all good Christians, and the sacrifice of millions of lives. I have followed the bloody path of Christian history through the expulsion of Jews from Spain, down to the recent expulsion from Christian Russia, and find Mohammedans far more civilized in the treatment of them. I have long ago read up the terrible Christian cruelties of the Inquisition; of the persecution of heretics, when they were themselves heretics to the Jews, who gave birth, foundation, and religious strength to all the religion they had. I have read of the terrible wholesale slaughter in the early days of Protestantism, and of both parties equally guilty as each had power, coming down to our own country, and its records stained with the blood of Quakers, mediums, called 'witches' and 'warlocks' in Christian Massachusetts. I have followed European history in constant war, with Christianity in both armies and plenty of chaplains on both sides, and fire and faggot for the poor unfortunate peacemakers, like Joan of Arc, when caught and given over to the Church. I still read of the standing armies and navies of Christian nations in readiness for slaughter the day that the least provocation is given, and yet these nations boast of civilization, which never can exist where armies and navies are. We come the nearest to it in this country, and even here we are organizing and drilling militia to put down the laborers when they strike or assemble to talk over their grievances. They must be peaceable, as they should be, and talk politics, which are not prohibited, and then they will escape slaughter, but not by riots, as they are then in the wrong.

"I watched closely the Christian war we had with that eminent Christian, Jeff Davis, and his Christian cabinet and officers, with the prayerful Stonewall Jackson and the many chaplains in both armies, and a sufficiency of prayers behind them; and though I could see plenty of the popular modern and ancient Christianity in both armies, I could discover no civilization, not even in Libby prison. It is true there were some noble women who went unarmed to the relief of sufferers, and these were civilized, but not the armed men and those who claimed to be Christians, no more so than atheists. If I could find the nation that Christianity has civilized, I should at once give it the credit. That Christian nations are the most enlightened I do not deny, but to me it seems that the wars even have done more toward civilizing them than Christianity. So far as I have been able to discover, no religion on earth (except, perhaps, Mohammedanism) has had as bloody, bloodthirsty, and cruel a historic record as Christianity, and certainly it is not done with blood yet, as it sings and prays and preaches the bloody code of washing and saving by blood. Spiritualism will civilize it if it ever gets the power, as the spirits do not murder in their world."

"HOLY DAYS.

"To some people one day in every seven, called a week, is more holy than the others. To me, all days and all time is holy, and we have no right to desecrate, abuse, or waste any of them or of it, and no one part is to me more holy than another, and yet I would have one day in every seven set apart for rest and recreation — not desecration. If one day in seven is holy, and the others are not, it would be necessary to know on what meridian line of longitude the holy day and what hour it began, which, I believe, has never been ascertained. Nor has it been settled which day in our seven, all named for heathen deities, is the holy one. It would require a congress of nations to settle that.

"Sunday is named for the sun-god, but it is the holy day of most Christians, but not of all of them. Its sacredness certainly could not be derived from the Jews and the command of Jehovah to rest on the seventh, as this is the first; hence it cannot derive any sacredness from the Old or New Testament, but get it all from decrees of the Catholic Church, which fixed the date of the resurrection of Jesus and took it from that fabulous event. Monday is named for the moon, and is the holy day of Greeks, and as sacred to them as Sunday is to Christians, and to me also. Tuesday is named for Tuisco, a deity of some little renown, and is the holy day of the Persians, and to them and me as holy as Sunday. Wednesday is named for Woden, a tutelary deity who is supposed to hold the winds and weather, and is the holy day of the Assyrians, and is also one of mine. Thursday is named for Thor, another little god worthy of a day name, and is the holy day of the Egyptians, and as sacred to them and me as Sunday is in our country. Friday is named for Friga, a goddess, and the only female in the list, except Luna, the moon, which is supposed to be an old maid, and Friday is the holy day of the Mohammedans, and very sacred to them, and me, as it is my lucky day. Saturday is named for Seator, another little deity, and is the holy day of the Jews and some Christians, as being the seventh in our numerical record, which is not ancient, and which was changed when not long ago we dropped out eleven days from the old style to begin the new style of counting and dividing the year. There is no way I can perceive of finding the holy day except mine of making all of the time sacred, and sacredly doing our duty every day and all of the time, and using it properly, and in it 'grow better and wiser as life wears away.'"

" RELIGIOUS RELICS.

"In analyzing Christianity and its creeds, symbols, ceremonies, and sacred objects, it is found to have very little that is new or original. Its holy cross is an ancient fetich with a sacred history of peculiar origin. It was not an instrument of torture used by the Jews, who never put criminals to death by crucifixion, and there is no historic evidence that they adopted it for Jesus. The Romans did use it before the Christian era and often nailed the bodies to it for exhibition after they were strangled and dead, but it is not at all probable that they crucified Jesus for blasphemy, as they were the rulers of Jerusalem, and not Herod, at the date of our era, and they were blasphemers of the Jewish God and had their own deities and despised the Jewish God and priesthood as much as he could. The cross derives no sacredness as a fetich for Christians from that event even if it did occur, of which there is no historic certainty, but it is a religious relic of very ancient date and made holy by the blessings of priests. The Hindoos have holy water made holy by priests as the Catholics have, and holy beads and other charms similar to our Catholics, but which the Protestants have largely dropped out of their list of holy things.

"High mountains were places of worship by the sun-worshippers, because they could see their god earlier and later from the mountain top and tower top and steeple top, and like Moses, who could not look his god in the face at noonday, could see his hinder parts as he was leaving at evening in the west. It is also probable that it took this sun-god forty days to harden the clay into stone on which Moses had inscribed in Egyptian hieroglyphics his ten commandments and which he so easily destroyed in his anger and renewed by forty more days of sun-drying. The towers and steeples of our modern churches are relics of the sun-worship and its mountains; they have no other use and are an expensive nuisance as a religious relic. That the Lord's Prayer is a relic of the sun-worshippers has long been known, and as applied to the Father of light and life which (not who) art in the heaven (sky) and gave our bread and the light to lead us out of the temptations of darkness by its light, and whose name was glorified or hallowed (haloed), shining and giving light, which is all there is to glory or halo.

"Prayers and supplications are modified relics of ancient offerings required by the priests and by which they keep control over the devotees and in return for which, so far as any change or variation in nature and its laws are concerned, or any special favors gained from beyond finite intelligences, there is no more than there was from the offerings of doves and bullocks. Asking God to bless the king and queen or the rulers, however wicked and cruel they were, was and is, a religious relic, first forced upon the people by tyrants as a religious duty, and kept up even in our free religious country and by our chaplains in legislative halls and the army. Blessing and thanking the Lord for every event in nature and its laws that is a blessing to us is a relic of religious tyranny which did not allow any complaints when calamities came from the same source, but taught the people to say, ' The Lord giveth and the Lord taketh away; blessed be the name of the Lord.'"

CHAPTER IX.

POETICAL SELECTIONS FROM AUTHORS KNOWN AND UNKNOWN, IN SCRAPS OF TRUE POETRY, AND IN JINGLE OF WORDS, WITH SUBJECTS FOR THOUGHT—VARIETY AS A SPICE IN LIFE.

" O wad some power the giftie gie us
To see oursels as ithers see us!
It wad frae mony a blunder free us
And foolish notion."

[A majority of the spirits that have written or spoken, even as far back as David and Solomon's time, have attempted to make poetry, and in our time some is beautiful almost beyond description, and a vast amount a mere jingle of words, unfit to print, and yet often there is in it some subject for thought. Much that I insert here is not from spirits, and some is, and I mix it for variety and preservation.]

ANNIVERSARY THOUGHTS.

OUR THIRTY-NINTH ANNIVERSARY.

THIRTY-NINE years since the angels of love
 Rapped at humanity's door,
Opening the way from the regions above
 Back to our error-dark shore,
Bearing a message from heavenly spheres
 Met with rejection and scorn,
Bringing a balm for earth's sorrow and tears
 Cursed on its fair natal morn.
Falsehood arose with its silvery tongue
 Quick to pervert and betray;
Slander went forth, and the vile song she sung
 Echoes around us to-day.

Thirty-nine years since the angels of peace
    Vowed at the altar divine
That the foul wrongs on the earth-plane should cease,
    Righteousness clearer should shine;
Vowed by the tears that they marked in their flow,
    Vowed by the ignorance too;
Vowed by the discord and terror and woe,
    The false should give way to the true.
Creeds should fall low with their teachings uncouth,
    Signs should be set in the sky,
And 'neath the radiant glory of truth,
    Dark superstition should die.

Thirty-nine years since the angels of might—
    Intellects worthy and strong,
Banded to bear the blest tidings of right
    Earthward through shadows of wrong.
To-day we would trace the sweet story again
    From where the effort begun,
Over and over with voice and with pen,
    How the great conflict was won.
To-day we would stand 'neath the sunshine agleam
    Out on the mountains sublime,
Looking once more down the shadowy stream
    That flows through the valley of time.

Thirty-nine years, and the liberal thought
    Shines over lowland and hill,
Lessons of beauty are everywhere taught—
    Brotherly love and good will.
Life is made grander and truth is made free,
    Fair recognition is won;
But in the light of to-day we can see
    Much that remains to be done.
'Neath its white banner so high and so broad,

Floating above every need,
Crawls the fell serpent of slime we call *fraud*,
Born in the bosom of *greed*.

Thirty-nine years, and to-day the demand
  Comes from its truths that endure,
That its fair altars so holy and grand,
  From this dark blot be kept pure.
To-day they are gathering from mansions of joy —
  Gathering with blessings untold,
This would they ask, "that no dross or alloy
  E'er have a place with the gold."
Rise! O ye workers, and wipe out the stain,
  Join hands with the ones o'er the way,
Lift up the truth to a holier plane
  On this *Anniversary Day*.   *Emma Train.*

WILLIAM DENTON.

A TRIBUTE TO ONE OF THE ABLEST AND BOLDEST ADVOCATES OF SPIRITUALISM.

WHO traced fair knowledge to its source
And followed it through all its course
And gave to science spirit force?
  William Denton.

Who found a sermon all unknown
Within each pebble, rock, and stone,
And preached it with unfaltering tone?
  William Denton.

Who saw in falsehood bitter foe,
And met it when the tide was low,
And gave back bravely blow for blow?
  William Denton.

Who read the strength of spirit power
Within each silent rock and flower,
And heard it in each summer shower?
    William Denton.

Who voiced the truth most strong and clear
And had for bigotry no fear,
But trusted to the angels near?
    William Denton.

Who left his home, with naught to mar,
To search for truth o'er lands afar,
'Neath burning sun and chilling star?
    William Denton.

Whose spirit sought the purer day
And left the garb of silent clay
Within a country far away?
    William Denton.

Whose form was laid in nature's lot,
Where grows the wild forget-me-not,
Without a stone to mark the spot?
    William Denton.

Who lives in realms beyond the skies,
And often when the daylight dies
Returns with thoughts all pure and wise?
    William Denton.

When Spiritualism comes to trace
The scroll that tells its leaders grace,
What name shall have an honored place?
    William Denton.
                    Emma Train.

PROGRESSION.

The gloomy night is breaking,
E'en now the sunbeams rest,
With a faint yet cheering radiance,
On the hill-tops of the West.
The mists are slowly rising
From the valley and the plain,
And a spirit is awakening
That shall never sleep again.
And ye may hear that listen
The spirit's stirring song,
That surges like the ocean
With its solemn base along.
Ho! can ye stay the rivers
Or bind the wings of light?
Or bring back to the morning
The old, departed night?
Nor shall ye check my impulse,
Nor stay it for an hour,
Until earth's groaning millions
Have felt its healing power.
This spirit is Progression,
In the vigor of its youth,
The foeman of oppression,
And its armor is the truth.
Old Error with its legions
Must fall beneath its wrath,
But blood, nor tears, nor anguish
Will mark its brilliant path.
But onward, upward, heavenward,
The spirit still will soar,
Till peace and love shall triumph
And falsehood reign no more.

Frances D. Gage.

HYMN OF THE BATTLE.

Can ye lessen the hours of the dying night,
Or chain the wings of the morning light?
Can ye seal the springs of the ocean-deep,
Or bind the thunders in silent sleep?
   The sun that rises, the seas that flow,
   The thunders of heaven all answer, No.

Can ye drive young spring from the blossomed earth?
The earthquake still, in its awful birth?
Will the hand on Time's dial backward flee,
Or the pulse of the universe pause for thee?
   The shaken mountains, the flowers that blow,
   The pulse of the universe answer, No.

Can ye burn a truth in the martyr's fire?
Or chain a thought in the dungeon dire?
Or stay the soul when it soars away,
In glorious life from the mouldering clay?
   The truth that liveth, the thoughts that go,
   The spirit ascending, all answer, No.

O priest! O despot! your doom they speak,
For God is mighty, as ye are weak.
Your night and your winter from earth must roll,
Your chains must melt from the limb and soul.
   Ye have wrought us wrong, ye have brought us woe.
   Shall ye triumph longer? We answer, No.

Ye have builded your temples with gems impearled,
On the broken heart of a famished world;
Ye have crushed its heroes in desert graves,
Ye have made its children a race of slaves.
   O'er the future age shall the ruin go?
   We gather against ye and answer, No.

Ye laugh in scorn from your shrines and towers;
But weak are ye, for the truth is ours.
In arms, in gold, and in pride ye move,
But we are stronger, — our strength is love.
   Slay truth and love with the curse and blow?
   The beautiful heavens, they answer, No.

The winter night of the world is past,
The day of humanity dawns at last;
The veil is rent from the soul's calm eyes,
And prophets, and heroes, and seers arise.
   Their words and deeds like the thunders go;
   Can ye stifle their voices? They answer, No.

It is God who speaks in their words of might,
It is God who acts in their deeds of right.
Lo! Eden waits, like a radiant bride;
Humanity springeth elate to her side. .
   Can ye sever the twain who to oneness flow?
   The voice of Divinity answers, No.

Thomas L. Harris.

A WONDERFUL thing is a seed,
The one thing deathless forever,
The one thing changeless, utterly true,
Forever old, and forever new,
And fickle and faithless never.

Plant blessings, and blessings will bloom;
Plant hate, and hate will grow.
You sow to-day — to-morrow will bring
The blossom that proves what sort of thing
Is the seed — the seed that you sow.

Anonymous.

WHY FEAR TO DIE?

WHAT if the seed put in the ground
    Refuse to sprout and grow?
Where should we see the mighty tree
    Or flower in summer's glow?
The seed must die, but in its death
    Feels an awakening power
That bears it on to higher life,
    In lovely plant and flower.
And if man might refuse to die,
    And still to this dull spot
Cling with unwavering desire,
    How wretched were his lot!
His clay must perish, but in death
    A changeless form is given,
In which the spirit germ unfolds
    Through its career in heaven.
Sordid the mind and dull the soul
    That never would go forth
Upon its upward, onward flight,
    Beyond this humble earth.
And low in being's scale it is
    To wish no higher sphere,
To be content with all the sin
    And shame that shroud us here.
To me earth seems a stepping-stone
    To higher worlds above,
A place where hate and wrongs are felt
    To teach the worth of love.
Decked in immortal forms we fly
    From sorrow and unrest,
To realms where hearts are sundered not,
    And love is ne'er unblest.

Owen G. Warren.

THE DEAD.

Say not the dead return to us no more,
When in the grave their withered clay is lying.
Think not communion with our friends is o'er,
When we have seen them close their eyes in dying.
Hath the soul then no other habitation
Than this pale clay, so feeble and so worn?
Must love, with that cold heart's last palpitation,
Die into night and know no waking morn?
Oh, no! we are not sundered by the grave;
The heart we loved is no cold night-watch keeping;
In that dark home o'er which the willows wave,
That loving heart is done with death and sleeping.
And o'er us and around us comes the spirit,
Wooing us still as erst we loved to love,
Through all our dreams its shadowy pinions bear it,
Near us forever wheresoe'er we rove.
Parted! — we are not parted — blind
And dull the soul that does not know it present;
That does not feel the influence soft and kind,
Though airy be the form and evanescent.
Ne'er would I look down in weeping sadness
Upon the grave and say the loved lies there:
'Tis but the clay cast off with joy and gladness,
By the freed soul now chainless as the air.
The one we love, whose absence we deplore,
Is with us, near us in our hours of sorrow,
Waiting to clasp us when our task is o'er,
And we, too, hail the everlasting morrow.
Then never be the brow in sadness shaded
When friends put off their worn-out robes of clay;
But with the eye of faith and hope be aided,
To see them newly clad in robes of day.

J. W. Spaulding.

NATURE'S GIFTS.

But for him whose cloudy looks
Are bent on law and ledger books,
Prisoned among the heated bricks,
The slave of traffic, toil, and tricks;
For him who worshippeth alone
Beneath the drowsy preacher's drone,
Where creed and text like fetters cling
Upon the spirit's struggling wing;
For him whom fashion's laws have tamed,
Till the sweet heavens are nigh ashamed
To lead him from his poisoned food
Into their healthy solitude,—
Such as these we leave behind,
Blind companions of the blind.
Little know they of the balm,
And the beauty, wise and calm,
Treasured up at nature's breast
For the sick heart that needeth rest.
C. P. Cranch.

He who seeks the truth and trembles
  At the dangers he must brave,
Is not fit to be a freeman;
  He, at best, is but a slave.

He who knows the truth and places
  Its high promptings under ban,
Loud may boast of all that's manly,
  But can never be a man.
W. D. Galligher.

COWARDICE.

The veriest coward upon earth
   Is he who fears the world's opinion,
Who acts with reference to its will,
   His conscience swayed by its dominion.

Mind is not worth a feather's weight,
   That must by other minds be measured;
Self must direct and self control,
   And the account with conscience treasured.

Fear never sways a manly soul,
   For honest hearts 'twas ne'er intended.
They — only they have cause to fear,
   Whose motives have the truth offended.

What will my neighbors say if I
   Should this attempt, or that, or t'other?
A neighbor is most sure a foe
   If he prove not a helping brother.

That man is brave who braves the world,
   When o'er life's sea his bark he steereth;
Who keeps that guiding star in view,
   A conscience clear which never veereth.

                              Anonymous.

THE DAY OF THE LORD AT HAND.

THE day of the Lord is at hand, at hand,
   The storms roll up the sky ;
A nation sleeps starving on heaps of gold,
   All dreamers toss and sigh.
When the pain is sorest, the child is born,
And the day is darkest before the morn
   Of the day of the Lord at hand.

Gather you, gather you, angels of God,
   Chivalry, justice, and truth ;
Come, for the earth is grown coward and old,
   Come down and renew us her youth.
Freedom, self-sacrifice, mercy, and love,
Haste to the battle-field — stoop from above,
   To the day of the Lord at hand.

Gather you, gather you, hounds of hell,
   Famine and plague and war —
Idleness, bigotry, cant and misrule,
   Gather and fall in the snare.
Hirelings and mammonites, pedants and knaves,
Crowd to the battle or sneak to your graves,
   In the day of the Lord at hand.

Who would sit down and whine for a lost age of gold
   While the Lord of all ages is here?
True hearts will leap up at the trumpet of God,
   And those who can suffer can dare.
Each past age of gold was an iron age too,
And the meekest of saints may find stern work to do
   In the day of the Lord at hand.

Charles Kingsley.

FRIEND OF MINE.

WOULDST thou be a friend of mine?
　Thou must be quick and bold,
When the right is to be done,
　And the truth is to be told.

Wearing no friendlike smile
　When thy heart is not within;
Making no truce with fraud or guile,
　No compromise with sin.

Open of eye and speech,
　Open of heart and hand,
Holding thine own but as in trust
　For thy great brother band.

Patient and stout to bear,
　Yet bearing not forever;
Gentle to rule, and slow to bind,
　Like lightning to deliver.

True to thy fatherland,
　True to thine own true love,
True to thine altar and thy creed
　And thy good God above.

But with no bigot scorn
　For faith sincere as thine,
Though less of form attend the prayer,
　Or more of pomp the shrine.
　　　　　" *Voices of the True-Hearted.*"

BE THYSELF.

Be thyself, my friend and brother,
    Do thy duty, faithfully;
Covet not to be another,
    Work thy way, and thou shalt see
There's a sphere of useful action
    Circling every son of man;
Spite of prejudice or faction,
    He who would be useful, can.

What though some may far outshine thee
    In the brilliant sphere of wit;
Be it so, nor yet repine thee,
    What thou art, that, that is it:
What thou art; aye, use thy power,
    Work with all the might thou hast;
Loiter not a single hour;
    Do thy duty to the last.

Do thy duty, act thy part,
    Labor with a right good-will.
Labor in the sphere assigned thee;
    Labor for thy brother man;
Labor, and success shall find thee;
    Do thy work: no other can.

If it be to ply the anvil,
    Or to break the virgin soil,
Or whatever else it may be,
    Seek not, ask not, lighter toil.
There's a secret thrill of gladness
    Waits thee when thy work is done,
Labor, tho' it be in sadness,
    Be thyself and labor on;
Nothing of thy work shall perish
    Nothing of the good and true.   *Anon.*

THE MAN I LOVE.

I LOVE the man who scorns to be
    To name or sect a slave;
Whose soul is like the sunshine free,
    Free as the ocean wave;

Who when he sees Oppression's wrong,
    Speaks out in thunder tones;
Who feels with truth that he is strong
    To grapple even with thrones.

I love the man who scorns to do
    An action mean or low;
Who will a noble course pursue
    To stranger, friend, or foe;

Who seeks for justice, not for gain;
    Is merciful and kind;
Who will not give a needless pain
    To body or to mind.

I love the man whose only boast
    Is wisdom, virtue, right;
Who feels if truth is ever lost,
    His honor has a blight.

Who ne'er evades by look or sign,
    In every place the same:
Methinks the glories are divine
    That cluster round his name.

William Denton.

HARMONY OF SPIRIT.

Nightly do my footsteps stray
In that valley hid from day,
Happy from ill cares to flee,
Where in peace I walk with thee.
  Overhead are smiling skies,
  Beautiful with rainbow dyes,
  While the soft enchanted air
  Breathes around us everywhere.
All the shadows of the day
By a spell are charmed away;
Not a doubt disturbs the hours,
Passed with thee in dreamland bowers.
  High the waves that roll, I ween,
  Walking *here* our souls between;
  But we pass them o'er and o'er,
  With one bound upon *that* shore.
There, as if by magic art,
Opes for me thy long-sealed heart,
And I read its fair leaves through,
Glowing, tender, strong, and true.
  Speech I have not, but to thee
  Of my soul I give the key;
  And as flowers unfold to light,
  'Neath thy gaze it grows more bright.
Then as thy soft, shadowy eyes
Ask of mine and give replies,
What care I, the world forgot,
That it comprehends me not.
  Thus, oh thus, when daylight grows
  Into silence and repose,
  Row I o'er that charmed sea,
  Where in peace I walk with thee. *Anon.*

THE TIME TO BE.

I sit where the leaves of the maple
And the gnarled and knotted gum
Are circling and drifting around me,
And think of the time to come.
 For the human heart is the mirror
  Of the things that are near and far,
 Like the wave that reflects on its bosom
  The flower and the distant star.

As change is the order of nature,
And beauty springs from decay,
So in the distant season
The false for the true makes way.
 The darkening power of evil
  And discordant joy and crime
 Are the cry preparing the wilderness
  For the flower and the harvest time;

Though doubting and weak misgivings
May rise to the soul's alarm,
Like the ghosts of heretic burners
In the province of bold reform.
 And now as the summer is fading,
  And the cold clouds full of rain,
 And the net in the fields of stubble
  And the *briers, is spread* in vain,

I catch through the mists of life's river
A glimpse of the time to be,
When the chain from the bondman rusted
Shall leave him erect and free
 On the solid and broad foundation,
  A common humanity's right,
 To cover his branded shoulder
  With the garment of love from sight.

Alice Cary.

ENTRANCE OF EDGAR A. POE INTO SPIRIT LIFE.

FIRST a harp of thrilling numbers
Roused me gently from my slumbers,
    And its tone
O'er my waking spirit stealing,
Kindling up a spirit feeling,
In its music sweet revealing
    Heaven's own.

Then a being pure and holy,
Through a door retiring slowly,
    Half disclosed
To my soul's enraptured vision,
Those eternal fields Elysian,
Where the blest, in full fruition,
    There reposed.

Then a being fairer, brighter,
Something smaller, something lighter,
And with raiment purer, whiter,
    Came in view.
Then her face was half averted,
Gazing back from where she started;
'Twas my lost, my loving hearted,
    Well I knew.

For a moment there she lingers,
And the beautiful white fingers
    Of Lenore,
Swept across the harp so shining,
Which the angel left reclining
    'Gainst the door;

Then as if some word receiving,
Half in doubt, yet half believing,
    Gazed around;
And at once she saw and knew me,
And at once she came unto me
    With a bound.

Oh! the rapture of that meeting,
Of that blessed spirit greeting,
    Is unknown.
They can never, till they pass the deep dark river
Which divides this world forever
    From our own,

Comprehend how hearts once blighted
In a world by sin benighted,
Are forever re-united
    On the shore
Of that river brightly glowing,
From eternal fountains flowing,
Where the tree of life is growing
    Evermore.

Inspirational; Medium Anon.

SPIRIT PRESENCE.

THE eye must be dark that so long has been dim,
  E'er again it may gaze upon thine;
But my heart has revealings of thee and thy home
  In many a token and sign.
I need but look up, with a vow to the sky,
  Where far off a bright vision appears,

And I hear a low murmur like thine in reply,
　When I pour out my spirit in tears.
　　　*　*　*　*　*　*　*　*
I know thou hast gone to the land of the blest;
　Then why should my soul be so sad?
To the land where the souls of the weary do rest,
　And the mourner looks up and is glad.
I know thou hast gone where thy forehead is starred
　With the beauty that dwelt in thy soul;
Where the light of thy loveliness cannot be marred,
　Nor thy feet be flung back from thy goal.

I know thou hast drank of the Lethe that flows
　Through a land where they do not forget;
That sheds over memory, only repose,
　And leaves behind only regret, —
To the land where the soul has put off at its birth
　The stains it had gathered in this,
And Hope, the sweet singer that gladdened the earth,
　Lies asleep in the bosom of bliss.
In thy far-away dwelling, wherever it be,
　I believe thou hast visions of mine,
And the love that made all things a music to me
　I have never yet learned to resign.
In the hush of the night,
　On the waste of the sea,
Or alone by the breeze on the hill,
　I have ever a presence that whispers of thee,
And my spirit lies down and is still.

T. K. Hervey.

DOUBT NOT; JOY SHALL COME AT LAST.

WHEN the day of life is dreary,
    And when gloom thy course enshrouds;
When thy step is faint and weary,
    And thy spirit dark with clouds;
Steadfast still in thy well-doing,
    Let thy soul forget the past;
Steadfast still the right pursuing,
    Doubt not! joy shall come at last.

Striving still and onward pressing,
    Seek not future years to know;
But deserve the wished-for blessing,
    It shall come, though it come slow.
Never tiring, upward gazing,
    Let thy fears aside be cast,
And thy trials, tempting, braving:
    Doubt not! joy shall come at last.

Keep not, then, thy mind regretting;
    Seek the good, spurn evil's thrall;
Though thy path thy foes besetting,
    Thou shalt triumph o'er them all.
Though each year but bring thee sadness,
    And thy youth be fleeting fast,
There'll be time enough for gladness:
    Doubt not! joy shall come at last. *Anon.*

SAMUEL TUTTLE OF SOUTH HARDWICK, VT., TO HIS WIFE SUSAN,

On the Thirteenth Anniversary of their Wedding, Jan. 2, 1866; now Both in Spirit Life.

Turn back life's book, review each page,
    My darling wife;
Thirteen short years is just our age
    Of wedded life.

Though much we've known of good and ill
    In life thus far,
Love's beacon light is on the hill,
    Our guiding star.

Now o'er the past fond memories crowd,
    Each claims a share;
Like summer's sunset on the cloud,
    Love's smile is there.

Our hearts have been with anguish torn,
    With grief and care,
When dearest friends were from us borne,
    We knew not where.

Since Bible times no one comes back,
    The preachers say,
Excepting on the Devil's track,
    Along the way.

We know our spirit friends return
    Our home to cheer;
And of the higher life we learn
    While churchites sneer.

Angels have thrown o'er death's dark stream
    A bridge of light;
The priests start up with nightmare scream
    And sad affright.

They know their tyrant rule and power
    Will soon abate,
And brimstone light and Devil lore
    Be out of date.

We've left old creeds all threadbare worn,
    For truth to search,
To often meet with slander born
    Within the church.

Let bigots like old driftwood float,
    Or deadwood sink;
We side by side will row our boat,
    And dare to think,

Until we join our gathered band
    On life's bright shore,
Among the flowers in summer land
    To part no more.

WRITTEN OF WARREN CHASE,

BY A SPIRIT THROUGH E. WALKER, MEDIUM, IN 1853.

HE speaks with a voice of thunder,
    Its echoes resounding afar;
He reads from the throne of Heaven
    And learns from the twinkling star.
He rose like the sun in the East,
    Proclaiming, My work must be done;

We sought him, and found in him truth,
   A standard to build upon.

Oh, when will man learn to be true,
   Both to himself and others?
For when he is true to himself,
   He will also be true to his brothers.
Why should we others' gardens weed
   When our own are overgrown?
No one is born so pure
   That he stands all alone.

Nor need we point to others' faults,
   That ours we may not see,
For in the very act we show
   That we are not quite free.
But let us strive to know ourselves,
   And in ourselves be strong,
But not deceive ourselves, and say,
   I am right, and all others wrong.

THE CRUCIFIED.

BY B. W. STODDARD, AN UNEDUCATED MEDIUM.
WRITTEN FOR WARREN CHASE.

BECAUSE I speak of man's deep sin, of woman's virtue lost,
And of the multitudes of souls, rude, by transgression tossed,
A legion of dark foes draw near to cast my plea aside;
By scorn and hate, envy and lies, my soul is crucified.

Because I speak of brutal vice, so rife among all men,
Who move unmindful of the law responsible with them,
'Tis then the spear of malice poised will seek to pierce my side;
My reputation by their blast is rudely crucified.

Because I speak of a reform upon this mundane land,
And wish the different sexes all in their true sphere to stand,
That on a true and normal plane our race be multiplied,
My heart by ignorance and sin is rudely crucified.

But oh, there gleams a brighter day; my words will not be lost,
And some poor soul may see the light while on these billows tossed;
And it may, as a bright star, rise o'er life's tempestuous tide,
And shower praises on the name that they have crucified.

Transfigurative power I feel, that God will on me smile,
That suns will pierce the darkening clouds that gather for a while;
That sorrows dim that enter in will all be moved aside;
Then I will work, although my soul be rudely crucified.

Sometimes confined, disconsolate, I see not Hope's bright stars,
And only blindly, as it were, look through the prison bars.
Quite weary of my sojourn here, I long to cross the tide
And seek the shore where high-born Truth is never crucified.

When a soft voice saith unto me, Let all such thoughts pass o'er,
And by thy labors here obtain admission to that shore;
By battling sorrows, cares, and woes, by fire thy soul is tried,
And as a star thy fame shall shine, though first 'tis crucified.

Bright angels come adown my path, while Wisdom's streamlet flows,

And light divine comes from above, and radiance round
    me throws,
That I may move the mountain, sin, that doth my joy
    deride,
And every day the voice that saith, Work on, though cru-
    cified.

A VISION OF BEAUTY.

Oh, such a lovely dream last night
    As o'er my vision swept!
Did white-winged angels bring to me
    Those beauties while I slept?
Or did my fancy roam
    'Mid scenes so fair and bright,
That painter's pencil could not sketch
    So beautiful a sight?

I saw at first a fairy group
    Of little children play;
Beside a silvery sparkling fount,
    Like diamonds fill the spray.
And laughingly they sported round,
    And shook their little curls,
Which fell in ringlets, soft and light,
    O'er shoulders white as pearls.

The air was laden with perfume
    Of more than earthly sweet,
And little, tiny, bright-eyed flowers
    Sprang up beneath their feet.
I listened, and such strains before
    Had never met my ear;
And wondering, I gazed around,
    But saw no minstrel near.

I looked again and saw a harp
  Of most exquisite mould,
And only zephyrs swept across
  Its strings of glittering gold.
And landscapes of such beauty rare
  My eyes have never seen;
And birds of loveliest plumage lent
  Enchantment to the scene.

Why are such pictures given us
  If they are nowhere real?
Or is there in some far-off clime
  A type of our ideal?
Or can the soul a heaven create,
  That doth nowhere exist?
Or is imagination's tower
  The summit of our bliss?

No; something tells me 'tis not so;
  The child must first be born
Before a picture can be made
  Of feature, size, and form.
And shadow ne'er was known to fall
  Without the substance near;
Nor is there in the heart a call
  That nature cannot hear.

* * * * * *

I fain would awake, I've fallen asleep;
I fain would awake where no calumny folds
Its dark pall of malice round innocent souls;
Where no scorpion sting can strike to the core
Of the heart that in anguish was writhing before;
Where envy and hate and scorn never dwell,
And truth, justice, and love weave a beautiful spell.

Lizzie Cone,
Mexico, N.Y., 1863.

FROM MY OLD SCRAP-BOOK.

I SEE a land of fadeless light
Arrayed in Truth's own armor bright;
So calm, so peaceful, so serene,
That all seems heavenly between.
I long to reach that fadeless goal,
Where rests the weary, waiting soul;
Where buds burst forth forever new,
In fadeless beauty's changeless hue.
I long to see that summer land,
To join that bright, angelic band,
To listen to those strains of love
Breathed by the angel choir above.
I sometimes think they beckon me,
Their shadowy forms I seem to see;
With open arms extended wide
They watch my pathway o'er the tide;
They bring bright garlands in their hands,
To tempt me o'er the silvery strands,
And harps of sweetest, softest sound
O'er the bright waters oft resound.
And soon my little bark shall be
All safely moored across the sea;
The boatman pale will land me there,
The beauties of that land to share.

Lizzie Cone,
Mexico, N.Y.

THE BROAD-SPREAD WALNUT-TREE.

I LOVE the mansion that was built
   Near fifty years ago,
Where my father spent his boyhood days
   And learned to reap and mow;

Where my mother came a blooming bride
   To share his destiny;
But dearer than those stately halls
   Is the broad-spread walnut-tree.

I love the playground where I danced
   When but a little child,
And the bubbling brook where oft I strayed
   With sister, meek and mild;
And the dear old swing — I love it yet,
   The barn where it used to be;
But dearer than those charms of old
   Is the broad-spread walnut-tree.

I love the orchard with its fruit
   That tempts the passers-by;
Beneath its shade and o'er its glade
   I breathed my childish sigh.
I love the spring, half down the hill,
   Where I drank in childish glee;
But the dearest charm of my childhood home
   Is the broad-spread walnut-tree.

I love the lake with its calm deep blue;
   I love its deaf'ning roar.
I love the little white pebbles that gleam
   And sparkle on its shore.
I love the trees that stand on the hill,
   That oft have sheltered me;
But the dearest charm of my childhood home
   Is the broad-spread walnut-tree.

Miss Emma H. Gilbert,
then *of Conneaut, O., on the shore of Lake Erie,*
now Mrs. Caswell, of Geneva, O.

ARE THERE THOSE IN HEAVEN THAT LOVE ME?

Are there those in heaven that love me?
   Sighed a broken-hearted wife;
In the skies that bend above me,
   Is there *one* I loved in life?
Bitter is this lonely anguish,
   All too dear the living — lost —
Sadly is the tempest wailing
   Through my bark so tempest tossed.

All the visions of my childhood,
   All the hopes of many years,
Faded when affection vanished,
   Leaving me to grief and tears:
'Twas the silent, lonely midnight
   When these dirge-like notes were sent
From the burning heart of sorrow
   Upward to the firmament.

Then with noiseless footsteps hasting
   Guardian angels to her side,
Bathed her soul in living waters,
   Fresh from love's exhaustless tide.
Round her form their white arms folded,
   Told her of a land of peace,
Where the beauty and the brightness,
   And the music never cease.

Then was changed her wail of anguish
   To a burst of joyous song;
And a new resolve was kindled
   Still to suffer and be strong.

Mary Fenn Love,
later Davis. *Written September*, 1853.

I KNOW THAT BRIGHT ANGELS ARE WITH ME.

I KNOW that bright angels are with me
In all of life's rough, thorny way;
I know that with love's hand they lead me,
And lead up to an endless day.

I see their sweet smiling faces,
When my heart is happy and free;
And I catch their low, sweet voices,
As they chant their sweet songs to me.

When the cloud of misfortune is dark,
And my heart cries aloud with woe,
O'er the dark rolling tide in their bark
Come the angels to their loved one below.

And I know that the angels are with me,
When in dreams at midnight I lay;
For their mantle of love is about me,
And the light of their smile cheers the way.

I know that bright angels are with me,
By the pity that flows from my heart,
For the sick and world-weary around me,
In this land where we meet but to part.

I know that bright angels do guide me,
As over the waters of life I float,
And that safely in heaven they'll land me
If I trust to their helm and my boat.

Clara A. Fogg,
Yarmouth, Me., 1865.

NEVER GO GLOOMILY.

Never go gloomily, man of a mind;
  Hope is a better companion than fear.
Providence, ever benignant and kind,
  Gives with a smile what you take with a tear.
    Look to the light,
    All will be right;
Morning is ever the daughter of night;
All that is black will be that which is bright.
Cheerily, cheerily, then cheer up.

Many a foe is a friend in disguise,
  Many a sorrow a blessing most true,
Teaching the heart to be happy and wise,
  Joys ever present and hope ever new.
    Stand in the van,
    Strive like a man;
This is the bravest and cleverest plan.
Trust in yourself while you do what you can.
Cheerily, cheerily, then cheer up.

TO W. C.

Thy pure love came as the early dew
  Comes unto drooping flowers,
Dropping its own sweet freshness on
  My life's dull, lonely hours.
As each pale blossom lifts its head,
Revived with blessings nightly shed
  By summer breeze and dew,
So my frail spirit rose beneath
Love's gentle dews and living breath
  To drink of life anew.

The author of the above was raised from a bedridden condition to health by my magnetism.

NOT LONG.

Not long shall demagogues oppress the just,
And trample Innocence beneath the dust.
Not long shall tyrants persecute the poor,
And Plenty drive the haggard from her door.
Not long shall Scorn and sickening Envy smile —
Their thoughts be daggers while their words are oil,
Might make the laws to gratify her spleen,
And talk of Truth her villany to screen.
Not long shall Pride in lowly aspect sneak,
The light look solemn, and the brutal meek;
Not long — not long — in these progressive days
When Freedom, Reason, Truth, and Science blaze, —
Shall burn the sparks of that Satanic zeal,
That piled the faggot and contrived the wheel.
Not long shall Neros and Domitians reign,
And savage Julians sink a world in pain.
Not long shall Lust the form of Love affect
And Malice wear the semblance of Respect.
Not long the gospel be a priest-made plan
Formed to delight, not sanctify the man.
Not long shall man with hypocritic face
Stab the fair cause of Piety and Grace;
Make moral Truth and spotless Justice bleed
And tear each righteous precept from their creed;[1]
Make faith a cloak their villany to screen,
And God Himself, a minister of sin.
Not long — not long — for Truth to manhood grown
Hath drawn her sword to cut the rebel down;
And every land amid this world's wide wave
Ere long shall blush to own she holds a slave;
War be no more, but olives proudly bloom
On Mammon's grave and Despotism's tomb.

C. B. Knowlton.

[1] As they did in Springfield, Mass., in 1887.

MERCY to him that shows it is the rule,
And righteous limitation of its act,
By which Heaven moves in pardoning guilty man:
And he that shows none, being ripe in years,
And conscious of the outrage he commits,
Shall seek it and not find it in his turn.   *Cowper.*

" Who noble ends by noble means obtains,
  Or, failing, smiles in exile or in chains,
  Like good Aurelius, let him reign or bleed;
  Like Socrates, that man is great indeed."

"In faith and hope the world will disagree,
  But all mankind's concern is charity."

" Disappointment lurks in many a prize,
  As bees in flowers, and stings us with success."

" Why should this gross encumbering crust of clay
    Seal up the vision of the spirit's sight?
  Why blind the soul to every spirit ray,
  And harshly drag this inner soul away
    From wond'rous gleamings of celestial light?"

" Love is to the human heart
  What sunshine is to flowers."

"One honest John Tompkins, a hedger and ditcher,
  Although he was poor, did not want to be richer;
  For this he was constantly heard to declare,
  What he could not prevent, he would cheerfully bear.
  And he said that revenging an injury done
  Would be making two rogues when there need be but one."

INTUITIONS.

I SOMETIMES have thoughts in my loneliest hours,
That lie on my heart like dew on the flowers,
Of a ramble I took one bright afternoon,
When my heart was as light as a blossom in June.

There are moments, I think, when the spirit receives
Whole volumes of thought in its unwritten leaves;
When the folds of the heart in a moment unclose,
Like the innermost leaves from the heart of a rose.

I know that each moment of rapture or pain,
But shortens the links in life's mystical chain.
Amelia.

THE VEILED FUTURE.

HEAVEN from all creatures hides the book of fate,
All but the page prescribed their present state.
From brutes what men, from men what spirits know,
Or who could suffer being here below?
The lamb thy riot dooms to bleed to-day,
Had he thy reason, would he skip and play?
Pleased to the last, he crops the flow'ry feed,
And licks the hand just raised to shed his blood.
Oh, blindness to the future, kindly given,
That each may fill the circle marked by heaven;
Who sees with equal eye as God of all,
A hero perish or a sparrow fall;
Atoms or systems into ruin hurled,
And now a bubble burst, and now a world.
Pope.

GEMS FROM GEORGE SHEPARD BURLEIGH,

IN HIS "MANIAC, AND OTHER POEMS," WRITTEN BEFORE THE
ADVENT OF MODERN SPIRITUALISM.

To him whose secret soul
Hath never dreamed of those diviner forms
Which people the bright realms of thought, or sighed
For the pure incarnation of his dream,
Love hath no language to reveal her deep,
Mysterious presence, or the workings of
Her prevalent spirit; but to one like him,
Whose heart from childhood bore an aimless fire,
While on the clear deeps of his gentle soul,
In hours of calm, were mirrored the serene
And lovely forms that hover over us,
Informing us with beauty — there but needs
One glance, when eye to eye lends fire, to hear
Her holiest revelation.

All things are transient save the Eternal ONE.

The veil is woven in the loom of life,
And every man fills up the delicate warp,
Between himself and those bright verities,
With woof of his own being, gross or clear.
Close by the heart of the serene and pure
Their warm hearts beat, and lend it holy strength;
But to the heart thick bound in earthliness,
No spirit pulse-beat sends its lifeful thrill.

Slowly descending from the fading cloud,
A being, beautiful beyond all thought,
Came o'er the wood; a star was on her brow,
And in her hand a coronal of flowers.

[From many compliments most gladly and thankfully received, and which I do not pretend to have deserved, I copy here for preservation a few retained, but many more as good are gone, or, having been given orally, were not reported.]

The following lines by E. Clementine Howarth, were published many years ago, a copy of which clipped from some paper was sent to me before I knew anything of the author.

RESPECTFULLY INSCRIBED TO WARREN CHASE.

FALTER not, O faithful hearted,
   Soldier in the cause of right;
From thy brethren thou hast parted,
   And art foremost in the fight;
For the fragile and the lowly
   Thou hast bared thy shining blade;
God is judge — thy cause is holy;
   Be not doubtful or afraid.

Falter not, thou faint and weary
   Toiler in the stony field;
Though thou seest no token cheery
   Of the harvest it should yield,
Sow thy seed, the winds shall speed it
   O'er the gardens far away;
Where no heavy feet shall tread it,
   It will ripen to the day.

Falter not, O brave reformer,
   Press thy cause with voice and pen;
Thou shalt have a greeting warmer
   Than the tardy praise of men.
Angels round thee, God above thee,
   See thee in thy manhood's might;
Lead the souls that trust and love thee
   Out of darkness into light.

A medium, under control of a spirit, dropped into my hand the following — I do not remember who it was — long ago: —

TO W. C.

TOILING in the field
    Where the laborers are few,
Sowing precious seed,
    Gathering in the new.

Where the battle rages,
    Foremost in the fight,
Fearless and undaunted,
    Battling for the right.

Your path is growing brighter
    As down the vale you glide,
Hand in hand with angels
    Walking side by side.

Work from early dawn
    Till the dews begin to weep;
You'll be glad that you have sown
    When the angels come to reap.

In 1887 Mrs. C. Laurens answered an article of mine in the *Spiritual Offering*, headed, " Where do I Belong?" stating that I stood between two fires, orthodoxy and atheism, etc., in these lines: —

I saw a man with honest brow and royal heart a king might grace,
Seeking among the creeds of men a worthy place his name to trace;
Where Superstition rears her head he cannot there his name enroll,

Nor yet among the class who say that man has no immortal soul.
Another class he sought, and found congenial minds; but even they would bind
His intellect to worship gods the proof of which he cannot find.
But now he sees a little band of men all pure and brave,
Who neither worship human creeds nor call on gods to save,
Who boldly fight for human rights with both tongue and pen,
Whose banner bears this motto fair, "We love our fellow-men."
He quickly seized the pen and wrote, as he a name did trace,
I stooped and read upon the page and found it, "Warren Chase."

TO WARREN CHASE.

THE years of thy pilgrimage are marching along,
But time floats onward with thee like a song;
For the music of truth with its rhythm sublime,
With its harmonies sweet and its heavenly chime,
Ever gladdens thy spirit with the freshness of youth—
Oh, such is thy power, bright, beautiful truth!

Brave Brother, in childhood's years I have read
Of the grand reformation thy spirit hath led.
"Life Line of the Lone One" made tender tears start,
And awakened deep interest for thee in my heart;
For thy name was enrolled to lead in the van,
As a great, and a good, and an honorable man.

Among the first who dared to say woman was free
In the realm of love, where as queen she should be;

And womanhood owes thee deep gratitude now,
And laurels we weave for thy venerable brow.
Long may'st thou live, humanity's friend,
And angels of ·love thy footsteps attend.

May thy heart ever beat with rejoicing and pride,
That the brave and the true now stand by thy side,
And spirits who dwell in the bright summer land
Reach down to earth's saviours the true helping hand;
And all the reforms for humanity's good
Soon unite all nations in true brotherhood.
Then thou wilt rejoice that thy help has been given
To lead human souls to harmony's heaven.

Sada Bailey,
now Sada Bailey Porter of Philadelphia, author of
"*Irene; or, The Road to Freedom.*"

ALLIANCE, O., Sept. 12, 1875.

CLOSING WORDS OF THOMAS SUTTON, WITH THE PRESENTATION OF AN ELEGANT CANE FROM THE SPIRITUAL SOCIETY OF WORCESTER, MASS., SEPT. 19, 1883.

VETERAN, walk on to your journey's rest,
With your true and honest bearing,
The bravest and the tenderest,
The loving and the daring.

LINES BY L. B. BROWN, EDITOR OF THE *Eastern Star*, AT THE CLOSE OF THE CAMP MEETING AT ETNA, MAINE.

Now let your spirit with ours blend,
While we speak of humanity's friend,
Who hath striven for forty years
To banish superstitious fears,
Preaching to the children of earth
Of Spiritualism's modern birth.

Travelling from State to State,
Oiling the hinges of Freedom's gate,
For Reason's light he hath striven ;
All these things he hath given
Cheerfully to the human race :
This veteran's name is Warren Chase.

Brother, your wrinkled locks portend
Your earth life is nearing its end ;
But well you know in Reason's light
You ever battled for the right,
And can with these kind friends sing
Memories that round our hearts will cling.

Brother, "The Life Line of the Lone One"
Will close in the rays of a spiritual sun,
Shining with light, progression true,
Shining because of men like you,
Lighting the paths of those who sing
Memories that round our hearts will cling.

TO WARREN CHASE.

AT HIS SEVENTIETH BIRTHDAY RECEPTION IN SAN FRANCISCO, CAL. BY ANNA D. WEAVER OF JAMESTOWN, N.Y.

ON this glorious star-gemmed evening I speed on wings of thought,
The shining silvery pinions that God in love hath wrought,
Across this grand old continent and join the festive throng,
Who meet to greet our hero with speech, and joy, and song.

Fall gently, O ye shadows ! his sun is in the west ;
And linger long, O twilight, in calm and peaceful rest ;

And spread a golden halo o'er the charm that memory
    weaves;
A valiant life is garnering its ripened golden sheaves.

We meet to place the milestone that marks his threescore
    years and ten,
And wreath it with the tributes of his own tongue and
    pen,
With the valiant love of liberty that sheds enduring fame
On him whose life-work ever is linked with Freedom's name.

For while old Ocean's surging breast draws long, dim,
    gray coast-lines,
And zephyrs play in palm-trees, and sigh in northern
    pines,
He is the truest hero who serves the sufferer's needs;
His prayers are ever answered who speaks in loving deeds.

Then let us grandly celebrate this birthday of our guest,
The foe of all oppressors, the friend of all oppressed;
At seventy strong, with armor on, fearless in power and
    might,
His grand, true words, the gleaming swords, defend the
    truth and right.

Then gently deal and kindly, and linger long, O Time,
And stay the mental vigor of our hero in his prime;
And when the shadows gather and sink down within the
    west,
Oh, bear him to his slumber, — place him tenderly to rest.

And when he beholds the Orient in the illumined east
Of that grander life but just beyond, and we gather to the
    feast,
The laurels which this birthday twines of purity and truth,
Our God shall place upon his brow with an immortal youth.

TO WARREN CHASE.

WRITTEN FOR, AND READ AT HIS 70th BIRTHDAY RECEPTION, BY MRS. SARAH A. HARRIS, OF BERKELEY, CAL.

If these few years of care and strife
Fill out the measure of our life;
If life, commencing with our breath,
Ceases with that which we call death,
How sad a thing it were to live,
How drear a thing to die!

If, like the wave upon the shore,
Life rings its chime and is no more;
If like yon bark, all tempest-tossed,
We stem life's tide but to be lost,
How vain a thing it were to live,
How hopeless then to die!

If we, like sunset so intense,
Which burns into the soul and sense,
Or childhood's dream and old folks' lore,
Could only live in memory's store,
Ah, then it were not joy to live,
For memory too would die!

If 'tween the cradle and the grave,
Where willows weep and cypress wave,
Come all there are of love's sweet dreams;
If from beyond no love-light gleams,
'Twere better far we had not loved,
Since that fond love must die.

If like the seed we live again
In summer bloom and autumn grain;
If like winter with frozen stream,
Death holds spring-time and summer green;

Ah, then what joy it were to live!
More joyous still to die.

If love which breaks the heart's repose,
Unfolding like the summer rose,
Lives on beyond death's sullen roar
And greets us from the other shore;
Then it were better we had loved,
E'en though the loved one die.

Seventy years! Life evermore!
A welcome from the other shore;
And now we hear the angels say,
"Walk firmly, for we light the way,
Which leads thee to a heavenly birth,
From all the joys and griefs of earth."
We trust thy future life may be
From every care and sorrow free.

A joy as full of light and love
As yonder star-ray from above;
As blest with hope as sweet spring-time,
As fraught with peace as days decline;
That into thy last eventide
Heavenly harmonies may glide
And waft thee to yon blissful shore,
While angels chant, " Life Evermore."

TRIBUTARY VERSES.

WRITTEN FOR, AND READ BY THE AUTHOR, GEORGE C. IRVIN,
AT THE SEVENTIETH BIRTHDAY RECEPTION OF WARREN
CHASE, HELD IN SAN FRANCISCO, CAL.

JUST threescore years and ten have passed
Since you upon life's sea were cast,
A tiny waif, to make your way,
From rosy youth to manhood gray.

To many this a trifle seems
Who spend their time in idle dreams,
Who down the stream so smoothly glide.
But never turn to breast the tide.

No silver spoon was made for you,
But poverty and work to do;
Whate'er of life's success you've found
You've gained a well-fought battle-ground.
Yours is a richer manhood for
The stern uncompromising war
You've made against Oppression's rod,
And Superstition's angry God.

At your head, anathemas
With hate and envy all ablaze,
Are hurled by bigots who would bind
To forms and creeds the human mind;
But like a modern ship of mail,
Impervious to iron hail,
These curses never harmed a hair,
But spent themselves upon the air.

Whate'er of truth your mind has grasped,
That to the world you've freely cast,
Nor paused to think just who 'twould hit,
Nor how the popular mind would fit.
A pioneer, you've led the way
'Gainst superstitions old and gray;
And crushing idols show the skill
With which you execute truth's will.

All sugar-coated shams in you
Have found persistent bitter foe;
But merit, worth, the cause of right,
You champion with all your might.

Dame Grundy you have often shocked,
The sanctimonious have mocked ;
But Virtue's face you much admire,
Believe true religion in pure desire.

Do not believe a lengthened face
Indicative of saving grace ;
But grace lies in one's willingness
To help a brother in distress.
In short, you take no stock in creeds,
That man's belief's best shown in deeds ;
The surest way to joys in heaven
To comfort hearts by sorrow riven.

And we are glad this night to say,
God speed you on your upward way ;
Continue still to spread the light
Till backward rolls dark Error's night ;
Till over every hungering soul
Refreshing waves of truth shall roll ;
Till might of right sway all mankind,
And hands of love more closely bind ;
Till spears to plowshares shall be beat,
And men no more their brothers meet
Like beasts of prey ; but each a friend
Shall comfort, joy, assistance lend.

Reward — if any you desire, —
Except that holy living fire,
That in each soul doth ever dwell
When life is spent in doing well ; —
You'll find it at the journey's end,
Where earth and heaven do sweetly blend,
And joys celestial greet your view,
When you have passed the portal through.

RETROSPECTIVE AND PROSPECTIVE.

WRITTEN FOR AND READ AT A RECEPTION TENDERED TO WARREN CHASE, ON HIS SEVENTIETH BIRTHDAY. BY MRS. LAVERNA MATHEWS.

As the babe born in the manger
Felt the cold world's scorn and hate,
So a helpless infant stranger
In a bleak New England State.

All unwelcome to the hearthstone, —
His only dower a mother's love, —
These the first years of " The Lone One."
Till mother passed to home above.

Then this helpless, homeless orphan –
What was there for such as he ? —
Cast upon the world's rough moorings,
Void of human sympathy ;

This poor outcast of creation —
Fatherless, motherless, was he —
Sent to earth in violation
Of the laws of equity ;

And the people we call " Christians "
Were the first to cast a stone,
At this poor despised orphan,
In the life line of the " Lone."

Bound in bondage by " selectmen "
Till the years of twenty-one —
Twenty-one was key to freedom
To this boy, who friends had none.

Labor — labor and exposure, —
Unproportioned to his years,

Beat and bruised until disclosure
   Found, at length, a list'ning ear.

Then there came a gleam of sunshine
   Whispering of liberty —
He would no longer bear such burdens;
   This boy determined to be free.

He ran away from cruel master,
   From the bondage he had borne;
His tired feet flew but the faster,
   As they bore him further on.

But why on sad memories linger
   In "The Life Line of the Lone"?
His angel mother's unseen finger
   Guides the footsteps of her son.

From out the damps of sorrow,
   Like the water-lily's bloom,
Thou hast risen in glorious triumph,
   Shedding light and sweet perfume.

Thou didst rise to bless the nation
   With thy counsel and advice,
And thy light has brought salvation,
   Dried the mourner's weeping eyes.

Thou hast plead the cause of woman,
   Thou hast bid the fallen rise,
Knowing every soul is human,
   And that none should we despise.

In the councils of the nation
   Thou hast plead the poor man's cause;
Shown the rotten, rude foundation
   Of our earthly man-made laws.

And when the "raps" at Hydesville
  First rang the reveille,
Sounding the glorious gospel
  Of the soul's immortality,

You were the first to catch its echo,
  And send it forth again,
And were never known to falter
  In sunshine or in rain.

But often in the winter,
  Through the storm, and cold, and sleet,
You have walked the weary distance
  Your engagements prompt to meet.

Very often not receiving
  Scrip enough to pay your fare;
But this blessed truth of heaven
  Must be spoken everywhere.

Thus you labor, all unselfish,
  By the help of spirit world,
Till Truth's grand and glorious banner
  O'er all nations is unfurled.

Oh, believe it not that heaven
  Is unmindful of her sons,
When she spreads such glorious banquet
  For earth's starving little ones.

As the babe in Bethlehem's manger
  Was born of low estate,
So this star from old New Hampshire
  Has risen good and great.

What though thy locks are silvered
  With the frost of seventy years;

What though thy feet have trodden
  Through sorrow's weight and tears;

The giant oak stands longer
  For the rough wind's cruel blast,
And human souls are stronger
  When the trial hour is passed.

What though old Time has silvered
  Thy locks of raven hair,
And with his silent fingers
  Has written wrinkles there;

The frosts of seventy winters
  But make the fruitage ripe,
And crown with radiant halo
  Your locks now silvered white.

And when you cross the river,
  Through heaven's pearly gate,
Across the bridge of silver
  Where loved ones fondly wait,—

You will find that all life's sorrows,
  Which seemed so hard to bear,
Will make a brighter morrow
  In your jewelled temple there.

WORDS OF CHEER.

WRITTEN FOR WARREN CHASE BY SUSAN M. RODGERS, MEDIUM.

THE tide of life is vast and deep,
  Its course is ever onward;
Down rugged cliff, up lofty steep,
  It keeps its course straight homeward.
The tide is sometimes deep and dark,
  And fearful we go forward,

Till brighter waters lave our bark;
    Then see our way straight homeward.
As needle to the magnet true,
    The soul will still tend upward;
Through storm and cloud of darkest hue
    It keeps its course straight homeward.
As storms will bid the magnet stray,
    So passions lead us downward;
But storm and passion pass away,
    And still we're tending upward.
To the ever-faithful soul
    Which ever looketh sunward
The path that leadeth to the goal
    Is short and leads straight homeward.

Mrs. Anna E. Kirk to Warren Chase.

THERE are gold-bright suns in worlds above,
    And blazing gems in worlds below;
Our world has love, and only love,
    For true worth and jewel glow.

God's love is sunlight to the good,
    And woman's, pure as diamond's sheen;
Friendship's mystic brotherhood
    In twilight beauty lies between.

TO WARREN CHASE.

SEND me one good April view,
Send me one sweet drop of dew,
Send me one fair fragrant flower,
Such as used to come from you.
Dig, oh dig around my heart,
Plant the seeds of love and truth;
Make the germ of goodness start,

While there yet is health and youth.
May I feel when life is o'er,
That it was not all in vain;
May a harvest line the shore,
As the sands that line the main.

      J. G. N.,
      Vineland, N.J.

"It is well she went before;
She'll be waiting at the door;
Over on the other shore
Ye shall walk the golden floor
Side by side forever more."

"No matter what part of life's hill you are on,
If you wish to mount up to the summit or top,
This motto observe, while you're trudging along:
'It is folly to whine and a sin to give up.'"

"Sorrow and joy, that interweave
 The raven with the golden locks.
Fall brings to those who sigh and grieve
 Their souls' autumnal equinox."

"A weary time thou'st been away,
 And yet I see thee, hear thee still;
Thy form is with me night and day,
 And thoughts of thee my bosom fill;
Thine image is to me like air,
 For it surrounds me everywhere."

"Responsive to our longing,
In the great future thronging,
Lost joys to man belonging,
 Beckon him to his home;
There, faith no more benighted;
There, love to love joy plighted;
There, sundered hearts united;
 There, all that buds shall bloom."

OUR OLD PIONEERS.

Yes, they are crossing and joining the ranks,
Gathered together on Jordan's fair banks;
Over the river, its shimmer and sheen,
Oft in a vision of glory they're seen,
Crowned with the light and knowledge of years, —
    These old pioneers.

Joining the soul life to which they have grown;
Sharing the harvest whose seed they have sown;
Throwing aside the old vestment of care,
Shining and beautiful garments they wear;
Lifting the veil without trembling or fears, —
    These old pioneers.

You should not mourn though you miss them to-day,
Higher the life that is over the way;
Earth cannot keep the pure spirits that rise
Back to the love reaching down from the skies.
They have no need of your sorrow or tears, —
    These old pioneers.

Back to your earth life they often will roam,
Bringing the light of their beautiful home,
Shedding a glorified radiance down,
Weaving for mortals a wonderful crown,
Transmitting truths from the heavenly spheres, —
    These old pioneers.

Hold you the ports that their valor has won;
Finish the work that their hands have begun;
Work as they worked for a purified cause;
Study, as they, into God's mystic laws;
Somewhere you'll meet in the love-lighted spheres
    Your old pioneers.
                      Emma Train.

CONTINUAL rivers make full seas;
Tumultuous streams are soonest dry;
Stars breed like birds, and multiply;
Death seasons food of richest taste;
Experience knows not haste or waste;
The surest boat hath pilots twain;
The womb of wealth grows big with pain;
Fires cure the cold, but love, heart chill;
Death comes from feebleness of will;
Roses take hue from lovers' lips;
Death ends, as does the sun's eclipse.
T. L. Harris.

IN the street the tide of being, how it surges, how it rolls!
God! what base, ignoble faces; God! what bodies wanting souls.
* * * * * * *
Passion, as it runs, grows purer, loses every tinge of clay,
As from Dawn, all red and turbid, flows the white, transparent Day;
And in mingled lives of lovers the array of human ills
Breaks their gentle course to music, as the stones break summer rills. *Alexander Smith.*

THE cloud which bursts with thunder
Slakes our thirsty souls with rain;
The blow most dreaded falls to break
From off our limbs a chain;
And wrongs of man to man but make
The love of God more plain,
As through the shadowy lens of even
The eye looks farthest into heaven,
On gleams of star and depths of blue,
The glowing sunshine never knew.
Whittier.

NEVER yet could I discover,
    Though I've struggled hard to learn,
That the rich could bolt out sorrow from the door;
    Or that wisdom, very wise
    In its own and others' eyes,
Did not nurse some little folly at the core;
    Never yet I knew a man
    Who made others' good his plan,
Who was not overpaid in peace of mind;
    Nor a worshipper of self,
    And a scraper-up of pelf,
Whose treasures were not scattered to the wind.
                            Charles Mackay.

CLOSE by the gate of the heavenly world,
An angel boy stood with his bright wings furled,
And an earnest light in his blue eye shone,
As he waited there for an absent one.
She came at last, and a shout of joy
Rang out from the lips of the angel boy;
It rattled through arches of heaven's high dome:
My mother! my mother! she has come! she has come!
                            S. N. Willard.

PROGRESS.

LET there be many windows in your soul,
    That all the glory of the universe
May beautify it. Not the narrow pane
    Of one poor creed can catch the radiant rays
That shine from countless sources. Tear away
    The blinds of superstition; let the light
Pour through fair windows broad as truth itself
    And high as God.

Why should the spirit peer
    Through some priest-curtained orifice, and grope

Along dim corridors of doubt, when all
　　The splendor from unfathomed seas of space
Might bathe it with golden waves of love?
　　Sweep up the debris of decaying faiths;
Sweep down the cobwebs of worn-out beliefs,
　　And throw your soul wide open to the light
Of Reason and of Knowledge. Tune your ear
　　To all the wordless music of the stars
And to the voice of nature, and your heart
　　Shall turn to truth and goodness, as the plant
Turns to the sun. A thousand unseen hands
　　Reach down to help you to their peace-crowned heights,
And all the forces of the firmament
　　Shall fortify your strength. Be not afraid
To thrust aside half truths and grasp the whole.
　　　　　　　　　　　　Ella Wheeler Wilcox.

A LOST CHORD.

SEATED one day at the organ,
　　I was weary and ill at ease,
And my fingers wandered idly
　　Over the noisy keys.

I do not know what I was playing,
　　Or what I was dreaming then;
But I struck one chord of music,
　　Like the sound of the great Amen.

It flooded the crimson twilight
　　Like the close of an Angel's Psalm,
And it lay on my fevered spirit,
　　With a touch of infinite calm.

It quieted pain and sorrow,
　　Like love overcoming strife;
It seemed the harmonious echo
　　From our discordant life.

It linked all perplexèd meanings
  Into one perfect peace,
And trembled away into silence
  As if it were loth to cease.

I have sought, but I seek it vainly,
  That one lost chord divine,
Which came from the soul of the organ,
  And entered into mine.

It may be that Death's bright angel,
  Will speak in that chord again;
It may be that only in heaven
  I shall hear that grand Amen.

Adelaide Annie Proctor.

WHAT IS NOBLE?

WHAT is noble to inherit?
  Wealth, estate, and proud degree —
There must be some other merit
  Higher yet than those for me!
Something greater far must enter
  Into life's majestic span;
Fitted to create and centre
  True nobility in man!

What is noble? 'Tis the finer
  Portion of our mind and heart,
Linked to something still diviner
  Than mere language can impart;
Ever prompting — ever seeing
  Some improvement yet to plan;
To uplift our fellow-being,
  And, like man, to feel for man.

What is noble? Is the sabre
　Nobler than the humble spade?
There is dignity in labor
　Truer than e'er pomp arrayed!
He who seeks the mind's improvement
　Aids the world in aiding mind;
Every great commanding movement
　Serves not one — but all mankind.

O'er the forge's heat and ashes,
　O'er the engine's iron head,
Where the rapid shuttle flashes,
　And the spindle whirls the thread;
There is labor lowly tending
　Each requirement of the hour,
There is genius still extending
　Science — and its world of power!

'Mid the dust and speed and clamor
　Of the loom-shed and the mill;
'Midst the clink of wheel and hammer,
　Great results are growing still!
Though too oft by Fashion's creatures
　Work and workers may be blamed,
Commerce need not hide its features!
　Industry is not ashamed!

What is noble? That which places
　Truth in its enfranchised will,
Leaving steps — like angel traces —
　That mankind may follow still!
E'en though Scorn's malignant glances
　Prove him poorest of his clan,
He's the noble who advances
　Freedom and the cause of man!

　　　　　　　　Charles Swain.

BEYOND.

It seemeth such a little way to me
  Across to that strange country — the Beyond;
And yet, not strange, for it has grown to be
  The home of those of whom I am so fond,
They make it seem familiar and most dear,
As journeying friends bring distant regions near.

So close it lies, that when my sight is clear
  I think I almost see the gleaming strand.
I know I feel those who have gone from here
  Come near enough sometimes, to touch my hand.
I often think, but for our veilèd eyes,
We should find heaven right round about us lies.

I cannot make it seem a day to dread,
  When from this dear earth I shall journey out
To that still dearer country of the dead,
  And join the lost ones, so long dreamed about.
I love this world, yet shall I love to go
And meet the friends who wait for me, I know.

I never stand above a bier and see
  The seal of death set on some well-loved face
But that I think, "One more to welcome me,
  When I shall cross the intervening space
Between this land and that one 'over there';
One more to make the Strange Beyond seem fair."

And so for me there is no sting in death,
  And so the grave has lost its victory.
It is but crossing — with abated breath,
  And white, set face — a little strip of sea,
To find the loved ones waiting on the shore,
More beautiful, more precious than before.

Ella Wheeler Wilcox.

www.ingramcontent.com/pod-product-compliance
Lightning Source LLC
Chambersburg PA
CBHW030741230426
43667CB00007B/795